THE KNIFE AND THE BUTTERFLY

THE KNIFE AND THE BUTTERFLY
A story of Jungian Analysis

Naomi Lloyd

Edited by
Corinne Henderson

KARNAC

First published in 2014 by
Karnac Books Ltd
118 Finchley Road
London NW3 5HT

Copyright © 2014 by Naomi Lloyd

The right of Naomi Lloyd to be identified as the author of this work has been asserted in accordance with §§ 77 and 78 of the Copyright Design and Patents Act 1988.

All rights reserved. No part of this publication may be reproduced, stored in a retrieval system, or transmitted, in any form or by any means, electronic, mechanical, photocopying, recording, or otherwise, without the prior written permission of the publisher.

British Library Cataloguing in Publication Data

A C.I.P. for this book is available from the British Library

ISBN-13: 978-1-78220-091-8

Typeset by V Publishing Solutions Pvt Ltd., Chennai, India

Printed in Great Britain

www.karnacbooks.com

ACKNOWLEDGEMENTS

Firstly, I wish to thank "Anna", my former analyst, for her invaluable help with Jungian theory, both before and during the process of writing, and without which this book would never have seen the light of day. Subsequently many others have been instrumental in helping me to bring this work to fruition over its three years of writing, editing and publication. This is also my opportunity to express my deepest thanks to them all:

Jacqui Lofthouse, my writing coach and mentor, whose advice and encouragement first gave me the courage to put pen to paper and who has been with me all the way. I owe her a huge debt of gratitude.

Voula Grand, novelist. Thanks to Jacqui Lofthouse, Voula and I met and formed a friendship, which helped to develop my self-belief as a writer. Her encouragement and support have played a vital part in the final success of this endeavour.

Rod Tweedy and Constance Gonvindin at Karnac Books, who have patiently helped me to negotiate the complex publication process.

Ben Hodges, whose artwork graces the front cover with such symbolic significance and sensitive understanding.

My many colleagues and friends, whose belief in this undertaking has enabled me to persevere through to the end.

My family, whose love and trust in the final outcome has never wavered. In particular, I would include my daughter, my son, and their partners—together with my dear husband, whose patience must have been sorely tried by the many hours of isolated work involved in this enterprise. My love and thanks to them all.

And finally, I end with another person whose contribution has been invaluable in enabling this book to see the light of day—my beloved sister Corinne. A psychotherapist in Sydney, Australia, her devotion to the process of editing has been unstinting, and has ensured that this work met the deadline for publication. For the part she has so lovingly played in this endeavour, I am proud for her name to appear as "Editor" alongside my own on the cover.

FOREWORD

This is probably the only book I will ever write—and without "Anna" I know that it would never have been written, because I truly believe I would not have been here to write it. I am convinced that I would have chosen to end my life many years ago. My continued existence, together with my professional journey into the world of psychotherapy, I owe entirely to Anna. In writing about our eight year journey together— in which we both battled heroically with my disturbing attachment towards death as the final solution to my despair—my purpose is to thank Anna for giving back to me the gift of Life. Inevitably, it is a gift suffused with the bittersweet paradox of joy and pain: the gift of life which a mother gives her child. And this is what Anna's gift came to signify for me within our analytic relationship. Now that I have "grown up" through the process of her nurturing, this book is intended as *my* gift to Anna. Through her, I was "reborn" in ways unimaginable when I first arrived on her doorstep in a state of profound crisis and life-threatening despair. During the course of analysis I felt reborn many times, but each time to an emotionally strong "mother", able to comprehend and contain both unknown and unacknowledged dysfunction from a past and present existence.

When the idea of writing this history first began to take shape in my mind, I knew that I wanted it to include academic and theoretical content rigorous enough to appeal to fellow professionals—since it is towards them that this book is primarily directed. Thus my intention was to describe the analytic journey from the perspective of the patient, but in parallel with the insight of the analyst whose work provides psychological, theoretical, and emotional meaning to the patient's presenting material. For this reason, my first hope was that we might write this history together. Though she gave serious consideration to this possibility, for reasons that included professional, ethical, and personal considerations, Anna finally decided against it. At the time, this was a huge blow. My training was not analytic, and I felt ill equipped to understand and explain Anna's perspective theoretically, or describe how she had chosen to engage with the many psychological challenges which my analysis threw at her. Even as my own training as a therapist was advancing, Anna remained circumspect about discussing my inner process in theoretical terms. Her concern was that I might feel this as a diminishing of the emotional content, were she to describe my experience by means of "theoretical explanation". And certainly in the early period of our work, this would have been neither appropriate nor therapeutic. But as the book began to form itself in my mind, my desire to "understand" Anna's perspective became an insistent need. Finally, it was her sensitive attunement which led her to recognise that we had to find a way to satisfy this need in order to effect a tolerable ending to our work—an ending which would leave me with "concrete evidence" of our relationship, and which contained the potential to continue the creative process of writing for which Anna had been the original inspiration.

In one highly significant sense, I knew that I had effectively already "written" the story of our journey. Very early in my analysis, I found myself overwhelmed by an urge to record every nuance of this experience in poetry. The words flowed from my unconscious in an irrepressible torrent. And once the urge had surfaced, it came to include dreams and letters to Anna, all of which initially felt "too dangerous" to speak about openly. As Anna's retirement approached and I knew that our work was nearing its end, I found myself reflecting on this vast collection of writing. I recognised that within this profusion of largely unconscious outpourings was contained the history of my analysis. Though I have chosen to explore the content of some poems and to preface certain chapters by their inclusion, it is not from any deluded belief in their literary merit. I see their value solely in terms of their psychological significance, which ostensibly promised enough potential material from which I might extract a meaningful account of my analytic journey. But without Anna's guidance, I felt unable to understand how her knowledge and training had informed this experience for *her*, as my analyst.

Ultimately, Anna offered me an exceptionally creative and generous way through this difficulty. For the last eight months of our work she offered me the possibility of recording our sessions, while guiding me through an "analysis" of my analytic journey by means of a detailed re-visiting of the writing. But this was a huge undertaking, and my concern was that we would run out of time. So in contrast to the more usual process of reducing sessions when working towards an ending, I found the courage to ask Anna if I might increase my sessions to three a week during these months.

By this time fully aware of the controversial nature of my request, I understood Anna's insistence that we consider the therapeutic implications together. Once she had reassured herself that this would help rather than hinder my process in ending, she agreed to increase our sessions. I recognise this as an entirely selfless gesture on Anna's part. If I were to use the recorded material to write a book, she wanted my "promise" that she remain anonymous. She did not wish to claim any public or professional acknowledgement of her contribution to this enterprise. I understood this altruism to be in my best interests. Her hope was that this might help me manage my painful struggle with the process of ending, by offering a formula through which she might be both "present yet absent" as I learnt to face the prospect of continuing my onward journey without her.

It is in this second sense that I wish to express my belief that this book would never have been written without Anna. In trusting me with the priceless gift of these recordings, I believe she gave me an opportunity to chronicle the process of our analytic work uniquely from our joint perspectives—something apparently missing for me in the current literature. True to her promise, Anna has willingly and regularly acted as "consultant", offering theoretical advice when I needed her guidance. But finally I appreciate that Anna was right in insisting that I make this next stage in my journey alone. This, after all, must be the ultimate aim of therapy. Anna *is* not, and *cannot* be "there" for me now, in the way in which I sense again her strong presence when I hear her voice speaking to me through the recordings. Inevitably I have felt the strength of her presence internally and alongside me as I re-visited our story in the course of my writing. At times, this has undoubtedly provoked painful feelings of loss. But finally, it enabled me to appreciate that Anna has left me with a gift, greater even than the recordings. In my holding of Anna as a strong internal object, I am reminded of "the map" of my inner world which we drew together, and which continues to guide me forward even when I occasionally find myself feeling lost. Sometimes I have felt the need of another helping hand, to guide me back to the path from which I have wandered. But held deep within me is the trust in my own power to return to the self-knowledge and understanding through which Anna taught me to believe, finally, in my strength to "know my own way".

Thus, in this written record of our journey, the reader will encounter the "voices" of both patient and analyst as accurate verbatim extracts taken from the recordings. My hope is that this will uniquely open up my experience of the process of Jungian Analytical Psychology to others. True to the process of therapy itself, I cannot offer the reader a comfortable ride. But I hope it will ultimately prove to be an honest and enlightening one.

*　*　*

It is hardly possible to imagine a detailed history of an analysis which does not also document the patient's personal history. And yet the reader may be surprised that so little information concerning my family background and history occurs in the ensuing account. This is not an oversight, nor is it a conscious attempt at resistance or denial—since I intend to rectify the situation here. However, my decision to largely omit reference to my personal history within the main body of this narrative merits explanation.

My intention in writing this book was to give an insight into the nature and workings of the analytic relationship—or at least, the analytic relationship as *I* experienced it in my eight years with Anna. As each chapter emerged, I kept telling myself that "soon" I would find an appropriate opening through which to introduce my family background, and the influential childhood experiences, which inevitably formed the backdrop to the crisis that finally led me into analysis. But strangely, this "appropriate moment" never emerged.

With hindsight, the reasons for this become apparent. My objective has always been to describe my analysis from the perspective through which I experienced it *at that time*. This was inevitably a perspective coloured by the effects of a major depressive disorder, accompanied by episodes of psychotic fantasy and suicidal ideation. Viewed from this standpoint, my hope is that the reader will be willing to endure the sometimes painful exposure to this experience in order to gain a deeper understanding—not only of the agonisingly isolating nature of depressive illness, but also of the profoundly challenging demands made of the analyst who offers to accompany their patient on the long journey back to recovery.

When I first began working with Anna, I believed my "problem" to be a long-repressed issue in my marriage relationship. This had emerged suddenly and dramatically in the course of couple counselling, and precipitated my spectacular descent into depression and psychological breakdown. What I could not have understood then was the significance this relationship problem had within the wider context of early attachment experience. Nor could I have understood how such early experiences continued to influence my way of relating, not only within my marriage, but within all other significant relationships, past and present. From the moment we met, this inevitably included the way in which I related to Anna, since—as every therapist knows—the therapeutic relationship invariably becomes a "mirror", reflecting the client's way-of-being in his external world. My personal analysis and my clinical experience have thus taught me never to trust that a client's view of his "presenting issues" will ultimately prove to be the fundamental focus of the therapeutic work.

But while Anna was alert to this, I was not. The crisis I was experiencing at that time seemed to concern only what was happening in the "present moment". And since it had shattered my sense of self into dangerously life-threatening fragments, I had lost almost all the inner resources necessary for survival. The word "almost" is important here. Evidently enough survival instinct remained to lead me to turn to Anna for help. But repairing my sense of self so that I would want to continue living was the painstakingly delicate work, which Anna knowingly undertook when I became her patient. The outcome of my journey—from darkness into the light—is contained within this narrative of our developing analytic relationship. Always subtle and sensitive, but also tough and challenging, Anna skilfully and lovingly negotiated a way through the minefield of my psychological fragility. This is the story I am choosing to tell—by taking the reader back in time, in order to expose them to an honest and intimate sense of this experience from the joint perspectives of patient and analyst.

Since my focus at that time was the present nature of my struggles with existence, the significance of my family relationships and childhood experience seemed less than relevant—and Anna's style of working rarely included asking direct questions. Her method was to wait for things to emerge, trusting that significant information would come to light as a result of the process. My recollection of our early therapeutic relationship is that I would throw in "bits of information" about my family background and early experiences quite casually from time to time, as if they didn't matter too much. Interestingly, several early dreams involved large family gatherings at which all my family were present. These dreams offered us the opportunity of exploring these relationships in more depth, as my unconscious was providing clear evidence of the need for this. But since my emotional instability made me resistant to talking about my dreams at that point, this opportunity had to wait until its re-emergence much later on in our work. Disconcerting though it is to admit, I recognise that, at that time, I could see no significant connection between my past history and my present psychological fragility. It would take much longer to understand the important influence of the past upon the present.

In the meantime, Anna waited patiently for the "bits and pieces" of my story to form a coherent narrative. Finally her patience was rewarded when a hugely painful piece of my personal "puzzle" fell into place through a casual reference I made concerning my maternal grandmother. As she interpreted to me the wider significance of this inadvertent illumination, I remember it as a moment of profound trauma, requiring all Anna's safe holding to contain its effects on my fragile ego. But it was also a moment of great revelation, after which I could not doubt the importance of my childhood history on my present way-of-being in the world.

But since this personal history does not emerge as an integrated account within this narrative, it seems necessary and appropriate to present it separately. I hope the reader will have the patience to follow this journey through to the later chapters, when the recorded material allows me to develop the psychological implications of my personal history into a more theoretical perspective.

INTRODUCTION

Those shadowy recollections,
Which, be they what they may,
Are yet the fountain-light of all our day,
Are yet a master-light of all our seeing;
Uphold us, cherish, and have power to make
Our noisy years seem moments in the being
Of the eternal silence: truths that wake,
To perish never....

—William Wordsworth
Ode: Intimations of Immortality from
Recollections of Early Childhood, 1802–1806[1]

I was the eldest of two children, born into a middle-class Jewish family in 1946. My younger sister was born four and a half years later. To the best of my knowledge, my paternal great-grandparents originated

---

[1] Wordsworth, W. (1802–1806). Ode: Intimations of immortality from recollections of early childhood. In: Nichol Smith (Ed.), *Wordsworth: Poetry and Prose, with Essays by Coleridge, Hazlitt, De Quincey.* Oxford: Oxford University Press, 1956.

from Lithuania and Poland. During the mid to late nineteenth century both countries were part of Imperial Russia. Permanent residency for Jews was confined to the "Pale of Settlement"—boundaries in which they were forced to live under Russian jurisdiction. These areas were often subject to devastating attacks by anti-Semitic mobs, whose violence was condoned by the Russian authorities. These attacks became known as *"pogroms"*, from the Russian word meaning "devastation". It is from these pogroms that my paternal great-grandparents escaped to England, where my paternal grandparents were born and grew up in poverty as the children of refugee immigrants in London's East End.

Nothing is known of my paternal great grandfather's former occupation in Poland, but by the time my grandparents met, my grandfather was working in his father's East End factory, making working men's caps.

My paternal grandmother's father had been a leather-worker and skilled saddle-maker in Lithuania. In England, like many immigrants, his diligent industry eventually enabled him to become the manager (or owner) of a grocery shop, in which my grandmother worked as soon as she was old enough. Following their marriage, my grandparents lived above a shop in Stoke Newington, selling my great-grandfather's caps. It was while living here that my father's eldest brother was born. By the time of my father's birth in 1915, his parents were living above their shop in Dalston, where their business had grown to include the sale of "millinery" and the designing and making of women's hats. By 1921, my aunt—their third child—had been born.

Though my father never talked about his early childhood, it seems certain that he spent his formative years growing up in this East End environment. But by the time he was seven, he had begun his education at a private preparatory school in Hampstead. By then, my grandparents had established a successful women's clothing retail business in the Dalston shop, and were living in comparative prosperity in a large family home overlooking Hampstead Heath. These were childhood years containing some fond memories for my father. They were years about which he *did* recount incidents of boyhood adventures, and misadventures, with some affection and evident amusement.

However, following the 1930s recession, a return to financial hardship necessitated selling the family home and moving back to the East End, to live again above the shop in Dalston. Though my grandparents eventually recovered some financial stability, this set-back had a lasting impact on my father and his siblings through the disruption which it caused during their adolescence and early adulthood. Recollecting the few memories about which my father did speak, they invariably focused on his experiences of the period spent in their Hampstead home. Reflecting on it now, I am convinced that our own subsequent move to a family home in Hampstead—when I was eleven years old—signified a reparative process for my father of this painful loss of his childhood home.

Concerning my mother's family, I know very little except that she described a comfortable German-Jewish background. Neither I, nor my sister, even know our grandmother's maiden name, so there is little possibility of tracing this side of the family. All I have is my "sense" of a story that my maternal grandmother came from "an educated and cultured background". An only child, my mother believed her father to have been the manager of a champagne processing plant in the Ruhr Valley. He died when she was eighteen months old, and my mother owned only one photograph of him, now in my possession. She learned that he was musical—an accomplished lute player and a lover of music and dance—musical talents which my mother inherited. He was not Jewish, but apparently converted in order to marry my grandmother. So with the growing threat of Hitler's rise to power in 1934, the non-Jewish family became antagonistic, and my grandmother "Oma" fled Germany for England with my mother, then aged thirteen. Throughout my mother's adolescence, she and her mother lived a precarious refugee existence in London as "enemy aliens". Required to report to the authorities every month to have their "permits" renewed, my grandmother lived in constant fear of being relocated to Germany. Never having worked before, she became dependent on her resources as a dressmaker to earn a living. She gained a reputation for making "trousseaus", and my mother was expected to help with the needlework after school and often late into the night. As a result of one such undertaking, my grandmother was invited to attend the wedding with her then sixteen-year-old daughter, which was where my parents met. They subsequently married on the day of the Battle of Britain—the 15th September 1940, when my mother was nineteen. By then World War II was in full flight and my father was in the army, having enlisted at the earliest opportunity. As children, we were told that the Rabbi had to be persuaded out of the air-raid shelter to perform the ceremony, because the air-raids in London were so alarming.

I remember my mother telling me that she refused to consider having a child until the war was over. Her understandable fear was that she might be left "a war widow". Consequently, I was born one year after my father was demobbed. Shortly after this, my parents bought their first home—part of a new housing development in an unfashionable suburb, built on the ruins of previous bomb-damage. My father struggled to re-establish his career as a barrister after more than six years in the army, and although he joked about having time to do *The Times* crossword, financial concerns always hovered close to the surface throughout my childhood. In fact, this was only one of many fears about the uncertainties of life, which I learnt to "tune into" from my earliest years. But until my analysis with Anna, I had no concept of how these largely suppressed fears—mostly as an inherited legacy of my family's refugee history—had been implicitly and unintentionally passed down to me. The ways in which I learnt to "sense" this fear of uncertainty arose from numerous childhood experiences.

In first talking to Anna about my childhood, I am certain that I would have painted a picture of a close, loving, and "normal" family. Throughout their lives, my parents remained deeply attached to each other in what I later appreciated to be an unusually loving and harmonious relationship. I experienced, and witnessed, great physical affection within the family, and viewed my childhood as having been devoid of any trauma or serious unhappiness. Indeed, I would have been able to say, with complete honesty, that I never witnessed any episodes of anger between my parents. My father's philosophy was that "anger" was an unnecessary and unproductive emotion, and whatever had prompted those feelings could be resolved calmly by "rational discussion".

I remember my father as gentle, sensitive, and highly intelligent. Much later, through analysis, I began to question whether he regarded his own sensitivity as "unmanly weakness". Childhood and adolescent memories seem to suggest that he struggled with aspects of this sensitivity—that it represented his "shadow" with which he battled in order to establish his place in the world. However, for me, he was a strong, protective, and loving role-model of "maleness". He was well read in philosophy, and though he would not have described himself as an Existentialist, he exhibited existential leanings in his belief in personal autonomy, freedom of choice, and the importance of taking responsibility for these choices. He was also profoundly aware of the uncertainty of life and the inevitability of death. Though I realised much later in my own life that he never finally came to terms with the impossibility of creating "certainty", preferring to hold onto the hope that, through choice and action, he might somehow transcend the "givens of existence"[2] by making numerous "contingency plans" designed to avert calamity, or at least to forestall its worst effects.

My mother's lack of English on her arrival in London as a child refugee caused a severe disruption to her education, of which she remained profoundly conscious throughout her life. As a result, she totally trusted my father's judgement on all matters. He offered her a love, protection, and security not previously experienced, and under his protection, she developed from a timid young girl into a socially confident adult with an enthusiasm for life. Together, my parents represented a perfect example of Jung's "compensatory factor" as it can manifest in relationships. A shy and modest man, my father's intellect was not matched by personal self-assurance. As his career flourished and he found himself increasingly forced into the spotlight professionally and socially, he battled to overcome his reticence and discomfort. Conversely, my mother loved nothing more than to be surrounded by people at a social gathering, where she would protect and reassure him through her natural ability to engage with warmth, charm, and confidence.

I would not wish to deny my good fortune in being born into such a close, loving, and secure family environment. There remains so much that I hold dear in my memory of my relationship with my parents, and much of what I learnt from my father's philosophy of life continues to be a guiding light for my own personal philosophy. However, it was the cause of great personal sadness to discover that "love" alone cannot protect a child from the influence of the "shadow" which lurks, however well-hidden, beneath every Jewish family history. In order to learn self-acceptance, my analysis inevitably required me to confront this "family shadow", from which my parents had striven so valiantly to protect me, but which inevitably emerged as a deeply unconscious aspect of my own struggles with life. Below the secure surface which my parents worked so hard to create, lay a history of uncertainty—the inevitable legacy of the refugee experience from which future generations cannot be protected. This psychological reality motivated a generation who had experienced the pain of persecution, exile, and homelessness,

---

[2] Yalom, I. D. (1980). *Existential Psychotherapy*, p. 8. New York: Basic Books.

to protect future generations from the knowledge of such traumatic experiences and losses.

Dr Paul Valent, an eminent Australian psychiatrist and psychotherapist specialising in generational trauma, was himself a child survivor of the Holocaust. Born in Czechoslovakia, he has spent over thirty years working with Holocaust survivors, researching and writing on its cross-generational impact. In his paper *Ripples of the Holocaust*, delivered at the International Holocaust Forum in Melbourne, 2006, he explains the legacy that his research leads him to believe is passed down to second-generation survivors—and beyond:

> From birth on, they absorbed feelings, images, sensations, behaviour that their parents carried in their beings. Thus, they said that they carried scars, but they did not know the original wounds. It was as if they should remember something, but they could not.[3]

In my own family, despite an openness on all other subjects, no significant "stories" concerning my parents' life history, or the history of previous generations, were passed down to us as children. What little knowledge I *do* have sometimes differs from my sister's account, since all such "knowledge" was gleaned from fragmented bits and pieces of information about which we had no evidential proof. There are no family photographs that date earlier than a few pictures of my parents in childhood, and of my grandparents at the same period. Neither my sister nor I possess any objects relating to our family history, other than one or two small items which were "wedding gifts" to my parents, and a few kitchen utensils—relics of my mother's childhood in Germany which her mother brought with when they fled to England.

Darren Sush, a Senior Psychologist at Metropolitan State Hospital in Los Angeles, is himself the grandson of Holocaust survivors. In his paper *A Final Solution with No End? The Trans-generational Effect of the Holocaust*, 2012, Sush writes that:

> Many survivors did not want to burden their children with memories of the past, and instead remained silent in the hopes of protecting their children's wellbeing. However, though the stories

---

[3] Valent, P. (2006). *Ripples of the Holocaust*. Paper delivered at the *International Forum on the Holocaust*, 2006, p. 4. Melbourne, Australia.

of the past remained silent, implicit memories were generally still conveyed.[4]

Sush refers to "a discontinuity of the historical legacy of the family" resulting from the lack of "photos, documents, and other objects of the family's past".[5] which may have been lost or destroyed. Paul Valent also highlights this point, explaining that:

> ... These children grew up enveloped in a parental cloak, saturated by memories, rent by grief, scattered with black holes of silence.[6]

Surrounded as we were by a loving family in my childhood, it did not occur to me to notice these gaps in my knowledge of our family history. Later on, when I was mature enough to start asking questions, I had already intuitively sensed that this subject was "out of bounds"—or, as Anna would later interpret to me, I recognised it as a subject "too awful to be talked about." Beneath my mother's charming social confidence lay an emotional vulnerability resulting not only from her refugee history, but also from the loss of a father she could not remember, and her experience of growing up with an insecure, fearful, and controlling mother, who relied on her daughter to provide emotional as well as practical support in her efforts to survive. Strictly speaking, my maternal grandmother cannot accurately be described as a Holocaust survivor, since she had the courage and foresight to flee Germany several years before the outbreak of war. Nevertheless, even subsequent German Governments have recognised that life for Jews during these pre-war years became intolerable. Fraught with traumatic evidence of increasing persecution, escape seemed a necessary defence against such life-threatening conditions—finally warranting reparation.

In England, my mother and grandmother became "displaced persons"; thus, not only "refugees" but also stateless, and consequently at the mercy of the authorities. In this sense, the effects on children of Holocaust survivors would also seem to apply accurately to my mother. Research evidence suggests that surviving parents often display a

---

[4] Sush, D. A. (2012). *Final Solution with No End?—The Transgenerational Effect of the Holocaust*. Paper published on the Internet, last accessed June 2013.
[5] Ibid., p. 3.
[6] Valent, P. (2006). Ripples of the Holocaust. Paper delivered at the *International Forum on the Holocaust*, 2006, Melbourne, Australia.

tendency towards over-involvement in their children's lives, which may include an anxious or overly sensitive response to their children's behaviour, and demands exacted on them to fulfil a particular role for the parents. It is thought that this may be the survivors' unconscious need for their children to restore or repair their traumatic losses.

Analysis provided an opening to look deeply into my childhood memories, and acknowledge for the first time the underlying threat which had been the only disturbance to my parents' happiness. Recollected incidents emerged as evidence of the ways in which my maternal grandmother's control had threatened to damage my parents' relationship over the years, as my mother felt constantly in the thrall of the heavy "duty" and gratitude demanded of her by her mother. I was a young adult when my mother finally found the strength to break this lifelong pattern of domination, which had most certainly been felt by me and my sister as children. But it was a painful process of change, and I came to realise the ways in which I had grown up intuitively "feeling" my mother's sadness and inner conflict, and my father's suppressed anger towards my maternal grandmother.

In my own internal world, these memories, and the childhood feelings surrounding them, had long been consigned to oblivion … or so I believed. But they finally found expression, painfully and unexpectedly, in a clearly remembered session with Anna in which I suddenly heard myself describing my maternal grandmother as "a witch". To my knowledge, I had never previously expressed this feeling openly to anyone. It emerged as a deeply held unconscious expression from childhood, and Anna was quick to appreciate the significance of this "revelation". The following dialogue is taken from my memory of this session, so I cannot claim it to be an accurate account—but I clearly remember sensing something unusually animated in Anna's response to my unexpected disclosure:

> Ah! … *Now* we have the answer to the question of where you learnt the model of "control". I couldn't really see that it had come from your parents—but now we can see that it came from your grandmother.

"Control" became my mechanism for survival following the breakdown in my marriage, described in detail later on in the book. The realisation of the unhappiness I had caused through my exercising of this control finally led to a psychological breakdown. But when Anna voiced these words, my first reaction was shock and disbelief:

> "That can't be right! My grandmother lived in America when I was growing up. I only saw her on occasional visits to England."
>
> "You learnt about her through the influence which you saw and felt in your mother's responses to her," Anna explained. "She became 'the witch' from whom your father wanted to protect her—and you *also* learnt that Mother needed to be protected."

Anna conveyed how, from my earliest years, I would have unconsciously absorbed the impact this problematic relationship had on the family—and this I could recognise and understand. But what I hadn't appreciated until then was how I had also absorbed my grandmother's role-model of "control" as a mechanism for my own survival. It was a deeply shocking moment to realise that, when my need to survive became paramount, I *also* became a "controlling witch", as contained within my family's perception of my grandmother. Since adolescence, I had learnt to hate her for the pain she had caused my parents by her dominating and manipulative behaviour towards my mother. Now I had to confront the horror of learning that I had effectively allowed myself to "become" her—with the result that I had also caused pain and hurt to my own husband and children. It was a harrowing revelation. Eventually, with Anna's sensitive support, I was able to work through the pain of this confrontation, and to feel compassion for the tragic events in my grandmother's life, which had led her to turn in desperation to such damaging means of survival. In time, and through this traumatic confrontation, I would also ultimately find compassion and forgiveness for myself.

Anna's perception had been accurate. Throughout our childhood, my sister and I received clear messages from our father of the need to protect our mother by not "upsetting" her. Any dereliction of this duty of care would meet with my father's sadness, and his thinly veiled "disappointment" that we had hurt her by not giving adequate consideration to her vulnerability. Inevitably, this also meant that we had hurt *him* through our insensitivity and thoughtlessness. With growing maturity and hindsight, I came to appreciate the ways in which my sister strove to resist this emotional blackmail by refusing to "play the game" of feeling responsible for our mother's emotional fragility. Perhaps her position as the second child made this easier. Already more than four years ahead of her, I had more or less accepted my role as significant "protector" of my mother's vulnerability. In an interview for Australian television in 1983, Dr Valent is reported as saying:

> ... One child can take the brunt of the family's [bad] experience and the other child might represent the hope of all the good things that should come in the new life ... It often happens that the oldest child is coloured by the Holocaust experience, whereas the youngest child escapes it, relatively speaking ...[7]

I subsequently realised that the effect of my sister's resistance to accepting this role led me to double my need to be my mother's protector. And when my sister finally escaped from the demands of this situation by choosing to live abroad, I found myself supporting my mother in helping her to come to terms with her guilt about this additional loss, which added a new dimension to my sense of responsibility.

By the time I reached adolescence, I had also sensed my father's protectiveness towards his own mother, while his relationship with his father seemed uneasy, for reasons I never fully understood since my father never expressed these feelings within my hearing. Only occasional incidents in later childhood and adolescence gave any indication of these suppressed difficulties between them. We visited our paternal grandparents regularly, and I never doubted their love for us—nor that of my aunts, uncles, and cousins with whom we maintained a close family connection.

In many ways, my father's attitude towards his "Jewishness" was ambivalent, and I found myself struggling to make sense of numerous contradictory "messages" about what "being Jewish" was supposed to mean—both to the family and me personally. Until the age of eleven, when we moved to Hampstead, the post-war housing development in which I had grown up since infancy consisted predominantly of Jewish families with young children. These children all attended the local primary school with me, and in deference to our numbers, a Jewish staff member would take us off each morning for "Jewish Prayers" while the rest of the school attended "Assembly". From this early experience,

---

[7] Valent, P. (1983). Interview Australian ABC Television.

I developed a sense that "being Jewish" made me "different", and part of a "special community".

And yet the attitude at home conflicted with this experience. Jewish children from school would play together outside in the street, whose parents all seemed to know each other. But while it was acceptable for me to attend school with these children, I was not allowed to play with them outside, or encouraged to invite them home to play. I soon learnt that my parents' choice was not to socialise within this community, and they made few friends amongst our neighbours. As a child, this attitude was incomprehensible to me. Though bound to accept their authority on the matter, it had the effect of leaving me isolated, lonely, and confused throughout my early childhood. During the long school holidays, I yearned for the companionship of these children, who I saw and heard playing together outside. But since I was forbidden to join them, I retreated into an inner world peopled with imaginary children in endless games involving "school"—the only place where it was apparently acceptable for me to be in their company. As soon as she was old enough, my sister would be pressed into participating in these imaginary games. Considering the disparity between our ages and stages of development, to be so dependent on the companionship of my younger sister did not necessarily benefit either of us—though I remain grateful for the close bond which my need created between the two of us, and which still continues to this day.

Through analysis, I came to appreciate how my childhood isolation revealed another significant legacy of the refugee experience of which I had been unaware. It surfaced as recognition of what I can only describe as my parents' "inability to play". I have almost no childhood recollection of them "playing with us" or of us "playing games together" as a family. In early childhood it was rare for a school friend to be invited home, as my parents seemed not to appreciate the value of childhood social relationships. Occasionally, accidental opportunities for play would arise when my parents' friends would bring their children to visits at our house. But these occasions were rare enough to make them stand out as exceptional in my memory. Almost always, my sister and I played alone at home, mostly inventing our own games and devoid of any parental involvement or interest.

When I first became acquainted with my husband's family, I was amazed to discover the various ways in which his family all "played" together. I learnt that during his childhood, his aunt and uncle would visit regularly each week for a family game of cards. At Christmas, board games would appear which the family had traditionally played throughout my husband's childhood. And as a young boy, childhood friends were constant and welcome visitors to his house.

Finally, since my husband is not Jewish, I came to understand this discrepancy in our childhood experiences as another legacy of my family's refugee history. As a descendant of parents and grandparents who carried this legacy and the scars of persecution, it is understandable that, for both my parents, their childhood experiences would have taught them that life was a serious business. For my mother particularly, it is likely that opportunities for "play" would probably have been no more than an occasional escape from life's fearful uncertainty. It has been interesting for me to reflect on the way in which I tried to repair this "playful" loss in myself by choosing to become a teacher of young children. This offered me magical opportunities to learn how to be a child again, through the natural and spontaneous example of the children in my care.

With their conscious avoidance of involvement in the social environment of my early childhood, what I sensed from my parents' attitude was something that felt like "disapproval" of the community in which they found themselves living. As an older child, I realised that they felt "out of place" in this overtly Jewish atmosphere. And yet it was clear that my parents identified themselves as Jewish, and that we regarded ourselves as "a Jewish family" in many ways. *The Jewish Chronicle* newspaper was delivered, and I would regularly see my father reading it. He subscribed to Jewish charities, and was professionally associated with several bodies, which promoted Anglo-Jewish relations between Jewish lawyers in other European countries. On important festivals in the Jewish calendar, my father would take us to synagogue, and later on, both my sister and I attended Hebrew classes on Sunday mornings. A significantly happy memory was the annual family celebration of Passover at my grandparents' home, where their small flat was magically transformed for the evening with candles, and a beautifully laid table, which had miraculously "grown" so as to accommodate the whole family. Wonderful and symbolic food—not seen or eaten at any other time of the year—would appear as if by magic from my grandmother's minute kitchen. An atmosphere of happiness and harmony permeates my memory of those occasions, when I could put aside my childish confusion about what it meant to be Jewish.

But my confusion was only to be alleviated temporarily by these family celebrations. Towards the end of the year, following shortly on the heels of the Jewish "Feast of Hanukah", we would get together for another family celebration which retains a magical quality in my childhood memory: this was Christmas.

In my fondest childhood memories of Christmas we are at the home of my father's sister and her husband. In contrast to my grandparents' flat, my aunt and uncle then lived in what appeared to me as a young child to be an *enormous* apartment—so huge that I can remember getting lost in its numerous "passageways". All the rooms seemed large, but especially the living room. Once again, I revelled in the sight of the large, beautifully laid table, shining with the best china, cutlery, and glasses, and adorned with Christmas decorations and crackers. But most magical of all was the Christmas tree, which, in keeping with everything else in my memory, also appeared to be the largest I had ever seen inside a room.

Throughout our childhood, we always celebrated Christmas together as a family—sometimes at the homes of my aunts and uncles; at other times in my own home. Always it was a magical time. And always there was a *real* Christmas tree. Like any young child, I anticipated this family event with excitement.

But the joy of Christmas soon compounded my sense of confusion once I attended school. Most likely, it was the morning ritual of Jewish Prayers, which alerted me to the fact that "Christmas" was not intended to be a time of Jewish celebration. "Hanukah" I learnt, was the thanksgiving holiday when Jewish families came together to give each other presents and celebrate. But my family hardly seemed to notice Hanukah, and it was only my attendance at Hebrew classes that taught me to appreciate the significance of this as a "family festival" in the Jewish calendar. Something alerted me to "keep quiet" about the way in which we appeared to have broken an accepted boundary by celebrating Christmas. At a very young age, I was left with a troubling question which gnawed away in my mind: did the way in which my family chose to celebrate Christmas mean that we couldn't *really* be Jewish?

I cannot recall trying to resolve this question by asking my parents to answer it for me—though I suspect that I *did* ask them. But the fact that I have no recollection of an answer explains why the question remained unresolved throughout my early childhood. Whether they intended to or not, my parents' attitude conveyed the idea that "being Jewish" was not something that need make us feel "different" in the world in which we lived our day-to-day lives.

Finally, it was with an adult perspective that I was able to make sense of these apparent paradoxes. By the age of twelve, I had begun to reflect on my own attitude towards religion. Though aware of contradictions in my father's response to his Jewish origins, he had not so far talked openly to me on the subject of his religious beliefs. Contrary to appearances, his reticence was in fact a mark of his openness. My father's personal philosophy was the belief that we each had an autonomous right to our own religious beliefs, without a "pressure to conform", which deprived us of freedom of choice. Unless questioned, he remained silent about his views on religion, and the subject of particular anathema to him was the concept of "missionary zeal"—I believe for precisely this reason—that it went against his personal belief in freedom of choice.

When I finally asked my father if he believed in God, he told me he was an agnostic. He explained that the concept of "God" took many forms according to different religions and periods in history. It was therefore not possible to believe or disbelieve, without first having arrived at a final concept of "the nature of God". And so, he informed me, he continued to question traditional beliefs, until such time as the nature of God might finally be proved beyond doubt. This remains as a powerful and poignant example of my father's philosophical openness. It is also an example of how his belief in freedom of choice inevitably encompassed the need to take responsibility for our choices. Long before I could have understood the philosophical implications, my father's role-model had already covertly opened me to an existential awareness that "freedom" and "responsibility" must inevitably become a co-existing problem for personal and philosophical consideration.

However, my father's explanation of his agnosticism did not answer my questions concerning the religious paradoxes of my early childhood. I still needed to know *why* he had taken us to synagogue on high holy days, and insisted that we attend Hebrew classes, despite the evidence that we were both bored by this uninspiring learning experience. And which "God" were we acknowledging in our family celebrations of both Passover and Christmas?

Ultimately, the answer to these questions was deceptively simple. During his mother's lifetime, his love and respect for her took precedence over his philosophical principles. It seems that my grandmother required evidence that he was instilling within his children a sufficient sense of Jewishness to enable us to share in the religious celebrations of our family's "adopted" culture without losing sight of our own Jewish origins. Once I came to understand my father's willingness to acquiesce to her wishes, I also learnt to respect and understand *her* need as a noble and appropriate aspiration.

Sadly, my father's internal religious and philosophical questioning, combined with the family's secrecy concerning the painful aspects of our history, could not finally be resolved for me by "paying lip-service" to our Jewish origins. Neither Hebrew classes nor visits to synagogue ultimately convinced me of my "Jewishness", apart from a vague sense of some sort of cultural connection. Moreover, my father's urgent need to re-establish his professional career on returning from a long war presented him with an additional problem of which I became unconsciously aware. He needed to gain acceptance into a profession largely governed by the attitudes of an elite, privileged, and traditionally conservative autocracy, which I imagine would have guarded cautiously against invasion from "outsiders". Despite a war having been fought against fascism, Jews were still regarded with suspicion in England after the war, and perhaps the label of "alien" can never finally be eradicated from the collective memory.

My father's attitude to this was to play down his Jewish origins publicly and professionally. This attitude was conveyed to us as children, so that while we did not hide our heritage, we also did not publicise it unnecessarily. Outside the immediate family, my parents did not join any Jewish social groups. What I finally understood from this was that we belonged to a wider cultural society, so that our Jewishness didn't really matter much in terms of "who we were".

Subsequently I have wondered whether my father's lack of a religious faith made it easier for him to manage this moral dilemma. Privately, he could continue to maintain a Jewish cultural allegiance, which perhaps eased his conscience about the well-educated public persona, which disguised his origins as a child from a background of uneducated and impoverished Jewish refugees. My father's need was to fit in with the demands of a society that comprised the elite of his profession. Effectively, this meant "playing the game according to the rules"—a message conveyed to me as a child in all sorts of covert ways. Now I can understand the true nature of his conflict—but it did little to help me manage the internal conflict that dominated so much of my early childhood.

Finally, and as a result of analysis, I am left grieving numerous profound losses for which I must allow my parents, and my family of origin, to take responsibility—even while I forgive them and they remain the object of my devoted love. But while I understand that their desire was to protect us from the pain of their own traumatic history, it has left me with another, equally profound pain. Probably it is one they could never have envisaged, otherwise I doubt that they would have left the next generation to bear the legacy of their story. This is the pain of "not knowing"—not knowing the origins of my family's history or the details surrounding the well-kept secrets from which they strove so hard, and so mutually, to protect us. My sadness is that this protection ultimately left me feeling adrift in the world, uncertain and insecure of where I truly belonged. Now I have children and grandchildren of my own. I feel guilt: guilt at the insufficiency of what I have bequeathed to them concerning the legacy of their Jewish heritage. At the same time, I worry about how much trans-generational trauma I *have* inadvertently and unconsciously passed down to them—a legacy about which they, in their turn, will know and understand so little.

It was Anna who helped me appreciate how much my origin as a Jew *did* matter to me—how it had always existed as an unconscious aspect of my being, as a form of collective trauma. With understanding, I was able to make sense of a feeling carried throughout my life: a sense of a deep, underlying sadness for which I was unable to account until I could understand it in Jungian terms as a collective unconscious memory. Anna's thought was that I might be "a conduit for collective sadness", without having any conscious awareness of the origin of such feelings. As I absorbed this perspective, I felt it resonate with every aspect of my being as a profound revelation. Though I had so little knowledge of my family's history, I could understand the way in which I was part of a "collective history", which connected me with "who" and "how" I was in the world.

But more than this, Anna's insight liberated a vital spiritual aspect of my being about which I had always been in denial, because I had previously assumed that "spirituality" equated with religious faith. Since the age of thirteen, I considered myself to be an agnostic, like my father. But—perhaps also like my father—I retain a powerful sense of Man's ability to rise above his physical and intellectual being—through great works of art, a love of humanity, and a generosity of spirit. In recognising this, I retain a "belief", not in religion, but in some kind of innate human potential, which has imbued us with the capacity to transcend the limits of our earthly existence. I retain a precious memory of Anna telling me that she saw me as "a very religious person without a religion." Her perception comforted me by the depth of its understanding.

Finally I learnt to understand my spiritual liberation in terms of Jung's "transcendent function", which mediates between the tension of opposites and expresses itself through symbolic representation. As Anthony Stevens explains:

> awareness of the Shadow means suffering the tension between good and evil in full consciousness, and through that suffering they can be *transcended*. If one can bring oneself to bear the psychic tension that the opposites generate, the problem is raised to a higher plane, where the conflict is resolved … Phenomenologically, the experience is one of liberation combined with an awareness of the inner strength that comes of reaching harmony … with something greater than mere ego. This is the essence of 'religious experience' …[8]

Personally, I know that my liberation from mental and emotional torment was finally reached through this process of suffering, integration, and transcendence, which Anna patiently and lovingly helped me to negotiate over many years. This is the path of individuation—a reconciliation that owes little, if anything, to rational or intellectual thinking: it is a purely symbolic process. From this personal journey, and my continuing work as a psychotherapist, I remain in awe of the huge complexity of the human psyche, the true nature of which remains a mystery always just beyond our grasp. Long may this be so! I believe it is this spirit of "un-knowing" which inspires the best and most creative work of psychotherapy. I view with dread contemporary thinking, which suggests that our psychological complexity can be understood and addressed in terms of "therapeutic techniques" whose efficacy may be "proved" by evidence contained in statistical data. Jung himself objected to the argument that psychological observations could (and should) be quantified and analysed statistically, believing

---

[8] Stevens, A. (1982). *Archetype Revisited: An Updated Natural History of the Self*, p. 277. London: Brunner-Routledge, 2002.

that: "statistics alienate us from our personal perception of life and prevent us from experiencing its meaning".[9]

The same dilemmas continue to re-emerge only to be reconsidered as if they were "new discoveries", and psychotherapy still questions the same arguments as disputed in Jung's lifetime. This is hardly progress—but rather regression to self-justification based on a fundamental human fear. In existential terms, this is a fear of the impossibility of creating "certainty". As I learnt to combine existential philosophy with a Jungian perspective in the course of my analytic journey, an acceptance of the uncertainty of life ultimately became liberating rather than fearful. Now, I choose to maintain a creative hold on the notion of our inherent complexity, by echoing the words of Patrick Casement:

> Just possibly there is something that lies entirely beyond us that will always defy definition, which cannot be grasped or owned. I have therefore come to believe that there is still a place for bowing before mystery.[10]

But these are thoughts based in the here-and-now, and I must return to the fundamental purpose of this history and begin at the beginning … for herein lies the "hidden story" with which I began my journey of analysis with Anna …

---

[9]Stevens, A. (1990). *On Jung*, p. 262. London: Penguin Books, 2002.
[10]Casement, P. (2006). *Learning from Life: Becoming a Psychoanalyst*, p. 194. Sussex: Routledge.

CHAPTER ONE

Today, my eyes don't want to open.
I don't want to experience painful sunlight,
Only soothing darkness.
I don't want today to happen,
Or
I don't want anything to happen today.

Today, I want to hide myself away,
Stay behind a closed door,
Lock myself inside my head,
Take myself away from this time
And stop it from being.

That big, gaping wound
Has started to open up again,
Raw and bloody.
And all I can feel is aching pain
And rising panic.

What can I do
To make this passage of time disappear
And myself cease to exist in it?

In the autumn of 2000, with no grasp of what was happening, I found myself in the grip of a deep depression for the first time in my life. The first and most terrifying sensation was the experience of disintegration. It was a profoundly physical sense of "splitting": firstly, my mind splitting from my body; secondly, my mind itself gradually but unmistakeably "fragmenting".

Though my inner and outer worlds were thrown into chaos, I could recall the precise moment when this process began, and the spoken words that were the catalyst. They embedded themselves deep into my psyche, and within the space of a few days I felt as though an almost total fracture had occurred. The most obvious effect of this, to those closest to me, was that my physical body ceased to matter. In fact, it became the object of my anger, with its inevitable demands for life to be sustained. In my attempt to extinguish these needs as important, the normal routines of life such as eating and sleeping were turned upside down, and became intrusive irrelevancies.

But this was merely the outer manifestation of what was taking place inside my mind. Here, the equivalent of an earthquake was happening, throwing into meaninglessness all former thought and feeling. In that cataclysmic moment when those words were spoken, I felt the "self" I knew collapse and disintegrate within me, driven to destruction by some unconscious process. This was the self upon which I had built and sustained my way-of-being until my fifty-fourth year. I recognised the experience as some kind of "psychological death". But what began as an unconscious process rapidly became conscious, powered by a force hitherto unrecognised, which demanded my subservience to its control. Much later, I understood that my ego had been overwhelmed by internal contents jolted out of the unconscious. A confrontation between ego and self followed, but since my sense of self had disintegrated, it could not save my ego from inevitable fragmentation.

The total collapse of my inner world signalled the start of an internal attack in the form of clamouring, angry, and accusing voices inside my head. But amongst the cacophony, one voice would often take precedence, insistently reiterating the theme of my "badness" for which I must be punished. Under its guidance, a new destructive world was born and grew out of the ruins of my shattered sense of self. It was the only voice which made sense to me in those war-torn regions of my mind. All around me lay the blackened and debased wreckage of what had formerly seemed my life's achievements. Most painful of all, the voice forced me to confront the "illusion" of loving relationships, which it accused me of having created. These were the relationships most dear to me, of which I had been most proud—my long-term marriage and my close relationship with my grown-up children. But the voice warned me that "nothing was what it had formerly seemed"—that these "achievements" contained vital flaws which my personal hubris had veiled. The voice commanded me to look at these deficiencies, take responsibility for their creation, and acknowledge the damage I had inflicted over the years to those I love through my human failings.

In the weeks that followed I submitted to the voice's guidance, without knowing or understanding from where, inside myself, its power had emanated. I could only feel its immense authority, and ultimately found myself forced to believe in the "truth" it told me. As I sat, hour upon hour, motionless in the silent darkness of so many nights, the voice spoke to me, unravelling the meaning of my former life, and finally offering it up to me as a "lie" upon which I had laid the foundations of much future destruction. Sinking deeper into a void of despair and guilt, there seemed no-one with whom I could possibly share the agonising pain of this mental anguish. By this time, I had long since given up all pretence of trying to function in the "normal" world. I no longer shopped, cooked or cleaned. I had given up my work as a teacher, and I could rarely leave the house. As soon as I was close to other people, my psychotic fantasy was the danger that I would "infect" them with the evil contained within myself. No-one was safe from me.

The only solution was to remain isolated from the world. Consequently, I began to turn the natural order of day and night on its head. Time and the outside world no longer made sense to me during nights spent in shadowy wakefulness. At least while the world slept, people would be safe from me. But while the world was safely and silently asleep, inside my head it was never silent. The voice continually demanded attention, bombarding me with accusations of guilt. If everything I had formerly believed and understood about myself was self-deception, this was much worse even than meaninglessness, since the purpose of my life now revealed having harmed others under the guise of virtuousness. With adulthood had come a growing sense of "vocation"—of wanting to give something to others which originated from the "best" aspects of my being. Now the voice forced me to question whether these choices actually signified some darkly self-seeking motives of unacknowledged egotism.

Such thoughts were my regular companions during these nights of mental torture, and no relief accompanied the light of the sun slowly filling the world with its warmth. This did not signal the end of my night-time anguish, but merely the beginning of my daytime fear—of the dangers created by my existence in the world. As dawn emerged I would creep back into hiding, to sleep away the day behind the darkness and safety of drawn curtains.

On one such night events took a dramatic new turn. Alone and awake yet again in the early hours, the unremitting clamour of voices reached a pitch of unbearable torture. Every fragment of my mind seemed to cry out for the pain to be silenced. What stays in my memory is the overwhelming feeling of tension, as if my mind was about to explode. No longer sensible of any capacity for voluntary agency, I submitted myself to the ominous inner force which took control of my actions. I found myself opening the kitchen drawer containing knives. I knew what I was searching for and chose a small knife with a long blade. Automatically, I then opened the box containing the knife sharpener; there must be no risk that the knife would not be equal to its task. Drawing the blade through the sharpening mechanism several times, I became aware of rising excitement. I felt driven by a sense of purpose, and yet it was as if I was standing outside myself—an interested observer watching a drama unfold from the wings. Resting my arm on the worktop, I dug the blade deep into my flesh, dragging it slowly and deliberately across the outside of my wrist. For some inexplicable reason, the pain felt pleasurable. As if in slow motion, I saw the skin part as the blade passed through. Blood oozed gently from the wound, forming a bracelet of bright red beads. In that moment, it seemed the most beautiful sight I had ever witnessed and I gave myself over completely to the unfolding action. I watched as the beads of blood grew, joining together into a half-circle, which trickled neatly from my wrist onto the worktop, forming a small but distinct pool of blood. At the same time, I became aware of a change taking place inside my body. The acute feelings of panic began to subside. My heart stopped pounding, and instead of hyperventilating I could breathe more slowly. The tension was lifting, and with this release the voices inside my head receded from a clamour to a background murmur.

But when I looked, the bracelet of blood had already begun to dry and crack. Terrified that the healing process would signal the return of the deafening voices, I took hold of the knife once again. Obviously I had not done enough to complete the job. What I now realise is that I developed a ritual, in homage to the superior yet invisible inner power which had assumed control over me. I began to elaborate on my "bracelet" by cutting a criss-cross pattern, which ran across the width of my wrist. In my urgency to do the job properly I doubled the pressure on the knife. The cuts were small, but deeper. This time there were no delicate "beads" of blood. The blood spurted out in a messy but distinctive flow from each wound—not pretty but effective. With immense satisfaction, I watched as the blood dripped haphazardly into several large puddles on the worktop. My perverted sense of logic determined that I needed to bring the ritual to a satisfactory conclusion if I was to earn the right to peace and mitigation from punishment, however short-lived. Gently, I placed some folded kitchen paper around my wrist, taking care not to wipe away the blood. The blood soaked through, creating its own unique imprint. I turned my attention to the red puddles staining the worktop. In a grotesque parody of childhood, I began to "play" at making shapes and patterns as if engaged in "finger-painting", smearing the bright red colour as far and wide as it would go. When I was satisfied with what I had created, I devised a further ritual around the process of "cleaning up". When this was over, I examined my ravaged wrist. Now the blood was drying into a thickly distinct pattern. I gazed at it once more before rinsing my wrist under running water. The pain was surprisingly and satisfyingly intense.

Once these rituals had been satisfactorily completed I could stand back and reflect on what had taken place—and on what was happening. Although driven to self-harm by a force outside my control, it seemed to guide me towards a specific destination. This no longer felt like "chaos", but promised "order" if only I would allow myself to be guided there unquestioningly. For now at least, I seemed to have been "rewarded" for my action: the voices were quiet, the painful tension had lifted, and a sense of peacefulness enveloped me like a warm blanket. For the first time in weeks, I could allow myself to spend the few remaining hours of darkness in sleep.

I hid my wound by wearing long sleeved clothes. Removing the dressing after several days, I was gratified to see the remains of my "bracelet" clearly visible as a scar on my wrist. The idea that I needed to mark myself permanently as a form of punishment took hold, and several times a week, when I found myself deafened by the voices, I took refuge in the peace which followed each ritual performance of self-harm. But it wasn't long before the voices demanded more. The ritual was too easy, the pain now a source of pleasurable release from suffering. Some small signs of "normality" had even crept back into my life. I managed the odd supermarket trip; I accepted some occasional supply teaching work; I sometimes found the courage to answer the phone instead of feeling threatened by its ring, and was able to conduct a half-sensible conversation with a friend. But the loudest and most insistent voice reminded me that I had not yet understood or fulfilled the purpose of the rituals, and that self-harm marked the beginning, not the end of the process of punishment.

A period of experimentation followed as I became increasingly "creative" in my efforts to quieten the voice, but it would not let me rest. Then one night, as I placed my arm in waiting for the first sharp kiss of the blade, something made me stop and turn my wrist over. I stared at the pale, unsullied flesh on the underside of my wrist—so white and innocent, unmarked by any signs of violation. Then I was drawn to the sight of the veins, raised, blue, and flowing with lifeblood. In that moment I suddenly understood the destination towards which the voice was leading me. The act of cutting on the *outside* of my wrist was only a practice for what had to follow. Once I had found the courage to repeat this process on the *inside*, the knife would cut across the main artery and end my life. Only then would I find peace … and perhaps forgiveness.

This grim and frightening insight into my destiny was not something I could share with anyone, and yet there was a bizarre sense of relief in having resolved the question of what was to become of my broken and despairing spirit. For now, I lacked the courage to take my own life. But as I increasingly dwelt on the idea of death, there was comfort in a project that seemed to promise a peaceful end to pain and guilt. From now on the wounding appeared to have a purpose, and every bodily attack strengthened my resolve, bringing me a little closer to a final resolution. Following this insight I gave up all efforts to return to a "normal" life. This had become a meaningless pretence in the face of what I now thought I knew.

Perhaps inevitably, this delusion soon encountered its first serious challenge when my terrified husband, Patrick, discovered I was self-harming. Uncertain of where to turn for help, he took advantage of the fact that we were seeing a relationship counsellor at the time. In our next session I found myself pressurised into telling her what I had been doing. We had been seeing her for several months. I had grown fond of her and had learnt to trust her. She had witnessed my trauma when Patrick honestly and unpremeditatedly uttered the cataclysmic words which had provoked my breakdown. Though I didn't *want* to share my secret with her, I assumed that she would understand the unbearable pain and know how to support me. Instead, she turned on me accusingly, informing me that she couldn't continue to work with us unless I made her a promise to stop self-harming. Bewildered, I provided her with the promise—but it was a lie. Now taboo, the subject was never mentioned again. Sinking deeper into depression I continued to self-harm secretly. In the sessions that followed I sat turned away from her and Patrick, refusing to talk. Though the sessions dwindled on painfully for a few months, the therapeutic relationship had foundered irretrievably on the rock of her fear, sinking ultimately to a messy end. This incident became further proof of my potential to harm others. I knew I had become a difficult and challenging client, but even from the depths of my despair, I struggled to reconcile my understanding of her role with what had happened. My depression had begun in her presence, brought about by her insightful intervention, which prompted Patrick to utter the words that signalled the start of my inner earthquake. Did this not make my sickness her responsibility? Wasn't it her role to care for and support me in my despair? To offer me help, not angry accusations leaving me feeling guilty for the vulnerability which I had exposed in her? But the message seemed clear: I was a dangerous and unmanageable client. I felt as though she had abandoned me and swum safely to shore, to watch me drown in the sea of my own misery. Even so, it seemed easier at the time to forgive her than to forgive myself, and I continued to mourn her loss through a prolonged and pathological period of grief that lasted many years.

With the benefit of hindsight, training, and experience, I have learnt to look back on these events with compassion and understanding ... but not forgiveness. This dramatic "abandonment" increased my psychotic fear that the powers of evil within me posed an even greater threat than I had imagined. The experience was an additional burden to the legacy of guilt that I already carried. But while I lived in fear of the harm I might do to others, the profound harm done to me as a result of this first counselling experience sent destructive shock waves through my psychic structure which it was to take many years of painstaking love and patience by another to repair.

* * *

Autumn transformed itself into winter with grey inevitability. Days and nights became merged in barely distinguishable gloom, and so it was in my internal world as my personal crisis deepened with autumn's death throes. Events began to move towards a crisis. The egotistical nature of major depression is that it has no concept of the pain it causes to others. As Patrick floundered beneath the heavy demands of full-time teaching and having to compensate for my deficiencies at home, I was oblivious to his pain. As he got up for work I would creep into bed, exhausted by a night of internal dialogue. When Patrick returned, I was often exactly as he had left me, hardly having stirred all day. And when the clocks moved backwards heralding the real onset of winter, I was comforted that the early disappearance of daylight made it easier for me to remain hidden in darkness.

Close friends were also deeply concerned by now. But helpless to do anything, they contented themselves with bombarding Patrick with "advice" about what *he* should be doing to help me—and I suspect that these "good intentions" only added to his burden. One such dear friend since childhood gave me the number of an analyst she had consulted. She lived and practiced in an area quite unfamiliar to me—and analysis sounded expensive. "It was worth every penny," my friend declared emphatically. I couldn't imagine getting myself into a car and driving myself to some unknown place, to talk to an unknown person about my mental anguish. Leaving the house had become a major undertaking, and it took all my courage to talk to the people I knew and loved. How could I possibly talk to a total stranger? And my difficult experience of relationship counselling had already convinced me that I was "an unmanageable client" who was damaging her counsellor. At regular intervals my friend would phone to ask if I had made the call. Patrick would reply that he didn't know, because I was hardly talking to him. On the rare occasions when she was able to speak to me, I told her that I had lost the number. Firmly she would make me write it down again, while I listened to further emphatic assurances about the immeasurable value of analysis and the skill of this analyst in particular. I think it took three repetitions of this scenario to convince my friend that she was wasting her time.

About ten days before Christmas, I did something to push Patrick's patience and fear beyond his powers of endurance. I can't remember what I did, except that Patrick declared that he was going to phone our medical practice and ask if a doctor would see me. It was a Saturday morning and I knew that only "emergency appointments" were seen on Saturdays. Anyway, I didn't believe Patrick meant what he said. Unlike some of my friends, it was totally out of character for him to take matters into his own hands, especially if this involved making a decision on behalf of someone else. But I underestimated the depths of Patrick's crisis—and how could I not have done? So wrapped up in my own pain, it had not occurred to me to consider how much he might be suffering. From another room, I realised that he was as good as his word. I heard him talking to the receptionist, who no doubt wanted a convincing reason for offering an emergency appointment so late on Saturday morning. I heard him tell her, "My wife is suffering from depression and needs to see a doctor urgently." Some more conversation, then he put the phone down and turned to face me. "They've told me to bring you to the surgery straightaway."

I recall a surge of emotions—a tidal wave of anger, pain, disbelief, confusion. What gave him the right to announce to the world that I had "depression"? Perhaps surprisingly, I hadn't even given my suffering a name, yet Patrick had taken it upon himself to make a diagnosis on my behalf. I was enraged. And yet beneath the anger, I was aware of a tiny, sadly despairing voice, which whispered with relief, "You *know* you need help. Perhaps this is for the best …" Nevertheless I refused to allow Patrick to take me to the surgery, angrily insisting that I didn't need his help to get myself there. When I walked in to see the doctor, he also became the target of my rage. But the fact that I went at all indicated my unspoken fear … the fear that I had crossed some hidden border dividing sanity from madness.

I will always be grateful to this lovely man for his sensitive handling of my pain, and the way he managed and understood my rage. His "medical explanation" of depression as "mainly a physical condition resulting from a lack of serotonin", was intended to reassure me that I was not going mad. Antidepressants, I was told, would help me to "cope better" by increasing the level of serotonin in the brain. I was deeply resistant, and resentful that my weeks of mental anguish had been reduced to a medical condition which could be controlled by pharmaceutical drugs. I expressed angry doubts about the label he was so eager to attach to me. How could he know what it felt like to be inside my head, and that this qualified as depressive illness? His response was reassuring. "I've got a very useful 'ruler' for measuring depression. Let's see what it tells us." He reached into a drawer and produced a ruler which, at first glance, looked like something a child might own. Initially I found myself amused by the row of "smiley faces", which seemed to decorate its length. "Which of these faces represents how you are feeling?" he asked me. Looking closely, I realised that the smiling faces gradually transformed from "happiness" to all the emotions ranging from sadness to despair. I was drawn to the very last face in the row: the saddest and most despairing. I liked its position, which suggested that it might "drop off the edge" at any moment … and land who-knew-where? But perhaps this was an over-emphasis of my despair. After all, if I truly believed my life was beyond hope I probably wouldn't have come to the surgery at all. So I pointed to the penultimate face, telling the doctor "I feel just one step away from falling off the edge." He grimaced painfully. "Well, I think that sounds like a pretty depressed place to be." Reluctantly I found myself agreeing with him, and also finally agreeing to take the antidepressants. Once again I experienced that small ripple of relief briefly washing over me. "But the questions I'm struggling to answer won't go away because I'm taking tablets." "No," he agreed. "I think it would help to talk to someone about how you are feeling. Do you know of a therapist? If not, I'll find someone for you." Guiltily, I told him that a friend had given me a name, but that I hadn't yet contacted her. I promised him I would do so as soon as possible, and he made an appointment for me to see him again straight after the Christmas break. As I left, I realised that we had been together for over an hour.

Naturally Patrick wanted to know what the doctor had said.

> "Well, it seems you were right," I confessed less than graciously.
> "I'm depressed. I've got to start taking antidepressants, and I've promised to phone the therapist."
> "Good."

This was the only word Patrick uttered, but it conveyed the unacknowledged sense of relief we both felt—that somewhere, out there, was the promise of support for us both, even though precisely what this meant remained shrouded in mystery. Rather humiliatingly, I had to phone my friend to ask her therapist's number for the fourth time. I had somehow managed to "lose" the details yet again. I listened to more reassurances, and tried hard to manage her thinly veiled gratification at my news. While I believed that I could trust her judgement about her analyst, I knew that I had now given her the ammunition she needed to be "on my case" with renewed vigour. I felt vulnerable and exposed, but tried to convince myself that her need to control my care came from a loving place. It took several more days to gather the strength and courage to make that call.

It was the week before Christmas. The voice at the other end was firm. "I'm not seeing any new patients before Christmas. You can try phoning me again in January when my practice re-opens."

CHAPTER TWO

Don't come too close—
Inside me it is reckless and damaging,
Full of danger and destruction.
All infectious and contaminated.

Stay
The other side of the fence,
Where at least if you don't know,
You won't be harmed.

This side is not safe,
For you or me.
Somewhere within these depths
I have the power to hurt and destroy.

On the surface all seems quiet.
But deep inside is a burning
Seething mass,
Constantly at war with itself.

Both a threat and a promise—
The power to devastate and demolish
Is only invisible for now.
It lies dormant, ready to burst out.

I grappled courageously with Christmas that year, but it was an uphill battle. By the time it arrived, the whole family knew that I was struggling with depression. Patrick was communicating regularly with our son living in Spain and my sister in Australia. Behind the scenes, I also knew that Patrick turned to his sister for support. I was grateful for her sensitivity in providing this so unobtrusively. I had invited Patrick's family to spend Christmas Day at our house, together with our daughter and her husband. Finally, I confessed to Patrick that I couldn't face the prospect of so many people. Gallantly and without complaint he phoned his sister and cancelled their visit. "We've been invited to join them after lunch instead," Patrick told me. "You don't have to go if you don't want to—but let's see how you feel." My "secret" now glaringly exposed, I felt the merest twinge of embarrassment but couldn't afford to dwell on it. Embarrassment was low on my list of anxieties. I wanted our daughter and son-in-law to come for Christmas lunch, and somehow a meal was produced, with my daughter lovingly holding the fort while I disappeared erratically to control several panic attacks. I had refused to commit myself to joining the rest of the family, but finally agreed to go. My absence would cause further concern, and I knew Patrick would be anxious about leaving me alone for fear of what I might do to myself. Several glasses of wine provided enough Dutch courage to face the rest of the family. At one point during the evening, amidst the noisy laughter, Patrick found a moment to put his arm round me and whisper, "You're doing really well." I wondered if he understood that this was the result of having numbed myself into a semi-stupor induced by alcohol and antidepressants.

The year laboured painfully to its close. The celebrations over, everyone's life gradually returned to normal—with the exception of my life. It was a relief to have survived the ordeal of Christmas, but it did nothing to lessen my profound misery. I was still adrift, unable to function in a world in which I no longer wanted to exist but without the courage to end it. Before Christmas my friend had checked up on me again: had I phoned her analyst yet? I told her the outcome of my call. At least this would guarantee me some peace from her pressing enquiries for a few weeks. But now January was here, and as I contemplated the prospect of making a second call my courage failed me. I had felt deeply rejected by the rather brusque, matter-of-fact voice which reflected no hint of compassion for my suffering. Did I really want to run the risk of further rejection? Then there was the fear that I might cause her harm, as I believed I had harmed our relationship counsellor. I couldn't face the responsibility of "infecting" yet another human being with my "badness".

Another phone call from my friend early in January, together with pressure from my doctor, convinced me that I must find the strength to make that call. I was increasingly desperate and knew of nowhere else to turn. Imagining that she would ask my reasons for wanting to see her, I practised my reply over and over again in my head. It sounded so messy and complicated. I didn't understand what had happened myself, and certainly wasn't confident that I could make sense of it to anyone else. I put her number next to the phone—a prominent reminder of what I still needed to do. But it took time before I finally steeled myself to make the call.

The ringing stopped and I recognised the voice that answered. My heart pounding, I stumbled through an explanation of who I was, my friend's name, my phone call before Christmas: "Yes, I remember," came the reply. A pause … "I think I need to see you … I need help." I waited fearfully for the inevitable questions. Another brief pause, then, "I can see you next Thursday morning at ten-thirty." The ordeal was over; no questions, except whether I knew her address. I cut this short by assuring her that my friend would tell me the way. I was struggling for breath and on the verge of another panic attack.

* * *

On a cold grey January morning, when day seemed barely discernible from night, I found myself on Anna's doorstep. I rang the bell ten minutes early, true to my mother's mantra that "it's always better to be early than late". I dreaded everything about this undertaking, including the journey to an unfamiliar place. Not only did I not know the way, I had hardly left the house for weeks, let alone driven any distance. On that morning, I also realised that I had almost forgotten how to dress myself appropriately for an excursion into the outside world. My alienated existence over recent months had turned such matters into irrelevancies. Knowing my fear of getting lost and being late, Patrick came to my rescue. A week beforehand, he offered to do a "trial run" to Anna's house. He also typed out precise details, so that when the day came I felt reassured that I wouldn't get lost. Nevertheless, I struggled to contain the rising panic as I found myself traversing unfamiliar territory. But thanks to him I had arrived safely—on the doorstep of this unknown being whom I needed to trust to put my fragmented and psychotic mind back together again.

Anna opened the door. I was immediately reassured to see that we were of a similar age. Until that moment I hadn't realised how important this was to me. I didn't sense anything overtly welcoming in her manner. Rather, her greeting was serious and business-like, as was her appearance. Leading me into a lobby area adjoining her consulting room, she asked me to take a seat. She then closed her consulting room door behind her. I experienced mortifying pangs of guilt about my early arrival. Inexplicably, my mother's mantra had let me down; on this occasion "arriving early" was evidently the wrong thing to have done. I felt humiliated, childish, and stupid. Had I already made some kind of *faux pas* that would influence her attitude to me? It would be a long ten minutes. Somehow I had to quell the rising panic. I decided to take in the surroundings. After all, this was Anna's home. There were bound to be all sorts of clues about the kind of person she was.

Briefly, I lost myself in this exercise. The first thing to catch my eye was an upright piano. Who was the pianist, I wondered? It had a solid, unfussy appearance—not shiny and polished, like my mother's baby grand remembered from childhood. This piano looked as if it had done good service over the years. Some music stood waiting to be played, but just too distant for me to discern the title. I noticed a shelf above which contained more music, some in hard-bound books. There was more musical evidence around the room, in the form of several unusual and exotic musical instruments. I hoped it was Anna who was musical. I had fond memories of listening to my mother playing the piano throughout my childhood. A fleeting thought suggested that it would be reassuring to have this sense of connection between Anna and my mother, though I had no idea why this should be so.

I turned to look behind where I was sitting. Above my head was another shelf containing photograph albums. I longed to get up and walk around—to touch the instruments, to peek at the music and the photograph albums. Instead, I scanned the room more closely, taking in the atmosphere. It had a comfortable, lived-in feel. I sensed that everything displayed there signified something special for Anna. A picture suddenly came to mind, of several pairs of different sized wellies by the front door—and a bicycle with a basket. I was convinced that this was a family home; that children had grown up here and that Anna's family were an important aspect of who she was. It was comforting to glimpse these imagined aspects of her other life.

Abruptly, my reverie was broken by the consulting room door opening. "You can come in now." Anna beckoned me in, indicating a large, comfortable couch. I sat at one end, suddenly feeling very small and lost. Anna sat in a revolving leather chair, diagonally facing me. Next to her was an imposing desk strewn with books, journals and papers. We looked at each other. Her direct, unflinching eye contact felt painfully exposing. My first encounter with analysis had begun.

* * *

Extreme anxiety rendered much of that first session a blur, but the opening minutes remain as clear as on that day, and will remain so forever. Anna began by offering some brief information about the way she worked. She sounded firm and authoritative. I felt scared of her and was reminded of my headmistress, instructing us all of the school rules on our first day. Too frightened to absorb most of what she was saying, I became aware of something that sounded important. Anna was explaining that this was "long-term, open-ended work", and wanted me to confirm that I understood and accepted this. Unable to express my huge relief I could only nod in agreement, silently grateful that I could stay with Anna for as long as I wanted to, with no threat of being told it was time to end.

Having completed this process, she handed me an information sheet and sat back in her chair. We now sat in silence. Time dragged interminably, Anna observing me closely while I waited for her to speak. Eventually I averted my gaze, unable to maintain eye contact any longer. Feeling bewildered and irritated, I finally spoke:

"Aren't you going to ask me anything?"
A pause: "You seem to want me to tell you what to say."

Anna's voice was now quiet and calm. Her expression remained impassive. She seemed to be waiting for something from me, but I was at a loss to know what it was. Trying to sound rational and in control, I responded:

> "Well, I'm not expecting you to tell me what to say exactly. But we've been working with a relationship counsellor, and she asked us a lot of questions at the beginning."

Anna's expression softened and I detected compassion in her voice.

> "This isn't the same as counselling" she informed me gently.
> "But you must have some questions you want to ask me?" I queried.
> Another pause; "I don't need to ask you questions. Answers will emerge in their own good time."

How would the answers emerge? How *could* they, if we continued to sit in silence? I felt increasingly bewildered by these unfamiliar responses. I had a sense of being engaged in some strange map-reading game in which I had to find my way without being given the map. Anna was offering no clues as to the direction I should follow. She seemed content to wait patiently until I was ready to start. And yet, despite my rising anxiety, I was in no doubt that Anna was "with" me—she had neither disconnected nor detached, and though I didn't know what was happening, I had a strong sense that Anna knew exactly what she was doing.
Seconds continued to tick by.

> "Well, I suppose I'd better tell you what's happened to me …"

Still no response. The silence had become extremely unnerving. It was obvious that nothing was going to happen unless I made it happen—and Anna wasn't going to relieve me of that responsibility. I summoned up the courage and blurted something out:

> "It's hard to know where to begin … It seems to have started so long ago … but we didn't realise at the time. And now it's all come back to haunt me and I don't know what to do about it."

Involuntarily, the tears began to flow. My mind floundered around, lost in the story of my pain as I struggled to think of where and how it had all started.

"You're shaking," Anna observed quietly.
"I know I am."

We sat in silence again. I could no longer look at her, but I felt and feared her penetrating gaze. The prospect of exposing myself to the pain of telling my story made me feel physically sick. I was acutely embarrassed by my shaking body and its visible expression of fear and distress. I needed to control what I recognised as the onset of a panic attack. As a way of deflecting my fear from thoughts of myself, I focused my mind on Anna and the present moment of our encounter. Instinctively, as self-protection, I heard myself asking her a question:

"Do you have any children?"

Anna absorbed this and looked away, as if contemplating somewhere in distant space. I would come to recognise this need to avert her gaze as evidence of serious reflection. I also learnt not to interrupt her at such moments. Now I felt able to watch her—wanting to witness the process of the formulation of her reaction. Seemingly endless seconds ticked by while she measured her response.

"You want to know if we share a similar experience of being mothers," she finally suggested.

She had understood precisely the significance underlying my question. I felt relieved and comforted. Yes, I agreed that this was important to me.

"I'm sure I couldn't work with someone who was not a mother themselves," I heard myself saying.

I surprised myself by the forcefulness and candour of this reply. Until I heard myself utter these words, I had been quite unconscious of any such need. Something in Anna's response had provided an opening—an invitation to recognise my hitherto unacknowledged need to share my experience of motherhood with someone who could comprehend it from direct experience.

"Yes, I *do* have children ... three boys, to be precise," Anna smilingly disclosed.

I was startled by her openness. She had given me more information than I had expected. I noticed how her smile softened her features and her eyes danced with humour. I felt sure that I had touched some vital aspect of Anna's being.

"That's a lot of boys," I reflected, half-humorously.
"Yes", she agreed.

Another silence followed. I needed to ask a follow-up question, stemming from the clues I had tried to piece together outside her consulting room. Anna's unexpected openness had fortified my courage.

"Did your children grow up in this house?"

This time I was aware of the briefest of pauses before her reply. "Yes," she answered—but without further elaboration. Some quality in her voice was enough to alert me to an invisible boundary surrounding further questioning on this subject.

* * *

Despite the anguish and discomfort of that first session, my most memorable recollections stand out clearly as the foundation on which my trust in Anna, and in the process of analysis, were built—though this was a slow and painful process. It is one of the many things I treasure from our relationship—her willingness to share aspects of herself. I continue to cherish this as evidence of her creativity and instinctive understanding of my therapeutic needs. The subject of self-disclosure remains a problematic one for psychotherapists, and perhaps more so for analysts trained in the classical tradition. And Anna always let me know, by way of a word, a look, a tone of voice, if she experienced a question as an attempt to cross an un-breachable boundary. These were the questions arising from mere curiosity. But "important" questions were always answered once Anna had explored and recognised my need to ask them: and she never once faltered in her ability to divine the significant need which had prompted them.

As I picture that first session drawing to its close, another significant memory emerges. I recollect nervously asking Anna:

"Am I your 'patient' or your 'client'?"

She paused, scanning my expression closely in an attempt to divine the unconscious concern beneath the question.

"My patient," she replied gently.

Without knowledge or understanding of psychotherapy, I was puzzled to hear myself ask that question. Where had it come from and why was I asking it? But in the instant following her reply, I understood my need to ask it. A wave of relief engulfed me as I gratefully accepted the implication in her response. Though Anna never openly pathologised my condition or spoke in terms of "illness", I believe we both acknowledged this reality in that moment. If Anna regarded me as her "patient", this implied her acceptance of my "illness" and a commitment to my recovery. I sensed Anna's strength to stay with me, wherever our uncertain journey might take us.

* * *

Within minutes of my return home, the phone rang. My friend had wasted no time in ringing to check up on me.

"Well, how did you get on?"

A minor interrogation followed, as I knew it would.

So how *had* I got on? More important than my friend's interrogation were the questions I needed to ask myself. The truth was that I had found Anna's physical presence disconcerting and unsettling. The evidence gleaned about her outside her consulting room seemed strangely at odds with the person I had experienced on the other side of that door. I tried replaying the session in my mind—the neutrality of composure reflected in her voice; her discomforting gaze which made me feel naked and defenceless. It was as though Anna's eyes had penetrated into the dark recesses of my soul, which I so feared to reveal. I was convinced that she had seen and understood everything about me, including those parts of which I remained unaware. And now there was nowhere to hide. I felt frightened by her. The contrast between her self-contained, dispassionate presence and my floundering vulnerability had left me feeling deeply exposed.

Then I allowed my mind to return to those glimpses of that "other" Anna—the one who existed in a different time and space outside the confines of her room. Occasionally, just for a few seconds, I had heard and felt that "other" presence—in the unexpectedly soft and tender resonance of her voice; in the smile, which hinted at humour in her reference to her "three boys". And if Anna had indeed perceived the blackness in my soul, she had not passed judgement on me—as our couple counsellor had done. I struggled to make sense of the bewildering paradox that was my initial experience of her. But despite these uncertainties, I had taken away something unique from this first encounter—something I couldn't yet put into words or understand. Shut away together in that surreal fifty-minute encounter, Anna's presence had conveyed a sense of "safety", and contained the strength I both feared and yearned for. As I thought of the many clues about the Anna who would leave her consulting room and return to her music and family concerns, they promised a resonance between our shared experiences. Though the pieces of these two disparate images refused to connect, I seem unconsciously to have resolved to make them fit at some time in the future. I was embarked on a project, and regardless of the anxiety and bewilderment, I knew I would continue to return to Anna, and the magic and mystery of her consulting room.

CHAPTER THREE

*There's a space in between my hands.
On either side my tears are falling
In time to the music.
But in the middle I can breathe more easily
And see more clearly.*

*If I were an artist
I would draw the space between my hands.
In that tiny gap lies the power for release.
But I cannot draw,
Only record in words how powerful the tears and pain
On either side of that space.*

*That is where I want to be—
Inside that space
With just enough room to grow and change,
If I am brave enough to face the challenge.*

*But for tomorrow
I am full of fear.
Tomorrow, again,
I will be on either side,
Hiding the tears behind my hands,
Frightened away by the freedom
Which seems to be on offer
In the space between my hands.*

Somehow I discovered the courage during that first fearful session to tell Anna my story, although the details unfolded gradually over time. In one of the many silences, a space emerged in which I rolled back the passage of years. I found myself describing all the agony and anguish of the young mother I had once been, whose love and trust had been betrayed during the pregnancy of my second child and in the year following his birth; a double betrayal, as "the other woman" was someone I believed to be a close friend. We had shared our first pregnancies and our children became regular playmates in the years following. Naïvely innocent, I offered her the safety of my home when she decided to end her unhappy marriage and had nowhere else to go. Gradually, and without understanding why, I watched my own marriage fall apart. Patrick withdrew from the children and me, or when not withdrawn, he would constantly find fault with me. Eventually, when I could no longer ignore the evidence, he acknowledged that they were having an affair.

Unwittingly, I had set up a "triangle" exposing our relationship to threat. I became the "third corner" of that triangle, alienated and excluded by the other two. Until this insight, I had never given credit to the truth in the saying, "two's company, three's a crowd". I learnt this truth the hard way. Overnight the bottom dropped out of my world. Instinctively, I was driven to call on all my primal maternal reserves, in an effort to maintain a semblance of "normality" for my children.

> "You were traumatised by what happened to you," Anna pronounced firmly.

Her words had a powerful impact. I had not thought of my experience in these terms before.

> "Are you sure about that?" I questioned tentatively. "Marriages break down all the time. What made *my* situation particularly traumatic?"
>
> "As a mother with a young child and a baby, all your maternal defences would have been aroused to protect your children."

Anna's words struck an instant chord with my memory of that strangely ambivalent emotional period. Despite everything, I had never doubted my love for Patrick. He was a good and loving father, and I loathed the possibility that our children might become yet another "casualty of divorce". I struggled with my desperate fear of losing him, both for my children and myself. I had never allowed myself to acknowledge the depth of this fear, and events so rocked my world that my unconscious need focused on building all my inner strength, so that I would never have to rely or feel dependent on anyone again. The world was suddenly dangerous, insecure, and full of hidden threats disguised as "love". Hearing Anna interpret my pain, I re-lived the memory of how I began to arm myself for battle in defence of my young family.

* * *

That summer I took the children to Wales for a month, leaving Patrick torn between indecision and unacknowledged guilt. We stayed with another close friend from schooldays with two children of a similar age. Her memory of that period is much clearer than mine, though I am left with a deep impression of how her love and support helped me to endure those first harrowing months. Years later I was shocked by her reminder of how ill I became, my repressed pain surfacing in huge boils all over my body. I recall how she would often tuck me up in bed in the afternoon, insisting that I sleep while she took all the children out somewhere. "I remember thinking how incredibly brave you were," she told me. I had no sense of "bravery" then, only the urge to survive with enough strength to support us through whatever ordeals lay ahead.

Patrick came to spend a week with us, but his inability to hide his emotional detachment from us all only made my task more difficult. On family outings, instigated by me, he would lag behind looking angry and miserable. The children began asking awkward questions: "Why isn't Daddy walking with us?" "Why isn't he talking to us?" I attempted to deflect their questions with some "safe" response. "Daddy's not feeling very well today." But I felt forced to overcompensate for Patrick's remoteness by summoning up enough emotional resourcefulness for the two of us.

During the years that followed Patrick's decision to stay with us, our relationship moved into a new, but no less damaging dimension. Continuing to hide my wounds behind the strength, which had enabled me to survive, I gradually turned this strength against Patrick with damaging and destructive force. Anna enabled me to recognise this as the unconscious expression of my desire for revenge and punishment. In Jungian terms, my *animus* was in full flight, and under its authority I grew increasingly ruthless and domineering. I described to Anna how I clearly remembered making two promises to myself at this time. Firstly, I swore that: "No man will ever make me feel insecure or vulnerable again." I determined to embark on a career that would allow me to be financially independent if I ever needed to be in the future. My trust in Patrick as my "protector" had disappeared, and by September I had begun a teacher training course. My second promise was more sinister and less conscious, and it developed a momentum of its own with the passing years. I resolved that if Patrick chose to stay with us, he would do so on *my* terms. I did not know exactly what this meant, but it was clearly linked to the first promise by its implication of "control".

In the course of analysis, I came to recognise how our repressed pain surfaced roughly every seven years. Another period of turmoil would erupt, causing us both to question our choice to stay together. Perhaps the space created between us once our children had grown up and left home finally forced us to confront the situation. I could no longer hide behind "young motherhood" as an excuse for avoiding our problems.

> "It's unfortunate that you didn't seek help at the time it all began," Anna reflected, with irritating logic.

Yes, I remember thinking: how wonderful is hindsight in enabling us to spot the error of our ways—generally when it is too late to rectify the damage it has caused!

> "I probably *would* have done, if I'd known then that couple counselling existed," I commented peevishly, "… but nobody ever offered or suggested it to us."

When another crisis erupted in the autumn of 2000, more than thirty years later, I presented Patrick with an ultimatum: either I would seek the advice of a solicitor, or we would go to couple counselling. He agreed to counselling, but, unsurprisingly, left it to me to make the first move.

* * *

I first met Gemma, our relationship counsellor, one evening in early November 2000, and immediately warmed to her. I saw her alone at first. Following my ultimatum, Patrick had made no further reference to his agreement to attend counselling. I had grown uncertain of his intentions and only told him of the arranged session as I was leaving that evening. I found it easy to talk to Gemma. She was a good listener and seemed able to empathise with my pain. I cried copious amounts of tears and was surprised by the relief and lack of embarrassment I felt. Gemma suggested that Patrick should also attend a first session alone, so that he could tell his side of the story. She then asked that we attend all future sessions together. I expected reluctance from Patrick, especially to the idea of attending a session alone, but instead he expressed his willingness. It is evidence of how little empathy I felt for Patrick that it never occurred to me that he also needed a space for his pain to be heard and understood.

Those Monday evening sessions rapidly became a significant focus of our week. Sometimes uncomfortable, and frequently painful, I nevertheless began to look forward to our fifty minutes with Gemma. It was a contained space where we could express our grievances towards each other safely, without our hurt feelings degenerating into an unseemly, deprecating feud. Despite this, after several weeks, neither of us had disclosed to Gemma the episode of Patrick's affair. With hindsight, I understand what blocked the revelation of such a significant event in our first experience of counselling.

In my own practice, clients often express bewilderment or disbelief at the idea that repressed pain resulting from a much earlier episode in their lives has surfaced—perhaps as projection, symptoms of illness, addiction, or a repeated behavioural response which has become a coping mechanism. Similarly for me, the truth was that it simply had not occurred to my conscious mind that an unhappy event over thirty years ago might be at the core of our current relationship difficulties. Learning that unconscious processes are beyond our control can come as a revelation, though the relief from such understanding may take a great deal longer to emerge. As we sat with Gemma, I had no way of knowing that the repressed, painful contents of my unconscious were now demanding to be acknowledged in consciousness.

Precise details of our discourse are lost to me now, but I recall one session in which Patrick was bemoaning my apparent indifference towards him. I remember the indignant debate that took place inside my head, before I turned to him angrily and declared:

> "Well, *you* were the one that had an affair, not me! I've never been unfaithful to you or shown an interest in anyone else."

My words brought a temporary halt to all conversation. Patrick looked down at the floor, avoiding eye contact. There was silence as Gemma looked expectantly from one to the other of us. I wish I could remember precisely what followed my cataclysmic disclosure. I think I went into shock at feeling myself suddenly submerged in acute pain, which had at last found an opening to emerge after thirty years. It was a decisive moment. In the following sessions, Gemma tried hard to give Patrick a similar opening to explain his experience of that time. But for him there was to be no such "cataclysmic revelation". Though he never denied the affair, he remained adamant in declaring that he had "lost all memory" of significant details. Gemma wondered if Patrick was guarding himself from the memory of his own painful experience. If so, it still left hanging in the air the many questions which had plagued me at the time, and which remained unanswered. Now they had surfaced again, if only in *my* memory. "Pandora's box" had truly been opened, and in the weeks that followed I began to re-live all the painful questioning of that horrific period. But before long, another piece of the jigsaw fell into place, when I finally understood how the emotional repercussion of these unanswered questions had led to the two decisive "promises" I had made to myself.

A few weeks later, I found myself recounting to Gemma an event recently told to me by our son, which I intended as an example of Patrick's "weak-mindedness". Our son had been talking to his father about our relationship problems. Patrick had expressed his unhappiness at my controlling behaviour. Our son had responded, "Then why don't you stand up to her?" to which Patrick eventually replied, "… Because it's not worth the bother."

On hearing this, Gemma turned to Patrick and asked,

> "I wonder what you were feeling when you expressed that thought to your son?"

There was a long pause. Patrick averted his gaze from Gemma, as he always did when her questions demanded difficult answers. Finally he responded:

"I suppose I just feel 'surplus to requirements'."

I recognised the attempt at jocularity in his tone and choice of expression—but it didn't fool me, or Gemma. What I heard in Patrick's words was an intense expression of his pain, and I suddenly understood how I had been the cause of it. In a split second, more than thirty years of troubled marriage flashed across my mind's eye. In that fateful revelation I saw how I had gradually but insistently used Patrick's guilt to deprive him of his "voice", until he felt that there was no space for him to express himself openly in our relationship, or in his relationship with his children. This was the meaning suddenly revealed in those "promises" I had made to myself. I had effectively pronounced a life sentence of punishing silence on Patrick ... and despite what he had done, I didn't believe he deserved this.

I experienced a violent explosion of grief—an expression of profound physical pain which erupted from somewhere deep inside the core of my being. In that moment, my mind and body united in an experience of affliction for which there was no adequate language of mourning. What I wanted in that instant was to disappear from the world—to cease to exist. But all I could do was to physically turn away from Patrick and Gemma, and give vent to my grief through inconsolable tears. These were agonising tears of guilt, destined to be shed throughout many years of future work with Anna.

But it was mainly from myself that I wanted to hide. In that moment, I understood how the strength on which I had learnt to place all trust in my survival had turned into a force for destruction. That strength had become my *animus shadow*, though I had no understanding of this at the time. It was a shadow which would continue to haunt me for years, in poetry and dreams ... and which still has the power to erupt unexpectedly into life. Internalised, it became re-born as my desire for self-destruction.

When we returned to Gemma a week later, I had sunk into a major depressive episode, which proved beyond her skill to contain.

CHAPTER FOUR

Today hurt, but it was good.
After it was over
I could feel your strength soaking into me,
Helping to mend and glue together so many broken bits
That hadn't seemed to fit together before.

Something in me is feeling brave ....
Brave enough to let you take the first few steps
Across what was a broken bridge,
Onto my island.
Now the dangerous fractures have been strapped up,
It is safe—
Safe enough for you to cross.

And I will be there,
Hearing, listening, watching,
Welcoming you and taking strength from your strength.
Waiting for that day
When everything is repaired,
And the bridge is safe enough
To let some others cross.

What Anna did in that first session was to free me to an acceptance of the repressed suffering which had made the deep wound of betrayal unable to heal. She had "given me permission" to acknowledge it as a traumatic experience. I felt strangely comforted. Though I could not have expressed it at the time, Anna was offering a safe space in which to probe the depths of my unconscious in a search for whatever lay buried in its darkest corners. In time, this "first story" would reveal roots reaching deep into the bedrock of my psychic structure.

But what Anna's words had *not* managed to do was to absolve me of the guilt I felt for the wounds I had inflicted on Patrick. By now Patrick was ready to forgive and be forgiven. But thirty years was *more* than a life sentence! I could not forgive myself, nor could I conceive of a time when I would be able to do so. As our sessions progressed, the theme of "punishment" was always sharply in focus. The punishment I had inflicted on Patrick now seemed so vastly out of proportion to his "crime" that the whole situation was turned on its head in my distorted perspective. Now *I* was the one who deserved to be punished, convinced that nothing less than a sentence of death would absolve me of guilt for the harm I had done.

We were meeting once a week in those early months, but before long Anna suggested increasing the frequency of our sessions. This was clearly appropriate in view of my precarious emotional state, which continued to urge me towards suicide. Nevertheless I was dismayed by the suggestion that I attend three sessions a week. In my ignorance, I assumed that every session represented a step forward in my recovery. Anna's words dealt me a sharp blow, which I immediately internalised as "criticism" of my efforts.

> "That sounds as though you think I am getting worse, not better," I retorted.

Unperturbed by my anger, Anna patiently explained that it was about providing the continuity and support that she considered necessary. It was not possible, she explained, to provide this in once-weekly sessions. I threw her support back at her because it sounded like an implication of "failure". I didn't voice these angry thoughts precisely; instead I made excuses, mainly about the additional expense. Anna brushed these aside, recognising them for what they were—deflections disguising my underlying resistance. I was fearful of putting my complete trust in her, and she would refer to this anxious pattern of attachment as "your fear of putting all your eggs in one basket." My conscious mind wanted to believe in her, but fear continued to throw obstacles in our way. Undoubtedly my earlier counselling experience was a trigger for this response, creating a block to my willingness to trust Anna.

* * *

"Falling in love with your therapist" is a frequent subject for humour—though rarely, I suspect, amongst clients whose therapists have mishandled the intensity of feeling that this can arouse. And it doesn't necessarily matter whether client and therapist are of the same sex. When we began counselling with Gemma I was very ready to engage in a therapeutic relationship, and was quickly drawn to her charismatic personality. She appeared warm, sensitive and humorous—an infectious combination which drew me irresistibly to her.

"It was like falling in love," Anna suggested.

She was right: that was exactly how it felt. Very rapidly I formed a powerful infantile attachment to her. While it is to be expected that this will develop during deep analytic work, it is unusual in couple counselling. Looking back, I can appreciate how disturbing this must have been for Gemma. It would not have been part of her training to work with the transference, and her response was to protect herself by rejecting me. This hostile rejection was profoundly damaging, and in the early dreams I brought to Anna she recognised that my unconscious need had manifested as a desperate longing for the closest containment possible, to prevent my ego from total disintegration. But I was now battling with a paradoxical double conflict: my fear that Anna would also ultimately reject me, together with the fear that if she did *not* reject me, I might also damage her with my "badness".

This conflict was conspicuous throughout our early work, as I lurched painfully between a desire to protect Anna and feeling angry towards her. In the beginning I struggled vainly to suppress this anger—trying to decide whether or not I "liked" her. Certainly I felt safe with her, but often I resented her strength, which made me feel pathetically disempowered and dependent. If I was to give in to this, I feared losing my own strength—the strength that had enabled me to survive. This was the self-delusion born out of internal conflict. The truth was that I already hated this strength because I now perceived it to be entirely destructive. And it was this hatred, turned in on itself, which was the origin of my desire for self-destruction. At times, I could palpably feel Anna's strength as a life force, willing me to live. But I didn't want to continue living, and so I jealously hung on to the shattered remnants of a fragile will, which urged me persistently towards death. In my projection, Anna became the personification of a new superego voice, telling me that I could not absolve myself of existential responsibility by taking my life. It was not a voice I wanted to hear then.

By June we had reached a compromise: I attended twice-weekly sessions. I did not trust our relationship sufficiently to confess the deep longing I really felt—how I yearned to stop fighting and submit myself, body and soul, into Anna's care. In dreams, I imagined her inviting me to come and live with her, telling me that she would look after me. If she had offered this I would have accepted, willingly giving over complete responsibility for my life. Instead, she had offered me three-times weekly sessions. This did not constitute the longed-for escape from my painful existence. So much of my life already consisted of the ceaseless internal dialogue being fought inside my head. I feared that the intensity of three sessions a week would result in the total loss of my ability to remain connected to the external world. At least, these were the arguments by which I attempted to rationalise my fear of trusting in Anna's offer of support. Frankly, three-times weekly sessions sounded "dangerous", and I told myself it was either "all or nothing". And since Anna was not offering "all", I would not submit to her alternative offer.

Because my dream could not be fulfilled, I generated another, "waking" dream, which met my need for self-punishment and self-destruction. I imagined doing something so damaging to myself that I would be taken into psychiatric care. This would be the ultimate rejection of Anna, creating a situation in which another "doctor" would appear who *was* prepared to take responsibility for my life. Often I longed for the peace of being locked up in a white painted room containing only a bed, a table, and a chair. This imagined room had a window looking out onto woodland. From the window I would watch tall poplar trees, their branches engaged in a violent and death-defying dance with the wind. I yearned to spend my days in silence, the voices in my head quietened, staring out at this imagined view which symbolised my internal struggle. An occasional visit from a psychiatrist would be the only interruption to this isolated existence. Fortunately for us both, I allowed this vision to live only as fantasy, into which I could escape relatively harmlessly from the pain of my internal world.

Reflecting as a psychotherapist on what these frequent confrontations must have been like for Anna, I can appreciate what a challenging and demanding patient I was—so fragile, vulnerable and unstable, and yet capable of such stubborn displays of resistant, and generally regressive strength, which would surface as angry self-sabotage, threatening to undermine the vital foundations of a relationship we had begun to build between us. My anger and resistance took various forms in those early months, some of which I recall with poignant clarity.

During our twice-weekly sessions, I continued to sit facing Anna, perched awkwardly at one end of her large couch. One day, she unexpectedly suggested,

"Perhaps you would like to try lying down on the couch?"

Since the start of our work I had found it excruciatingly painful to voice my feelings spontaneously in Anna's presence. Clearly she was trying to help me overcome this barrier, perhaps with "free association" in her mind. But I didn't regard her suggestion as helpful. Instead I felt angry at what I perceived to be another attempt to disempower me.

"Why is it better to lie down than to sit up?" I questioned resentfully.

Anna explained something I barely understood: something about the lack of eye contact allowing for more free-flowing expression. My recollection is that I launched into an angry tirade.

"I can't talk to you without looking at you," I declared indignantly.

Watching Anna's expression and body language had become vital to my enterprise of getting to "know" her. Not that she gave much away, but it enabled me to hold onto some sense of personal control. How could she *not* have understood this need? I felt fiercely disappointed. Anna seemed to be trying to fit me into some "theory" of analytic practice which only alienated me. A long angry silence followed. In retrospect,

I realise how often I would remain silent in Anna's presence, frequently when it felt "too dangerous" to express my angry thoughts openly.

During this particular silence I thought defiantly about my reluctance to "lying on the couch". My reason for perching awkwardly at one end was that the indentations left by other bodies reminded me of the many other clients who had "lain down" there in my absence. But this was not jealousy. What I had not summoned the courage to tell Anna was how frequently I feared being overcome by the hidden pain, which I sensed to be contained in those indentations. Often I glanced at them, longing to remove the evidence by plumping up the cushions; but so far this had remained a secret. Now my anger gave me the courage to express this:

> "Why would I want to lie down on your couch anyway? It's full of other people's pain."

This angry response seemed to take Anna by surprise. I thought she looked startled, and there was an ensuing silence.

In more than eight years of analysis I only rarely "lay down" on Anna's couch—mostly in response to feelings of deep distress. Instead I chose a compromise—though it would take several more years for this to become a regular occurrence. Finally I allowed myself to sit curled up in one corner, my shoes removed, and my feet tucked under one of the cushions. Anna interpreted this as my effort to "ground myself safely"—so I assume that she must have understood something of the anxiety which underpinned my reticence. Certainly she never questioned me again about "lying down". And she continued to allow me the opportunity of making eye contact with her if I wanted to.

It is interesting for me to reflect retrospectively on the importance of this experience. Since having my own couch and my own clients, I invariably found myself needing to plump up the cushions before each new client arrived. Even so, on occasions, clients have referred to their own sense of "the pain and tears" which they assume to be secretly contained within the "memory" of my couch. It is an anxiety with which I can deeply resonate.

I recognise how much of that early anger stemmed from my need for Anna to "feel" my pain. I needed to hurt her so that she could feel and understand the depth of my hurt. I needed to reject her, so that she could understand my own painful feelings of rejection. But unconsciously I was also throwing out to her another challenge—how much could or would she take from me before she would feel bound to reject me as an impossible and damaging client, as Gemma had done? I still believed that this would only be a matter of time.

What confused me during those dark months was Anna's ability to contain my fear. Month after month, as I talked endlessly about my black despair and the terrifying "badness" inside me that beckoned me relentlessly towards suicide, Anna listened to my outpourings with no evident sign of emotional agitation. Ungrateful though it now feels, I perceived Anna's composure to be evidence of emotional detachment. It is true that she tried all kinds of "arguments" to help me understand the gravity of what I was contemplating. In different ways, she would invite me to reflect on the traumatic loss that would be felt by my family if I was to take my own life. But her calm, non-judgemental delivery and impassive expression only conveyed emotional distance. I envied her this degree of control, and struggled to understand what "magic spell" enabled her to achieve it. Finally I told myself that it must be her training, which had taught her to remain "unmoved" by whatever horrific stories assailed her senses.

What I failed to recognise was the vital distinction between "feeling something deeply" and "being able to contain it for the good of the other", as opposed to "not feeling anything at all". Of course Anna felt my terror. I already had ample evidence of her capacity to empathise with this. But it would hardly have been helpful or containing had she disclosed her fear to me. Much later, she explained that her training had given her the strength to separate *her* fear from *mine*. I understood that if she had not found the inner resources to accomplish this, our combined fear might have overwhelmed her and been defensively projected back onto me—as had happened with our relationship counsellor. She had taught me an important lesson.

But this is all hindsight. At the time—and it saddens me to confess this—I concluded that Anna's training had taught her to become an "unemotional robot", able to absorb without feeling whatever hideous confessions I chose to hurl at her from the depths of my destructiveness. Once I had reached this conclusion there was no holding back. I threw at her the pain and hurt of my dark inner world in all its virulence. When Anna described the potential trauma to my family of my suicide, I coolly pronounced that ultimately, they would all be grateful that I had relieved them of my existence. I truly believed this, and though Anna attempted to steer me towards a less distorted perception, I would return, time and again, to the same argument.

Then, one day, a dramatic exchange occurred which fundamentally changed the nature of our relationship. As I desperately repeated my conviction that I would be "doing the best thing for my family" by ending my life, Anna lapsed into a long silence—long enough to force my deranged imaginings away from my own pain. I turned to look at Anna. She was staring into that remote and distant space—the place where I knew I must leave her silently to her thoughts. I sunk back into my corner of the couch, my mind drifting away once more on a tide of self-destructive fantasies.

Probably only seconds passed, but when she finally spoke, Anna's voice appeared to come from some deep place inside her which resonated with the full power of her love. Very quietly, she asked me a question:

"And how do you think *I* would feel if you took your own life?"

I felt and heard the undercurrent of emotion in her voice, matched only by my own intense experience of her in that moment. So bound up in my own pain, it had never occurred to me that it might matter to Anna whether I lived or died. There was another silence as I absorbed the implication behind her question. I was deeply moved by her words, which awoke my mind to the realisation that Anna really *did* care what happened to me. And however implacable I remained in arguing that my death would ultimately benefit my family, it was manifestly clear that *she* would only feel it as a tragic loss.

It proved to be a life-changing episode in my analysis and in our relationship. From then on, I could no longer doubt the depth of her care. And because I could now recognise that my death would be a tragic loss for her, I was also forced to confront the realisation that it would most certainly be a loss for my family. Chastened and subdued by this experience, I felt ready to promise Anna that I would not take my own life.

This was just the beginning, and many desperate and demanding challenges still lay ahead for us both. But we were now embarked on a new stage of our journey—one in which I could start trusting in Anna to lead me away from the yawning jaws of death and back into a commitment to life.

CHAPTER FIVE

*You might have something to say,
But me, I don't need to talk.
I've said it all on paper.
There's no more to add.
—Just let the written words speak for themselves.*

*What is important
Is for you to read and keep them for me.
Wherever I am—
Wherever you are—
There is protection
For all those injured bits
That have started to heal.*

*Where will all these words be,
Far into the future?
Wherever you are
It will be a safe place.*

Despite my newly emerging trust in Anna, an extremely precarious period lay ahead. We were approaching summer and Anna had given me notice of her four-week summer break. It would be my first long separation from her, and in the weeks leading up to the break this trust was severely challenged by my *inner daimons*, who forced me to question whether this separation equalled "rejection and abandonment" in a disguised form.

By July the poems had begun to surface, seeming to emerge from nowhere and driven by a force for which I hardly felt able to claim ownership. I hadn't written any poetry since adolescence, but the depth of Anna's concern for my life had released something. A "hidden hand" appeared to control the pen from which the words simply flowed forth, almost without thought or effort, and suddenly the urge to write overwhelmed me like an addiction. Once I had started I could hardly stop, often completing several poems in one sitting. The power of this force scared me. It seemed to be beyond my control—and yet I was aware of an intense release, as all the terrors and anxieties found a medium through which they could be expressed. Now, the lonely night hours were spent in communicating my deepest fears in a written form, which gave substance to their existence. What I hadn't been able to say to Anna, I was now able to give to her—the concrete reality of my pain.

In one month I wrote forty-three pieces of work—mostly poems, but also several early dreams and a "letter" written to Anna during her absence. Now, each session would begin with my "pushing" a large bundle of writing at Anna, which I was unwilling to discuss at the time. My need was for her to "look after it". Therapeutically, I was giving my most fragile and fragmented parts into her safe-keeping. My psychic survival depended on her willingness to accept this unconditionally— and thankfully she recognised this need—for the time being, at least.

As I contemplated the prospect of Anna's four week holiday another desperate need emerged, generated by the terrifying fear that I might "lose" her through some fatal accident. Though this fear would never abate entirely it was particularly prevalent at this period, and on this first occasion it felt overwhelming. Finally, as her holiday drew closer, I was driven to express this terror obliquely by a question:

"Are you going abroad or staying in this country?"

I had prepared myself for the inquiry which I knew would follow. Anna observed me closely, her eyes narrowing in quizzical scrutiny of my expression. When she replied, her voice was firm, though not unkind.

> "I will answer your question, but first I'm going to ask why it's important for you to know that?" she questioned.
> "I need to know because … if I hear there's been a plane crash, I will be worried about whether you are on it."

Anna immediately grasped the depth of my fear and did not question me further—either then, or on the many future occasions when I so desperately needed to ask this question.

Over time, because it felt safe enough for me to be open about my terror, my questions became more searching. When would she be leaving the country and for how long? Who was going with her? Would she be safe? Gradually what emerged was not simply my fear of losing her, but my need to create an "internal picture" in which I could safely contain her physical presence during her absence. This picture would help me to survive our separation, and when it included spending time with her family, I experienced enormous pleasure in contemplating this image. Initially, Anna was sceptical about my professed lack of jealousy of her family relationships, but ultimately she understood that it allowed me to weave a narrative in my mind which, over the years, became fleshed out with "knowledge" gleaned from both overt and imagined sources. Gradually I pieced together a "film" of her life outside the consulting room, which I replayed over and over, to reassure and support myself when we were apart. As many dreams subsequently revealed, I would "invite myself in" to this internalised picture, through which we would share the unconscious needs, fears, and anxieties being played out during these "dream visits" to Anna's imagined family world.

* * *

I had now promised Anna that I would not take my own life—a promise I intended to keep. In amongst the angry feelings was a deep love for her. The infantile transference attachment which I had developed towards Gemma had begun to transfer itself to Anna as my trust gradually grew. The difference was that Anna understood and knew how to work with these feelings.

But now she was threatening to leave me unsupported and vulnerable for four weeks. How was I to make sense of this seeming abandonment, in terms of her expressed care and concern for my life? My "adult" mind repeated reassuring messages: of course Anna was entitled to a summer break. I had begun to recognise that she must need time and space to renew her energies from such demanding work. But my "vulnerable child" could only feel panic-stricken at the loss of her physical presence. As I foundered between these ambivalent feelings, the poems became the vehicle through which I was able to give vent to my fear and anger.

I now recognise that an unconscious process was struggling to communicate the unbearable fear of disintegration which threatened me in her absence. The torrent of words dramatically illustrates shifts in mood which would swing from hope for some future return to "normality", only to be submerged minutes later by a black despairing hopelessness presaging impending psychological death in the wake of our separation. Years later, Anna would reveal that the most challenging aspect for her, was "picking up on your terror that your ego was about to fall to pieces."

The urge to self-harm was immense at this time. And yet my promise to Anna implied an assurance that I would try to stop myself doing this. If I no longer intended to end my life, then the act of self-harming had ostensibly lost its purpose. But such rational thinking failed to remove this powerful urge, heightened by the prospect of our imminent break. The self-harm had continued sporadically during these early months, but it was now bearable to share with Anna the events and feelings leading up to each episode, and to "show" her what I had done to myself when she questioned me. By now, I had learnt not to misinterpret the lack of an emotional reaction as a sign of "detachment". Though uncertain of what she was "doing" with these revelations, I trusted her strength to contain them safely. But still, my growing love for Anna made me want to stop self-harming, perhaps as reciprocal evidence of my love. I felt driven to try and find a way of achieving this before our four-week separation.

* * *

The resolution happened quite unexpectedly—though, I'm convinced, synchronistically. One day when out walking, I spotted a tiny shop which I must have passed hundreds of times without noticing its existence. It was easy to overlook. It had an air of dark and suggestive secrecy, its window half obscured behind black painted panels designed to prevent passers-by from looking in. The shop door was also painted black. It looked firmly closed, although the sign mysteriously declared it to be "open". That day, something drew me inexorably to its blackly adorned mystique. I stopped to read the large, bright red letters on the panels, which proclaimed *"Custom Tattoo"* in ornate lettering. Underneath, more blood-red words declared boldly, *"The only local professional tattooist and body piercer!"* followed by the offer of various affiliated "services" available to anyone courageous enough to enter the doors of this shadowy hinterland.

I stood there reading and re-reading the words, which beckoned me with the same eerie power I had felt as a child, drawn to the horror and fascination of Grimm's fairy tales.[1] I found myself gripped by the conviction that to enter that door would signify some "rite of passage" into another, hitherto unacknowledged dimension of existence. I remained transfixed, aware of the sound of footsteps as people passed by on the pavement behind me. Did I imagine hearing their footsteps quicken as they approached the shop, as if anxious to hurry past the challenge of its murky interior? I didn't have the courage to walk in then. Instead, I wrote down the phone number. The sign promised that "private appointments were available".

Walking home, my head was full of the symbolic significance of this "discovery", which suggested an answer to my dilemma. I wanted to stop self-harming because I knew that it denoted my desire for self-destruction. But the conflict for me lay in my continuing need to "mark myself" as a reminder of the "wrong" I had done. Suddenly, having myself tattooed offered the possibility of bridging the destructive past with a creative and healing future. Now I could choose to "mark myself" with a symbol containing the hope of possible redemption—though this revelation was no more than an unconscious instinct at the time.

I arrived home and immediately made the phone call, fearful that any delay would mean a loss of nerve. A gruff male voice answered. When questioned, he revealed that he was "Carl", the tattooist. I explained that I would like to make an appointment. There followed numerous questions for which I was unprepared: did I know what design I wanted and where on my body I wanted it? How large and detailed did I want it to

---

[1] *Grimm's Fairy Tales* (1948). London: Routledge & Kegan Paul.

be? Or did I have a design of my own that I wanted him to create? His questions unnerved me. I hadn't the faintest idea how to answer him. I told him that this would be my "first time"—that I thought I wanted some small design, as yet unknown, but probably on my arm. Did he have any designs from which I might choose?

> "No need for an appointment," the gruff voice responded. "Just turn up. You can choose something then. I'm not open on Mondays."

Abruptly the receiver was replaced and I found myself unexpectedly listening to the dialling tone.

* * *

It was an inauspicious start, but the following Tuesday, while Patrick was at work, I returned to the mysterious little shop on my secret mission. It was a hot summer's day, and this time the black door was ajar, a beaded curtain covering the entrance. I heard voices, and was disconcerted by the sight of two young girls already inside. Obviously friends, one was being tattooed while her friend chatted and watched. A lot of nervous giggling went on between them. I felt acutely embarrassed to have invaded their privacy, but I needn't have been. Although the shop was even tinier from the inside, nobody paid any attention to me. Relieved, I sat next to the young girl whose friend was "in the chair". Briefly and furtively, we exchanged sidelong glances, our attention quickly reverting to her friend.

It was the chair which first seriously occupied my attention. There was something quaintly outdated about its black leather appearance. It reminded me of the dentist's chair I remembered having first sat in as a very small child. Or did it resemble a barber's chair? I hastily brushed aside unwelcome thoughts of Sweeney Todd. The girl was being tattooed on her back. Carl was sitting hunched over her on a revolving stool, and both had their backs turned to us. It was impossible to see what was happening, but there was something suggestively erotic about their huddled physical closeness. There was a recognisable noise like an old-fashioned dentist's drill, which issued from some implement that Carl was holding. I was mesmerised. The drilling conjured up horrible memories of early pain, also linked to my first unforgettable experience of dentistry as a five-year-old. But the girl being "drilled" emitted no audible sounds of pain. I decided to turn my attention elsewhere, to distract myself from the disturbingly incongruous connection between dentistry and eroticism which had begun to trouble my thoughts.

Looking around the tiny space, I noticed that along one wall were a number of large, hanging frames containing designs. These were obviously the designs to which Carl had referred, and from which I could "choose what I wanted". Pleased to have an appropriate source of distraction, I got up to examine them. Immediately, I found myself immersed in an alarming and fantastical world—a fairy tale nightmare certainly reminiscent of Grimm's imagery. Eagles, lions, dragons, and devils stared back at me, starkly aggressive and insinuating in their grotesquely bright colours. Other frames contained images of strange amorphous creatures—unrecognisable beings from another nightmare realm of existence. I felt inexplicably drawn to this metaphorical vision of such a darkly alternative world. Violence, fear, sex, love, childhood, nostalgia—everything and anything contained within the collective unconscious memory of Man—seemed to be on display within the confines of this tiny museum to the fallibility of the human spirit.

But *my* need was to find an image that would signify my intention to re-invest in Life. Relieved, I finally came across a frame containing softly seductive images of butterflies and birds, flying free and optimistically into some bright space which suggested future hope. I was attracted by a design of two swallows flying in unison. They spoke to me of hopefulness in my relationship with Patrick. I decided instantly.

By now, the two girls had left the shop and Carl turned his attention towards me. It was an unnerving moment. He was a short, heavily built man, probably in his late fifties, and dressed entirely in black. His open-necked shirt and rolled-up sleeves revealed another dramatic invitation into that darkly alternative world, and in that moment, Carl manifested himself to me as its physical and tangible "representative". What was visible of his arms, hands, neck, and chest was completely shrouded in elaborate, brightly coloured, and intertwining tattoos. No unmarked skin found space for expression here. My mind was momentarily lost in a vision of the images that I imagined might cover the rest of his body. It was as if his head and face emerged as a separate entity, reclaiming his existence in the "real" world.

I stifled my initial feelings of alarm and indicated my choice of the two swallows. He opened a drawer beneath the counter, which revealed a carefully ordered filing system of every design contained on the frames. Flicking through it, he brought out a "blueprint" of my design and told me to sit in the chair. Our conversation throughout was very limited, but at this point Carl asked where on my body I wanted the tattoo. I indicated a place slightly below the bend in my left arm. He took hold of my arm, stretching it out, and questioning me about the positioning of the design, while moving it around for my approval. I realised that what he was showing me was an "upside down" view of the swallows, from my perspective. This was not what I wanted. I took hold of the blueprint and placed it on my arm the other way up.

"If I do it that way, it's going to be upside down," he informed me gruffly.

"It's not upside down to me," I explained, "and I need to be able to look at it the right way up."

I was surprised by this sudden display of assertiveness in the face of all my secret apprehension. Carl didn't argue. I imagine he was used to "individual requirements" relating to his work. But his words made me realise that, until that moment, I hadn't fully appreciated the significance of what I wanted for myself. It seemed that for most of Carl's customers, a tattoo was something intended for others to see—hence the need for them to appear "the right way up". But I was not concerned about this. My swallows were intended as a reminder to *me*—of where I had been, and where I hoped to go in the future. It mattered not a jot whether they appeared "upside down" to anyone else who might happen to look at them.

My decision made, Carl pressed the blueprint in position. Effectively it was a transfer. When he removed it, the design was ready for the next stage of his work. I was so fascinated by watching his preparations for this procedure that I lost all sense of fear. From amongst his tools, Carl produced something that resembled a small gun, inserting into it a sort-of needle with a sharp point. Then he wiped over my arm with a cloth that smelt of disinfectant. He flicked a remote switch and the dreaded "drill" noise started up again.

Now Carl began his work, holding my arm steady with his large, powerful hand. As I watched, our profoundly physical contact made me aware, once again, of the disturbingly erotic merging of physical closeness with pain. Slowly and carefully, Carl followed the transferred design with the needle of his "gun", creating a permanent outline of the birds in dark blue ink on my arm. I was surprised that it felt no worse than a needle being dragged superficially across my flesh. It was bearable. There was only a little blood, and when he had finished he wiped away the transfer design with more antiseptic solution. I looked down at my arm. My heart sang in celebration at the initial sight of the two swallows, whose unified birth was taking place while I was a witness to their creation.

Lost in my reverie of "new birth", I was suddenly aware that Carl was asking me another question: what colour did I want for my swallows? He produced a selection of different coloured bottles of ink. I chose a turquoise blue, and the next stage of the work began. Now Carl changed to another "gun". I watched as it inhaled the turquoise ink from the bottle, my arm stretched out in readiness. Once again, Carl's strong hand maintained its firm, steady hold on my arm.

Initially I had expected pain, but I had been deceptively reassured by the relative painlessness of the first stage of this process. Now the pain really began, as the colour was slowly forced, drop by drop, to emerge through my flesh precisely within the confines of the design. Even now I don't understand how this process was achieved. I simply watched it taking place before my eyes. But the pain took on a special significance, and while I gripped the arm of the chair in my effort to maintain a stoic silence, it felt appropriate that this "marking" of myself should be an unforgettably painful experience. It signified "punishment", and I welcomed that it had involved me in suffering. I was also gratified that, this time, there was a lot of bleeding. I watched as my red blood mingled curiously with the vivid blue ink, creating a cacophony of colour that seemed to embrace both life and death in its surreal merging.

There was not much time to invest thoughts and feelings in the visual significance of this experience. Having completed his work, Carl quickly wiped away the bloody evidence with more antiseptic lotion. He then plastered a sterile dressing on my arm covering my swallows, and I was given an "after care" instruction card. The whole endeavour had taken no more than half an hour.

* * *

This proved to be the first of many significantly timed visits I was to make to Carl's shop over the ensuing years. But in those few weeks before and during my first long separation from Anna, a collection of butterflies and birds came to life on both my arms. As in real life, their birth involved necessary suffering while also signifying life-affirming hope for the future. Undoubtedly, the pain and bloodiness of the enterprise was a vital feature, and even then, I recognised that there were aspects to this ritual which had their beginnings in my original desire to self-harm. At certain momentous stages in my analysis, the urge to "mark myself" would re-emerge. Carl began to recognise me, and we became strangely united in an improbable relationship born out of our secret and mutually symbolic connection, which I was to record in a number of poems. On one such visit, I was surprised to be given an unexpected "warning":

> "You know that this can become addictive," he gruffly informed me.
> "Yes ... I think I've come to understand that," I conceded.

But I was touched by this emergence of a sensitivity which made him want to protect me from the dangers of a human frailty with which he was well-placed to empathise, both personally and professionally.

The final and most painful tattoo was created within the three-year period when I knew that my time with Anna was limited. Our focus necessarily had to include all the suffering and loss that combined the past, present, and future as an inevitable aspect of our ending. I knew precisely the symbol that would signify the painful, yet magnificently "circular" journey we had made during our years together. I returned to Carl for one final visit. Above the "butterflies and birds", he created a design of "thorns" containing one red rose. This design formed a complete circle around the top of my left arm—the arm on which the swallows had first commenced their journey six years previously. Symbolically, it had begun to feel as though the wheel was nearing full circle.

CHAPTER SIX

The birds are special and different.
They were the first to be born.
They fly together and touch together
For a few brief, exhilarating moments.
But the image is not reality …
Nothing is really forever,
And when they have attained their object
They, too, must fly separately
And survive.

Butterflies and birds,
Separate and together;
Learning that to need
Is not necessarily to be wanting.

Give me what I need.
Then I will be empowered to fly alone
And achieve. A whole world will be within my grasp.

An important aspect of this undertaking was that it should not be shrouded in shameful secrecy. I needed to have the courage to show my first tattoo to the world—most significantly to my family and those closest to me. Amongst that number I now included Anna, and perhaps predictably, I needed her to be the first person to bear witness to it.

In the last few months of our work together, Anna allowed me to record her dramatic recollection of that session seven years earlier, in which I revealed my first tattoo to her. What intrigued me about her account was the marked difference between the emotional impact of this event on each of us at that time. Anna's ability to contain my painful feelings could still mislead me into underestimating the intense impact it could have on her. I simply trusted in her strength to "manage everything", with little concept of the heavy emotional demands I was making on her. Though I still didn't understand where this strength came from, I now firmly believed that it originated from a compassionate concern for me. But conflicting feelings towards Anna continued to battle in my deeply troubled internal world.

My own recollection of that session is curiously devoid of emotion—almost a sense of "blankness", with no feeling-toned quality. I suspect that I dissociated from the feelings in fear of Anna's response. And probably this defence contained the hope of remaining in control of my narrative while bringing to her the evidence of what I had done. But effectively there was no "narrative" to be controlled. I recollect choosing a few words carefully and dispassionately, and finally what I announced to Anna was that I had found "a more acceptable way of marking myself." My intention was to offer to show her my solution, but my memory is that her rapid response forestalled my words:

"You've had a tattoo done," she guessed almost instantly.

Unusually, I have no memory of her tone or the feelings she conveyed. Instead, I remember wondering how she had managed to anticipate my disclosure so accurately, and I recall a sharp sense of disappointment. Was I *really* so predictable? Anna's ready anticipation seemed to diminish both me, and the uniqueness of my revelation. In hindsight, this is a powerful illustration of how "misunderstanding" would arise when I was at my most vulnerable. At such times, I would project my feelings of self-condemnation onto Anna, and "assume" that her response must be similarly judgemental, even in the face of all the evidence to the contrary.

I know now that this was a total misreading of Anna's reaction. Seven years later, her recorded recollection of that session revealed that she retained a vivid and intense memory of the experience quite at odds with my own recollection, which painted a very poignant picture of its significance just before the summer break:

> "What sticks in my mind is the *way* you showed me your tattoo. You came into the session and were very short of words—but you were making it clear that something had happened. It was at the time when you were still cutting. You found it very hard to say what it was you had done, and you didn't know how to tell me. It was *very* scary. You started to roll back your sleeve, very, very slowly. I hardly dared to imagine what you were going to show me, but I thought you were going to show me a big cut. When I actually saw that it was a tattoo, I was relieved. That's the feeling I remember ... You were communicating to me something of the terror of what it was that you were making visible."

Those first tattoos were my way of trying to contain something which felt hugely dangerous. Without understanding why, I knew they needed to be physically visible. An unconscious warning suggested that if the terror went "underground", into some deeply inaccessible layer of my psyche, it threatened to be much more damaging. I sensed menace from my shadow, and was trying to find a way of holding this within my conscious control. And by implication, this would also allow Anna access to this fearful aspect of my internal world. Once we had explored the motivation behind my need for that first tattoo, Anna had no difficulty in recognising it as creative and life-affirming. Contrary to appearances, this was not a destructive act but an attempt at self-preservation. To my knowledge, she was unique in this insight at the time.

Years later, as we reflected on that dangerous and delicate time in analysis, Anna's words finally enabled me to comprehend the unconscious process which had driven me to "act out" the terror I was struggling to contain:

> "I recognise that it was a way of trying to hold onto life ... because cutting was about death," I heard myself reflecting to Anna. "But I don't know how I even thought of the idea of having a tattoo, or where it came from."

"Well, that's what was so creative," Anna emphasised. "Your mind just served you up something which was so *much* more creative than cutting yourself, even though it contained some of the same essential elements. But you turned your fear of your shadow into 'birds' and 'butterflies'—symbols of the spirit and the self: something which could fly and be joyful, and which contained the hope that they might actually be transformative."

As a psychotherapist, I can appreciate how the difficulty in verbalising my terror placed us both in a precarious position. Anna's only way into my internal world was to try to "interpret" my written words and actions—because of my fear that expressing thoughts and feelings from the darkest place in my shadow had the power to damage her. And yet it was vital for Anna to get some of that terror expressed in the room, "… so that I had some chance of making it different," she would later explain. Despite tentative beginnings, the visual images with which I had chosen to mark myself now offered an opening into my internal world which we could talk about together: a uniquely symbolic record of my psychic struggle for survival.

* * *

The weeks while Anna was away heralded other equally creative, though similarly precarious beginnings. I found myself with a lot of time to fill, and appreciated that I had a choice about whether to use this space constructively or destructively in her absence. I could choose to turn my anger at Anna in on itself, internalising it into the self-loathing capable of sabotaging everything we had begun to build between us. Or, I could internalise her life-force and try to hold onto the powerful evidence of an undeniable love, despite my darkest moments of self-doubt. Even in the face of extreme vulnerability at that time, I knew that, finally, I *had* to take existential responsibility for my choice. It was not a choice for which I could hold Anna responsible.

In the event, I resolved to maintain hope of a "future time" when Anna and I might "pick up the pieces" of our relationship. And if I had not destroyed everything during the intervening period, there would be hope of future healing. In writing about this period, I am struck by how insensible I was of the inner strength which Anna had left me holding in her absence—though wrestling in the weeks ahead with the tension between the positive and destructive energies it contained would prove a battle. But once again, synchronistic events transpired which appeared to point a way forward.

As my love and trust in Anna grew, so too, did my struggle to resolve the painfully ambivalent feelings surrounding my two very different experiences of therapy. As a result, I became intrigued by a desire to understand the process from a theoretical perspective. That summer, a local adult education college advertised "short summer courses". Amongst what was on offer was a six-session course entitled "An Introduction to Psychotherapy and Counselling". I recall feeling intense excitement at reading the course details—it was as if my barely conscious need was being acknowledged in the clearest possible terms. Without hesitation, I enrolled myself on the course.

Those six sessions proved to be another life-changing event. The tutor was inspirational, and by the final session I had convinced myself that my future lay in training to become a counsellor. We were informed that the college ran a two-year Diploma Course, and that acceptance involved the satisfactory completion of a preliminary "Certificate" year. When Anna and I met up again in September, I informed her that I had applied for the Certificate Course and was waiting to be interviewed.

How had I expected Anna to respond to this news? The timing was hardly propitious, and I could not honestly hide my own awareness of this. Amongst the hefty bundle of writing which I thrust at Anna when she returned, was a "letter" in which I described how close I had come to taking an overdose during her absence. And despite my life-affirming tattoos, occasional incidents of self-harming continued during the months ahead. There was no doubting how ill I had been, nor the fragile emotional state in which I still struggled to maintain my hold on life.

Not surprisingly, Anna greeted my news with a resounding silence. It was an extremely delicate situation, and in the recorded recollection of her thoughts at that time, she explained her difficulty:

> "I didn't know … I just *didn't* know … Soon after this, we had a session in which you threatened to self-harm again. Just as it was ending, you told me, 'You've got three minutes to say something to stop me' … So, *of course* I didn't know … So I know I didn't say much. I couldn't find any good enough reason either to encourage or discourage you … In the end, I just thought we had to go on in faith."

Poor Anna! My heart goes out to her now, when I think of the venomous and hostile poetry which emerged during this period—the result of dark battles which I assumed myself to be engaged in with Anna. Her silence led me to fear that she was "telling me indirectly" that I was unfit for counselling training. But the "doubts" that I assumed Anna to be harbouring were as much a projection of self-doubt about the timing of this undertaking, and I knew that it was appropriate for Anna to be harbouring similar doubts for herself. Ultimately, the unexpressed paradox of which we were both silently aware was that if she *had* expressed encouragement, I would not have believed her. On the other hand, any discouragement or reservation, however sensitively expressed, would have left me feeling rejected and angrily defensive. And so she kept silent, explaining to me,

> "A large part of me thought that it was an experience which you probably had to go through ... because I was getting a sense of a very determined part of you, that perhaps actually *does* just have to 'go in there and find out'—rather like the little girl who wasn't allowed the bicycle, but who was damned determined to 'have the bicycle' as an adult."

And so, while Anna quietly "kept faith" in the future of our journey, I was forced to reflect for myself on the powerful and persuasive arguments for and against my future training as a counsellor.

Throughout that early period of analysis, my struggle to manage the pain of rejection by our relationship counsellor, Gemma, was never far from the surface. It emerged regularly in poetry, but also lurked as a dangerous undercurrent, which frequently threatened to undermine my relationship with Anna. Secretly, I still longed to understand why two therapists had responded to me so differently: why my self-destructive behaviour had resulted in rejection by one, yet loving care and containment by the other. There seemed only one way to find out what I so desperately needed to know—by entering this mysterious profession myself. But I came to realise that there was a deeper resonance that drove me towards this undertaking—one which had its origins in childhood.

* * *

My love of reading developed very early, and one of my fondest childhood memories is of weekly visits with my father to the local library every Saturday afternoon. He would leave me in the "Children's Library" and disappear upstairs into the "Adult" section. But in the mid-50s, the children's section was a far less vibrant place than it is today. By the age of ten, with a considerable personal "library" of my own at home, I began to feel that I had exhausted what was on offer in the children's section. The day came when, bored and uninspired by the limited choice, I wandered up the impressive staircase into the main library in search of my father. With difficulty, I pushed through the heavy doors which opened onto this secret adult world. I recall the vivid thrill as I gazed up in awe for the first time at the tall and seemingly endless rows of groaning bookshelves. There was a moment of fear. Suddenly I felt very small and overawed by this daunting glimpse into the adult world. And yet ... I could hardly believe the Aladdin's Cave of treasures into which I had gained entrance. So many books to choose from, all demanding to be read! I think, in that moment, I experienced a sense of myself as "a second-class citizen". Books, it seemed, were important and available without limit to adults—but not to children—at least, not then.

When I eventually found my father, I explained sadly that there was "nothing left for me to read" in the children's library. My worry was that this would mean an end to our shared library trips. Instead, it marked a new beginning. My father had always encouraged my love of reading, but what I did not appreciate as a child was the pleasure that our shared love of books also afforded him. It seems that this was not a pleasure that he was prepared for either of us to relinquish, and unexpectedly he found a way to resolve my difficulty:

> "I have more library tickets than I need," he explained, in response to my sad appeal. "Take one of my tickets, and then you can come up here, with me, to choose a book."

With sensitivity and insight, he liberated me from the dreary and limited confines of the "Children's Library". In opening up this vast and enthralling new "adult" world, he gave me the freedom to roam unrestrained amongst its many treasures.

Though my father always vetted the books I chose for their suitability, he never discouraged me from pursuing my own inclinations. I'm sure I must have read a great deal of second-rate rubbish in my rather unsystematic search for "interesting books". The sheer volume of subject matter alone was enough to overwhelm me. Perhaps a little guidance from him might have been helpful. But then this would have diminished my excitement in the freedom he offered, which made me feel very "grown-up" and autonomous.

Finally, from the vast expanse of reading material, only one book remains as a significant memory, though its title does not suggest an immediate or obvious appeal to a child. The book was entitled, *An Outline of Abnormal Psychology* by William McDougall, originally published in 1926.[1] I think I was twelve years old when I read it, and I can still picture the edition clearly. It was a huge, thick book—the biggest, heaviest, and most lengthy book I had ever undertaken to read—and it had a bright yellow cover, which was probably what first caught my eye. My father looked it over and seemed content with my choice. I tucked it under my arm, elated at being allowed to carry home such an important and grown-up volume. I devoured it avidly, desperately trying to make sense of the psychological arguments surrounding the many fascinating and moving "case studies". I remember asking to renew that book many times—as many times as I was allowed—because I hated the thought of having to part with it. Undoubtedly, there was something about its invitation into the hidden recesses of the human mind, which left a lasting impression buried deep in my psyche. It was a memory which remained hidden for over forty years, until events in my life signalled my unconscious to release the memory once again. Now I firmly believe that this was a response to my quest towards individuation.

As I struggled to make sense of the many-layered arguments for choosing to train as a counsellor, that vivid childhood memory of William McDougall's book enabled other pieces of personal history to fall into place. On one level, I could quite appreciate how my decision seemed to be the result of a sudden impulse, based on a need to understand and repair the damage caused by my first painful experience of counselling. But this merely represented the surface layer of reasoning. Beneath that, I recognised a deeper, unconscious layer, now recognisable as a "goal" towards which I felt that my life had been quietly but inevitably moving … from William McDougall in early adolescence, to my love of the "psychological literature" of Henry James which began in later adolescence, to my first job as an Editorial Assistant in a book

---

[1] McDougall, W. (1926). *An Outline of Abnormal Psychology*. York: Methuen.

publishing company in my twenties, and the subsequent training in my thirties to become a teacher of young children, with its absorbing focus on human psychology and child development. I was suddenly able to view my past, present, and future as a coherent drive towards psychic understanding, and after so many months of destructive energy which had threatened my "sense of self", I now saw my decision to undertake counselling training as a step towards psychic integration. I felt it as a deeply powerful drive demanding to be acknowledged, despite all the obvious challenges that it raised in terms of problematic timing.

CHAPTER SEVEN

"…. At this stage in therapy, when all the doors have been opened, it's a bit like a very stormy love affair—it has that degree of intensity about it."

—*Anna*, recorded in October 2008

While my "adult" mind had resolved the difficult question surrounding my future, I was unprepared for the onslaught from my "inner child" that now surfaced. It took the form of a huge battle, which I increasingly perceived myself and Anna to be engaged in following her return from the summer break. My interpretation of her silence around my decision to begin training caused the first rumblings of suppressed anger. Then a series of events catapulted our "battle" into the open, and contained the familiar internal conflict of trying to reconcile my feelings towards her.

In early October, Anna announced that she would shortly be going into hospital and would have to cancel my sessions that week. She gave no further explanation, though she did emphasise that she only expected to be in hospital overnight. This was insufficient to subdue my extreme anxiety at her news, but the unspoken message I implied from her words suggested that it was inappropriate for me to question her further. I began to fantasise that Anna was "hiding something too awful to reveal". This anxiety stemmed from a family history of "protecting me from bad news", and was a painful trigger to events surrounding my father's death. In order to save me from unnecessary worry, he had told me casually about his "brief stay in hospital" the day before it was scheduled. I was emotionally unprepared for the tragedy that followed—so if Anna was "protecting me", I did not want to be shielded from the full story.

There was a sense in which I was justified in feeling this. Anna would later confirm that her deliberate intention was to keep herself "very separate" at this stage, because of my fear that I could or would damage her if she came too close. Maintaining her sense of separateness was deliberately intended to deny my fantasy that we might be "merged together", which she recognised not only as a desire, but as an unconscious aspect of my fear:

> "... Because so much about our early therapy was about feeling a closeness which you were unable to separate into the two of us."

This was the idealising transference, which made Anna's intention to be "different from me" feel like rejection or abandonment, and threatened my sense of security. As Anna recollected:

> "It was a very changing situation for us at that time—because sometimes it was hugely good, but sometimes it was awful ... There was this huge dichotomy. On the one hand you were terrified that you could 'get in' and control me—and that was a tremendous fear. But on the other hand, it felt very damaging and excluding if you couldn't 'get in' to some degree, to get something which felt safe enough to hang on to ... I would expect, at this stage in our therapy and with the material coming up, for us to have a battle—because you needed to test out whether I *was* strong enough to hold you, or whether you *could* damage me ... And I needed to hold a boundary in order to establish myself as a 'separate person' with my own way of being—and because I *also* needed to check out that I could hold you too."

However, my anger surfaced gradually. On the day that Anna told me of her imminent operation I had brought with another bundle of poems. Concerned and solicitous at her news, I questioned whether I should give them to her. Though she did not seem troubled, I assumed she was hiding this from me. And so, *my* need was to protect her.

My resistance to reading or discussing the poems still remained a major unresolved issue at this time. For months Anna had tried gentle persuasion and encouragement, but I remained adamant that neither she nor I should read the poems aloud. What I couldn't comprehend then was that until I explored the terror that the poems held for me, there was no possibility of integrating these split-off fragments of my psyche. Somehow, it was vital that Anna find a way to remove this stumbling block that was preventing us from moving forward.

That day something different happened. When I expressed reservations about giving the poems to Anna she became thoughtful, then replied,

"Ok … Let's just leave it for now."

I remember feeling her words as powerfully as if she had dealt me a physical blow. In that moment, what my disturbed mind "heard" was Anna telling me that she no longer wished me to give her any more writing. Fearing that my safety net had been withdrawn, I felt suddenly exposed to a world that I had few inner resources to manage alone, and this gave rise to unspeakable terror … truly unspeakable, since Anna's news left me unable to voice these terrors openly. She was shortly to undergo an operation—and perhaps she was ill, or in pain. In the transference Anna had become an "emotionally strong mother". But now she appeared vulnerable, and I responded to this as I had learnt to respond to my real mother—by suppressing my own vulnerability in order to protect her from my pain. For the first time, I didn't give Anna my poems but took them home again. But my inner world had reverted to a threatening and dangerous place as I imagined the nightmare of her safe holding withdrawn from me.

"It was *such* a dilemma," Anna later reflected. "You didn't want to own those split off parts of yourself. But if you could just give them to me—so that you'd kind-of 'evacuated them' into me—it reinforced your terrible fear that you were being damaging. But if I tried to get us to talk in order to make some sense of it, then it felt as though I was being damaging to you. At that point you felt I didn't want to hold what you were giving me … so it was all about us trying to work out the difference between a 'container' and a 'barrier'."

"So when it wasn't appropriate just to give you the poems, it *did* feel as though one or other of us had damaged something," I queried.

"Because then if I don't read them, I'm actually confirming the idea that something about them *is* damaging or unacceptable. So at this point you're not sure about whether or not to trust me—and you're uncertain about whether *you're* dangerous or *I'm* dangerous."

Anna was right. I struggled to answer the question of "which of us was the more dangerous". Often I saw her as powerful and felt scared of her power, and in our recordings Anna reflected on that aspect of my conflict:

"I think you experienced me as powerful because I seemed to have the capacity to stand up to you—to hold you and not to waver … You were in the grip of something powerful, and if I was holding that, you were going to think that I was hugely powerful. You were scared of your own power, so if you feel that *I'm* powerful you're going to be scared of that too … but there's no point in having a therapist who hasn't got the power to hold you, because that's what happened with Gemma … At that point in our work, I don't think it was possible to avoid that difficulty."

For some reason Anna's operation was delayed for two weeks, but I continued to write—the poems graphically documenting my desperation. I floundered around trying to find another source of safety: firstly from my doctor, and then from an alcohol counsellor who he recommended in response to my concern about my increased drinking. Later, Anna highlighted the conflict I was struggling to resolve:

"… If I think analytically about this, you had to keep me as the 'good enough mother' to keep you coming to therapy. By taking some of your problems to someone else, like the alcohol counsellor, you could keep me as a 'good enough object' by minimising anything which you felt was conflictual between us. It's a sense that we are not in complete empathy …"

The ultimate note of desperation is captured in the only poem I ever wrote directly to my deceased mother, recalling how, as a very young child, I would curl up in a big armchair to listen to her playing the piano. What dimly emerged was a link between "mother" and "music", which conjured up feelings of safety and security contained in these childhood memories. Time would prove this to be a significant connection, and as Anna reflected,

> "When you're in a space where you feel so desperate and disintegrating, and everything has become so difficult and disturbing, you flail around trying to do whatever you can. You move into 'survival' mode."

Although the poems persisted, I now told Anna that I no longer intended to bring them or discuss them with her. I was torn between wanting both to punish and protect Anna by "excluding" her—a mirror to my feeling that she was excluding me. But on the day that she went into hospital I was consumed with anxiety. I wrote a poem to her entitled *Hospital*, which described my intention to "keep you safe inside my head." I spent the day fantasising about what might be happening, finally unable to resist phoning her husband to check that she had come through the operation successfully.

* * *

What happened next was an illuminating example of how the unconscious has the capacity to throw up solutions emanating from the self-care system, with the intention of preserving the psyche from destruction—though I recognised that the origin of this solution had lain buried in my history, simply awaiting a trigger for its release.

During the dark days and nights of those early months when my world had been shrouded in silence, I was increasingly disengaged from an outside world, which felt both threatened by and threatening to my existence. Before this period—a time of "normality"—I had been a radio lover; but now all my favourite programmes whose companionship I had previously enjoyed became equated with the accusing psychotic "voices" inside my head, bombarding me with discordant messages which endangered the remnants of a sanity I was struggling to hold on to. And so, in switching off the radio, I effectively cut myself off from the last lifeline linking me to the outside world. It was my daughter who sensitively came to the rescue, telling me of "a lovely classical music station" which she thought I might enjoy. One silent afternoon, I plucked up the courage to switch the radio back on. Either it was fortunate timing or another example of synchronicity, but that first listening experience after so many months contained piano music which re-connected me instantly with childhood, and which I associated with having heard my mother play. And so, throughout those painful early months, music became my constant companion as I battled with my troubled internal world, soothing and holding me with its connection to childhood memories. As my unconscious memory threw up the musical connection between Anna (my "mother" in the transference), her piano, and the memory of my real mother playing to me in childhood, I remembered telling Anna in that first session:

> "My mother was a talented pianist. We had a beautiful baby grand, and she could never dust it without sitting down to play … And as soon as I heard her I would appear, and curl up in a big armchair to listen. I never wanted her to stop, and always felt sad when she closed the lid and went back to her dusting."

Now music emerged as something which might mend the split which I feared would divide us. One day, I brought Anna an Enya CD that had been played on the music station. Anna told me she was familiar with Enya's music, and suddenly it became possible to discuss together the meaning of the words contained in the songs, which expressed my tormented feelings as powerfully as if they had been written *just* for me. Anna later speculated on what she believed had happened in that important session:

> "You were needing a 'containing mother' and the armchair to curl up in—somebody to hold all those fragmented bits of you. And I wonder whether that was where music came in. Music came up as a symbol for you. It was something which we could 'be in', and which would bring us together … because by bringing me something which wasn't your creation, you didn't have to worry about whether it was damaging, or whether I'd want it. It was something we could share which helped to unblock you from that very 'dug in' place … something really containing, soothing—a feeling of being surrounded with love and warmth … My piano was there

in the room that you first came to, with music around it. So that gave you an identification of me with 'mother'—and in the midst of everything that felt so scary, and wondering about whether I was 'disapproving', there was also this very warm, powerful link."

Following this session the healing process began, making it safe enough to give Anna the poems again. But more significantly, I resolved to find the courage to begin reading them aloud so that we could talk about the material they contained. Throughout my analysis music remained an important symbol, and Enya was the first of several CDs, which I gave to Anna. Each piece of music corresponded with some aspect of my internal process that I was also attempting to convey through the poems. But as Anna understood, I no longer felt myself alone in experiencing these feelings, since they also appeared as the subject of another's creative expression. There was comfort in this shared experience. It pushed the fear of insanity further into the distance, making it easier and safer to talk to Anna about my dark internal world.

Relief also came from Anna's explanation that "not taking the poems" had not been an intention to reject me or my writing. Earlier, I had resisted her offer of a third weekly session. Now she returned to it again, believing we needed "more space, so that we had time to work on the material you were working so hard to express through the poems." If I was now prepared to share this material openly, we really needed that third session to explore the huge backlog that had been silently piling up over previous months.

* * *

But this was not to happen. Though I no longer felt threatened by Anna's offer of a third session, I had effectively arranged my life to conspire against this possibility.

I had recently attended an interview for the first year of counselling training. With no prior information about the interview, I had little idea of what to expect. When I arrived at the college, I was directed to a classroom. Though early, the room was already quite full of people sitting silently—waiting uncertainly for something to happen. The room appeared to be organised in readiness for an examination, each table placed at a mathematically precise distance from its neighbour. I found an empty table and joined the silently waiting applicants. Sitting quietly a frightening thought crossed my mind: that we were, indeed, going to be asked to sit an "entrance exam" for this course. I began to worry about what sort of questions such an "exam" might contain, and why we hadn't been given advance warning to prepare for it. But before my anxiety could take hold, the silence was interrupted by the entry of a tutor. Having introduced herself, she talked with gravity about the nature of the training, and the serious commitment required in undertaking such a course. She explained that to pass from the Certificate Year into the two year Diploma, there would be a continuous process of assessment, which included written assignments. Her tone left me in no doubt about the seriousness of the undertaking, enhanced by the nervous atmosphere that had by now descended on the room.

We were then required to complete a form giving personal details and our reasons for wanting to apply for training. The forms did indeed bear a resemblance to an exam: our "papers" in place, we immersed ourselves in our task. Once completed, we were required to present the forms to the tutor, who would use them to conduct a personal interview with each prospective trainee.

They seemed to take me forever to complete and contained challenging and demanding questions requiring careful thought. But after a time I became aware of movement, as people began to present themselves for interview. To my alarm and embarrassment, I suddenly realised that the room had emptied, and that I was only one of a handful of people remaining to be interviewed.

Only one question endures in my memory: this was a question requiring us to answer honestly whether there were any mental health issues likely to affect our ability to manage this rigorous and demanding training. The form emphasised the need for personal responsibility in managing self-care, and that if we had any doubts these must be discussed with the tutor undertaking the interview.

It was a fearful moment, knowing that I had to share the information that I was attending analysis as a result of serious depression. With my strong sense of the unspoken doubts that I feared Anna to be harbouring—and which had forced me to question my own motives and timing—I now dreaded rejection. I remember being closely questioned about the nature of the therapeutic support I was receiving. Then, as if to reassure me, it was explained that the "most demanding" aspects of the course did not really begin until the first year of the Diploma. In the event, I was accepted onto the course on condition that I remain in analysis for the duration of my training.

I was to record this interview experience in a poem entitled *Beginnings*, in which the final verse acknowledges to Anna that "I had to vouch for you in your absence." It is painful for me now, to appreciate the extent to which these words presumed on Anna's willingness to stay by my side on this journey, and I hardly dare to imagine what went through her mind when I explained the condition on which I had been accepted. Anna's own training had involved a different route into the profession, both lengthy and demanding. Although I was entering the profession through another door, I'm certain she would have anticipated that aspects of the course were likely to make huge demands on both of us to maintain my mental and emotional well-being. What helped to reassure her, she told me later, was the knowledge that I would not be expected to work with clients until my final year. For now, time was on our side. But in view of the struggle we were trying to resolve, it was truly a precarious time for me to embark on entry into the profession.

But whatever doubts or concerns Anna might have had, she indicated nothing but her continued willingness to support me. I feel greatly moved when I reflect on such evidence of love, patience, and courage, especially since—once again—I was obliged to refuse her offer of a third session. Effectively I had a choice: I could attend three sessions a week with Anna or embark on the training, which involved a major financial commitment and a day's attendance at college each week. I explained that my choice meant I had neither time nor money to attend sessions three times a week: a less than gracious response to Anna's offer of increased support at such a difficult period. Ultimately Anna concluded that I had found another way to get "a third session" through my engagement with the group of trainees accompanying me in that first year.

* * *

Despite the large number of people who had attended for interview, I was surprised and delighted to discover that when we began, we were only a group of five.

The tutor's assessment of the first year as the least demanding proved correct—though it opened up a significantly different way of relating to others which was not without its emotional demands. Apart from learning some basic theory, the course was a gentle introduction to the concept of "personal development" as a significant aspect of the training, and the process of "sharing ourselves with the group" at a level of depth and honesty was often a painful experience for us all. I recall how this personal honesty was modelled by our tutor, when he chose to tell us that he was "a gay man", and that this was an important aspect of his way of being-in-the-world which he felt we should know. I saw this as a courageous disclosure to make to a group who were little more than strangers at that point. His honesty helped set the tone of what we were all there to do … and we did not remain strangers for long. We were to experience the nature of empathic, non-judgemental relationships, which gradually enabled us to trust in the safety of the group as we found the courage to expose our vulnerabilities. These were Carl Roger's "core conditions" in action, and the impact of this experience created a close bond amongst our small group, unlike anything I had previously experienced.

I soon found myself forced to question my own willingness to be personally honest in such a public arena. So far, I had said nothing about my twice-weekly analysis, or the events leading to it. It is interesting to reflect on how significant this felt at the time, as I contemplated sharing such highly sensitive information about myself. It would take all my courage to manage it—and yet now I feel intrigued that it caused me so much anxiety. I believe this was due to shame at having to confess to lived experience of "mental illness", combined with a fear that the group would find it impossible not to judge me, and that the tutor might decide my presence was inappropriate and unacceptable. Clearly these were all projections of my own fears, heightened by the doubts with which I assumed Anna to be questioning my decision.

What enabled me to overcome these fears was a session with Anna, on the day when I decided to share my "secret" with the group. The poem *Strength'* recounts how Anna's words gave me the necessary courage, and left me "feeling better now than I have done in months." At the end of that day, one group member told me that I was "brave, to say what I did," and that she knew I was not alone. I had experienced the power of a loving and non-judgemental relationship with Anna—now I felt this power in action within the group. It was a moving experience, which I was to take into my future training and work as a practitioner.

Not only had I found an alternative way of getting a "third session". Anna clarified another important aspect of that group experience:

> "I think there was something about trying to link the 'inside' and the 'outside'. Because therapy was very much about 'inside stuff' at

this point—about 'inside feelings' that were getting enacted in our relationship … and this made it easy to think that 'ordinary people' wouldn't understand this one little bit. They'd think it was crazy. So telling the group about your therapy was a way of starting to link the 'outside' with the 'inside', to make it feel less crazy. It was a way of getting a third session which felt grounding and safer, and which re-engaged you with the outside world—because part of the illness was that you felt very disconnected from everybody, and your fear about a third session was that it would increase your sense of isolation … So in the end I felt we just had to check out what this need was about, but then to go with your own instincts."

It is evident from this final comment that Anna had understood a need of which I was barely conscious: this was to do some of the work of therapy for myself and to have some control over the process of my own recovery. In Anna's words:

"You knew that you needed therapy, and that you needed whatever it was that I could give you. But it was also very important for you to feel that there was an independent bit that could do some of the work for yourself too. And I think that part of the story of our therapy has been about how to bring those two things together. You found the medium of the poems, and we had to fight and negotiate how we were going to use them—but then you found Enya's music. And then you found the counselling course, which was kind-of like your third session, only you were doing it in a different way … You really needed to find your own ways to think about what was going on for you."

Anna recognised that I had come to appreciate how analysis offered opportunities to think about my internal process—but analysis proceeded slowly. By now, it had become important to find theoretical interpretations that would help me towards a quicker understanding. It is a testament to Anna's dedication and skill that she remained resolute in supporting me through these risky excursions into uncharted territory, which remained a significant feature throughout our on-going journey.

CHAPTER EIGHT

Christmas

*I hope this will be
A special time for both of us.
A time to forget and to remember.
So many conflicting emotions
Race through my mind—
Pain and joy mixed
In a volatile cocktail.*

*I wish I knew what this time means for you.
My mind is full of imaginings—
None of them linked to reality.
But still, there is comfort
In the picture I have created.*

*Now my heart is full of love.
This time, I hope it will help
To raise me above the doubts and difficulties,
To build a new structure
On top of the dismal framework
Of last year.*

Christmas 2001 was an unexpectedly happy time. The New Year felt like a "marker". As I stood on the threshold of my second year in analysis, I recognised the importance to our therapeutic relationship of so many shared experiences. By now I was convinced that it was this relationship that was enabling me to survive, however fearfully, in the outside world.

Looking back over our first year together, some of these experiences had become important connections linking us closely together in my mind. Notable amongst these was the discovery that Anna and I were both to become grandmothers in the same month. In contrast to the previous Christmas, with its destructive thoughts of death, this Christmas held the promise of new life and hope. I desperately wanted to project this symbol of hopefulness into our continuing relationship. Knowing that Anna was also spending time with her family, I was able to maintain a fantasy about her activities which contained the quality of a shared experience. Unlike the summer break, this holiday appeared to be holding us together rather than tearing us apart. A poem written at the time conveys a mood of dreamlike unreality in which I "floated" through my own family Christmas that year. Nevertheless, in my memory it stands out as a time full of good things. To re-experience these feelings after so many months of bleak hopelessness was a relief in itself.

* * *

With stark inevitability, the New Year heralded a return to reality. Inside my head things sometimes felt better, though I fluctuated disconcertingly between ambivalent "existences" in my insubstantial world. Perhaps antidepressants were partly responsible for this. It was as if I was rehearsing for a play, or playing a part in someone else's dream. Not that this was particularly unpleasant. Aspects of this existence felt promising, and I had begun taking tentative steps back into the outside world which seemed to mark an improvement in my mental health. I took on a new job, as part-time administrative assistant at the local adult education college, which fitted conveniently around the two sessions a week with Anna and one day at college. Life was busy and demanding once again.

But it was still early days … and the benefits of analysis often take time to materialise. Reflecting on that work experience, I recognise how I drifted through it as if in a reverie. Somehow my inadequate computer skills, which had slipped through the net at interview, soon became apparent once I was actually doing the job. My usual response would have been panic, followed by guilt and a sense of failure, leading me to practise secretly in order to make up for my deficiency.

In fact, none of this happened—simply because, in my strangely disembodied world, none of it seemed to matter. This is not to say that I "didn't care"—just that it wasn't possible for me to care, because it wasn't my world which felt "unreal", but *their* world. Eventually things came to a head when my Line Manager invited me to attend a "Personal Development Interview". Sensitively highlighting my lack of computer skills, she informed me that to continue, I must commit to a comprehensive computer training programme. Uncharacteristically, I experienced no pangs of anxiety in declining her offer, telling her that I had committed to a new career and had begun the training. Shortly afterwards—with an unaccustomed lack of concern—I handed in my notice without a backward glance.

* * *

By now I had completed my first term of training as a counsellor. I had loved almost every minute of it and unlike the administrative job, I had coped with many challenges. But other aspects of my day-to-day world remained far from easy. While close friends loyally stayed in contact, I mostly preferred to avoid social exposure. When this wasn't possible, I felt horribly conscious of invasive and inquisitive gazes seeming to search my psyche for signs of illness or recovery. Though I knew that these "invasions" stemmed from a loving concern, they threatened the fragile equilibrium that I was barely able to sustain. I became acutely aware of appearing odd in company, either by my behaviour or my conversation. Somehow, I had learnt to adopt the persona necessary to survive in the work environment, where no-one had any knowledge of what was happening in my internal world. These people were unlikely to threaten my tenuous stability by intense questioning or inquisitive looks. But amongst close friends who knew about my "mental health problems", there was no protective emotional armour behind which I could shelter. The only environment which felt safe was the one in which I could speak "the language of therapy". There, I could say whatever came into my mind—or say nothing at all—without being judged, misunderstood, or finding myself a focus for concern.

It was evident that my external world had shrunk whilst my internal world had grown. Apart from Anna, only my colleagues on the training course felt safe enough to allow into this inner world—perhaps because of the shared experience of vulnerability in which we were all equal, in some sense at least. I now recognise the importance of this place of safe holding in gradually enabling me to encounter others less fearfully. Each group meeting inevitably introduced me to the many and varied worlds which my colleagues inhabited during their "normal" existences. Though a vicarious connection, it was nevertheless a vital one—something with which I had lost touch over the preceding months. Increasingly I felt hopeful of a time when I might also fully engage in this existence, free from fear or the need to create a "false self".

But for now, external appearances did not look particularly promising to those closest to me who were unaware of these internal processes—and this included Patrick. The way in which unresolved issues of the past had threatened the total disintegration of my psyche had become, of necessity, the main focus of my analysis. And since the blackness in my soul was life-threatening, Anna's first priority was to save me from the worst excesses of my shadow. But something had begun to shift my perspective on these problems, as Anna helped me to acknowledge the deeply repressed hurt and anger around Patrick's original betrayal. It was becoming possible for me to accept that he shared responsibility for our troubled relationship; that it wasn't simply about the damage which I had inflicted on him, but the damage which we had both inflicted on each other. My poems show how I lurched precariously between feelings of love and resentment—the significance of which Anna emphasised in our needing to talk about the poems, so that she could explore this evidence of my troubled internal world.

As New Year began, Patrick and I found ourselves experiencing yet another problematic period in our relationship—though precisely why is hard to remember. But I can well imagine that my emotional fragility did not make me easy to live with.

I also wonder whether Patrick was struggling to understand my continued need to isolate myself from him and others, while managing a training course which signified the start of a new career. Perhaps this had given him hope of my imminent return to normality. Certainly he had supported and encouraged me, so possibly it came as a profound disappointment to him, to find that at the end of my first term I was still intent on remaining emotionally and physically isolated from him and our social world. Since I had been in therapy for a year, I can imagine

Patrick's frustration at the sleepless nights during which I continued to sit in darkness listening to music; at my continued inability to manage trips to the supermarket, phone calls, social engagements; and at my fear of leaving the house except to drive myself to work, to Anna, and my counselling course. My inner world was still in turmoil, and my relationship with Patrick was often haunted by the ghost of our earlier problems, and by the additional complications created by my mental instability. Emotionally, we were both out of our depth in knowing how to negotiate a way through these difficulties. And then, in January 2002, my anxiety emerged in a dream:

> It was Christmas time and we were at home. Suddenly the doorbell rang, and a couple of old friends were standing there. They said they had come to visit, and that they were returning some things we had lent them a long time ago. They began to bring in mountains of big, bulky furniture and objects, mostly broken or damaged. As well as furniture, there were paintings, ornaments, vases, bowls, children's toys. They kept bringing more and more things into the house until we had no space left. The house began to feel dusty and dirty, and looked like some horrendous junk shop. Patrick was desperately trying to find places to put everything, but things were arriving faster than he could deal with them, and objects ended up being piled high all around us. It all seemed to be part of our past that we thought we had disposed of, but which had somehow been resurrected. Now it had come back to haunt us and was threatening to take us over. It felt as though we were drowning in a sea of broken objects.

Years later, when Anna and I found a meaningful context in which to explore this dream, I recognised the couple as old friends in real life. Anna reflected:

> "You had shared a past …. And at this point you were finding it impossible to see old friends so it was all very difficult, and you were feeling that 'something was broken'. There's a lot of fear in the dream, and a sense in which your present mental state is so 'full up' with what feels like broken, unusable things from the past that you can't yet sort through … And here we were, at the beginning of a new year of therapy, with so much to sort through—and

a feeling that you and Patrick also still had a lot of sorting out to do."

Several other significant dreams surfaced, which soon led to another difficulty over which Anna and I were to wrestle. With reluctance, I had finally agreed that we would read my poetry aloud, though often the strength of feeling which emerged would make it impossible for me to continue. Then Anna would take pity on me and continue the reading. I found the whole process extremely painful, though I understood why it was necessary to find a way to bring this evidence openly into the space between us.

But the thought of reading or discussing my dreams still felt impossibly dangerous, and so far I had refused to do this. As had happened with the poems, I was writing them down and giving them to Anna—with the expectation that she would "tell me what they meant" without wanting me to contribute anything. By treating her as "the expert", I could relieve myself of responsibility for adding anything which might prove harmful to her. From her recorded account of those gruellingly painful sessions, I have gained an invaluable perspective on what was happening between us:

> "It was a real tussle for us to think about the meaning. You wrote them down in a very polished way, so that what you'd written became an object in itself—and to try to tease it out or to make sense of it felt very difficult. And one of the things I would usually try to do with dreams is to use the way it's *told* to me, to make extra sense of it. But if you read a written version you can't do that—and you weren't wanting me to do that. You'd said it all on paper; you'd chosen the words, and it felt as if quite a lot of 'editing' had gone on—so that I mustn't hear the tone of voice, or I mustn't be able to feel anything about the dream."

"So I was feeling that you'd much prefer it if I'd come and talk about the dreams. But I was wanting just to write them down and not to talk about them?" I asked.

"Yes. You didn't really want to talk about the dreams at all ... And what I was trying to do was to move us on from you giving them for me to read and to tell you what they meant—because this was very paralysing. It stopped any communication. But of course at that point, you felt that I didn't want to have them at all.

So I thought we needed to go through a period of you not giving me anything, and just talking me through them ... but we had to battle that one out—and I think it was about fear, wasn't it? You were very scared ..."

"Yes, I was—because they felt so damaging. And yet you were saying, 'It's okay. I can manage it.' So I got it into a form where it felt a bit more contained, but then you were telling me to 'uncontain' it again—and that felt very dangerous."

"Yes, you did feel it was dangerous—and you thought I was dangerous ... And there were a lot of sessions with very long, heady silences ... And you would imply that there was masses going on—but you weren't going to tell me about it. There was a lot of 'tantalising'."

"Yes, I think I found the 'you' inside my head easier to talk to than the 'you' in the room—because in my head I could make you say what I wanted you to say—but it wasn't like that when we were together ..."

"... So your psyche devised this wonderful way of keeping me well out, and having a kind-of 'do-it-yourself' therapy!"

Though with hindsight we could be amused at this situation, the outcome of this "tussle" was that I stopped bringing Anna any dreams, and a period of hostile silence followed. Then a dream emerged about which I was able to talk without having first given Anna a written version. We subsequently referred to it as "The Wedding Dream":

I was getting ready for my wedding, but nothing was as it had been in reality. I was in a strange, little, modern semi-detached house which I didn't recognise. None of my family was present. I was upstairs, and a close friend from my schooldays, Louise, was helping me to get dressed in a typical, white wedding dress with all the trimmings. Suddenly we heard a commotion from downstairs. Louise went down to see what was happening. A crowd of guests had arrived early to see me. Louise argued with them, telling them to go away and wait for the wedding to take place. I was hiding, but watching and listening from upstairs. I didn't recognise any of the people. They all looked well-dressed but seemed rough and aggressive. Eventually Louise managed to get rid of them. Now there were just the two of us. At this point I became very aware of my surroundings and my clothes. Everything felt wrong. Nothing seemed to be what I was expecting and I suddenly didn't know where I was.

At that time, I felt myself to be under protest in telling Anna the dream. I expressed feeling "extremely disconcerted" by the experience, because if felt "much easier to write than to talk."

"... Because when you write," she suggested, "you don't actually have to manage the reality of the other person. You've got the 'internal me' that you're writing to, without having to manage all your anxiety around the 'real' me."

Years later we were able to openly reflect on a likely interpretation. My feeling of being "forced into a marriage"—signifying my relationship with Anna during this period—was evident in the constraint suggested by the "strange, little semi-detached house", and my discomfort with my "traditional wedding dress with all the trimmings". Perhaps this also reflected concern with what I sometimes imagined to be restrictive aspects of the analytic model of therapy. The "gang at the door" are aggressive strangers, alien to my world—which might indicate my fear of Anna as an aggressive intruder. I am protected by Louise, who sends away the threatening intruders. In reality, Louise was the friend who had looked after me when I escaped to Wales with my children following the initial breakdown of my marriage. During that early period in therapy I was aware of Louise's desire to "protect" me, and her consistent mistrust of Anna and the process of analysis. This made her an appropriate guardian against Anna's threatened invasion in my dream. Significantly the dream suggests no "husband". He is totally irrelevant, because "the wedding" actually reflects the struggle in my "marriage" with Anna. And since this was also a stormy period in my relationship with Patrick, I was desperate for something like a "marriage" which felt supportive and reassuring.

* * *

Any therapist of a Jungian persuasion reading "The Wedding Dream" will perhaps accord with Anna in making a connection with the "mystic marriage", or *coniunctio*, described by Jung in *The Psychology of the*

Transference.[1] In this extraordinarily illuminating work, Jung explains how the work of fifteenth and sixteenth century alchemists symbolises the development of the transference in the analytic relationship. This symbolism is explained through detailed interpretation of a set of alchemical pictures taken from the *Rosarium Philosophorum*, an anonymous collection of alchemical writings, which describe the highly paradoxical processes involved in the chemical transformation of matter.[2]

From a scientific standpoint, the alchemists knew that the attraction of opposites would eventually lead to "conjunction", and thence to the emergence of a new substance—but in a different form from its originally base and worthless components (the *prima materia*). Through many further processes, the new substance would finally emerge in its purest form—sometimes referred to as "the philosopher's stone", which alchemists believed would be capable of turning base metals into gold. The "birth" of this pure substance also contained within it the hope that Man might ultimately achieve perfection and enlightenment.

Since no such pure substance actually exists in nature, Jung deduced that alchemy needed to be viewed from a symbolic rather than a scientific position. In each alchemical process, he divined a psychological parallel, which led him to regard these alchemical writings as "a prefiguration of modern depth psychology".[3] According to James Hall:

> A famous alchemical dictum, "dissolve and coagulate," suggests the repetitive psychological process of realising that a hard "substance" of the mind—for instance an apparently insoluble conflict—is really capable of solution, only to be replaced by another "substance" that in its turn requires dissolution.[4]

From his intensive study of historical documents, Jung provides evidence that later alchemists understood that their work also

---

[1] Jung, C. G. (1954). The psychology of the transference. In: G. Adler & R. F. C. Hull (Eds.), *Collected Works of C. G. Jung, Volume 16: The Practice of Psychotherapy*. Princeton: Princeton University Press, 1985.
[2] Frankfurt, A. M. (1550). *Rosarium philosophorum. Secunda pars alchimiae de lapide philosophico very modo praeparando ... cum figuris rei perfectionem ostendentibus*.
[3] Hall, James A. (1983). *Jungian Dream Interpretation: A Handbook of Theory and Practice*, p. 96. Canada: Inner City Books.
[4] Ibid., p. 97.

described a process of personal transformation, and that their search was as much for a "gold" contained within the possibilities of psychic transformation, as within the transformation of base metals. Andrew Samuels *et al.* describe how:

> The alchemists projected their internal processes into what they were doing, and, as they carried out their various operations, enjoyed deep, passionate emotional experiences along with spiritual ones.[5]

In considering the symbolic significance of the attraction of opposites, Samuels *et al.* point out:

> Male and female struck the alchemists as ... the most fundamental representation of the existence of psychological opposites. Because the outcome of intercourse is a new entity derived but also different from the parents, we can see that human beings and their development are being used symbolically to refer to intrapsychic processes and the way in which an individual personality develops.[6]

Alchemy, therefore, becomes "a metaphor which illuminates how a relationship with another person promotes internal growth, and also how intrapsychic processes fuel personal relations".[7] In human form, this alchemical transformation was symbolised in the *Rosarium Philosophorum* by the archetypal figures of the King and Queen. According to Jung, their "wedding" (*coniunctio*) signifies the "supreme union of hostile opposites",[8] through which they become, literally, joined into one person. They must experience seven principle processes of transformation, amongst which is their descent into a black, shadowy chaos (the *nigredo* or *tenebrositas*), equivalent to a place of hell, in which a painful division or dismemberment (*disiunctio*) into their elemental parts take place. Their death, followed by corruption and decay, leads

---

[5] Samuels, A., Shorter, B., & Plaut, F. (1986). *A Critical Dictionary of Jungian Analysis*, p. 12. London: Routledge, 1997.
[6] Ibid., pp. 12–13.
[7] Ibid., p. 13.
[8] Jung, C. G. (1954). The psychology of the transference, p. 211. In: G. Adler & R. F. C. Hull (Eds.), *Collected Works of C. G. Jung, Volume 16: The Practice of Psychotherapy*. Princeton: Princeton University Press, 1985.

to "purification" through fire and water,[9] "the return of the soul",[10] and finally the emergence of "the new birth"—since "no new life can arise, say the alchemists, without the death of the old".[11] The spiritual significance of this unifying process is seen in parallel with the scientific and chemical processes, so that the King and Queen become the archetypal manifestation of both aspects, representing the union of opposing elements through a loving affinity.

This, then, is "a *symbolical* relationship whose goal is complete individuation (wholeness)".[12] Extraordinary as this alchemical parallel may appear—and I do not pretend to do justice to it here—Jung gives us painstaking proof of its relevance to the practice of analysis:

> Everything that the doctor discovers and experiences when analysing the unconscious of his patient coincides in the most remarkable way with the content of these pictures. This is not likely to be mere chance, because the old alchemists were often doctors as well ... In this way they could collect information of a psychological nature, not only from their patients but also from themselves, i.e. from the observation of their own unconscious contents which had been activated by induction.[13]

As I return again to Anna's perspective on the "Wedding Dream" in the light of Jung's writings, her connections seem unquestionable:

> "We were getting into the *nigredo* during this period—the really black awful place ... And there were things that had to be 'burnt off' or 'discharged' in some way. And you're getting married, so there's something about the relationship between you and me, but I'm not there in the dream—because we're not nearly there yet. We're in too constricted a place, and there's still a whole lot of stuff that needs 'getting rid of' first ... And Jung has this image of *coniunctios* at different stages of the therapy ... but sometimes they can only be there briefly—they have to 'separate', because a whole lot of other stuff that has to be 'burnt off' before you can unite. It's

---

[9] Ibid., p. 273.
[10] Ibid., p. 283.
[11] Ibid., p. 257.
[12] Ibid., p. 261, my addition of parentheses.
[13] Ibid., pp. 200–201.

about the relationship uniting and then breaking down again … And when you have the symbol of a marriage right in the middle of a dream, it's always going to make me think of that connection. Of course, there are many ways to think about a dream, but perhaps the most grounding way is to start to think about it in relation to the transference—it's like a 'window' into it, which helps it to make more sense."

According to Hall:

> Observing the appearance of *coniunctio* imagery in a dream … can give clues as to when the reconciliation of a particular pair of warring opposites may be expected … Much of the work of analysis, indeed, seems to be to maintain a steady and reliable containing structure in which preparations for the *coniunctio* can safely take place.[14]

As Anna surmised, though I had decided to talk about the dream it felt as though I was being "constricted" into giving in. Without doubt, I felt angry—but importantly, I began to let go of the obstruction blocking us from a truly therapeutic "joining together". Though the process of transformation had only just begun, this small breakthrough signified a "little marriage" between us which promised hope of future synthesis.

Reflecting on the many blocks through which we stumbled during the early analytic process, we were both aware of the huge fear of my shadow from which these blocks emanated. As it had overwhelmed me, so its power to overwhelm all who ventured too close became a further source of anxiety. Perhaps this was not an altogether psychotic response to my perceived danger, since Jung himself poses the question: "How can man live with his shadow without its precipitating a succession of disasters?" This suggests a warning, whose intention is to remind us that, "Recognition of the shadow is reason enough for humility, for genuine fear of the abysmal depths in man … The man who recognises his shadow knows very well that he is not harmless …" (p. 239).[15]

---

[14] Hall, James A. (1983). *Jungian Dream Interpretation: A Handbook of Theory and Practice*, p. 99. Canada: Inner City Books.

[15] Samuels, A., Shorter, B., & Plaut, F. (1986). *A Critical Dictionary of Jungian Analysis*, p. 239. London: Routledge, 1997.

CHAPTER NINE

Now I am feeling very low.
Some sort of crisis seemed to hit me tonight.
Was I challenging you,
Or was it the other way around?
Did we have what you call 'a tussle'?
Because now I feel completely drained,
And I have sunk to the bottom of a big, black hole.

I know you tried to hold me
Somewhere safe—to let me know
You understood how I was feeling.
But right now it isn't working,
And I am crying tears of pain and regret—
Sorry for what I said,
But knowing I had to say it.

What will happen next time?
How will we begin?
Issues of 'control', you talked about ...
That makes me very frightened.
Now I don't want to win—only lose.
Control is a terrifying word for me.
But something reassures me that you will keep hold
Of what is happening, helping me to understand.

Listening to recordings of what was happening between us during my second year of analysis, it is clear that Anna had begun to challenge me to open up my material in a number of ways. Firstly it concerned the poems; then it moved into a battle to get me to talk about my dreams. By Easter 2002, the focus of Anna's challenge concerned my wanting her to start the sessions, rather than being willing to risk this for myself.

In my own clinical work, I often witness the huge discomfort clients experience in opening the session. In the initial silence, I regularly encounter the gaze that explores my face, looking for signs to gauge my mood that day. If I resist responding, the gaze might transform itself into a look that seems to plead with me to speak first. Sometimes the silence may be broken by a question: "Are you well?" This question might be just an "ice breaker", a desperate attempt to fill the discomforting space. Or it might be a "polite question", since this is an appropriate social response in relationships outside the consulting room. It would be easy to explain away clients' difficulties in such terms. But as Anna taught me to appreciate, answering a client's question too quickly might be to miss its significant "unspoken" message. Most important to consider is whether the question—or the silence—might be hiding anxiety about my response to the client's recent material, and my capacity to contain this safely. Opening a session for the client, or accepting a question at its face value, may actually be evidence of the therapist's defensive need to protect herself from the client's anxiety. Whatever is going on for the client, it is my job as the therapist to explore the anxiety underlying a client's difficulty in opening the session.

And so, inevitably, it was also Anna's job to notice and respond to this difficulty in my own therapy. The process of analysis is tough, and perhaps in contrast to the more humanistic models, it does not set out to be overtly "reassuring" in the normally accepted sense. By now, we had been working together for fifteen months. For many other models of therapy, this would have been regarded as long-term work. But this is not so with analysis. There were undoubtedly times when I longed for some comforting words of reassurance about my progress—to hear Anna tell me that I was "doing okay"; that she had faith in the final outcome of our work. Many of my poems contained "questions", indirectly inviting her to respond to this need. But I learnt that the role of the analyst was not to reassure my anxiety, but to explore and work with it so that we could try to make sense of it. Ultimately, through this process, I would find a much deeper, more lasting "reassurance" born out of greater self-knowledge and understanding.

The poem opening this chapter is entitled *Crisis*. Written in-between our first two sessions following Anna's Easter break, it expresses my painful questioning concerning this latest challenge to our relationship, and became the subject of a uniquely enlightening session during our recordings. It was Anna's focus on this poem which gave her the opportunity to explain in detail, not only the nature of my psychological struggle as she perceived it at that earlier period, but also her analytic response to my situation in terms of her theoretical thinking. For the benefit of our recording, six years later, Anna had revisited her notes and reflected carefully on her own process at the time, which led to the decision to bring into the open my anxiety about starting the sessions:

> "It had become an issue by then, so it felt as though if I started the next session, you'd won—and I didn't think that would be good, because, as you said in the poem, you 'only wanted to lose'. But if I didn't start the session, then the battle continued. I thought long and hard about this and in the end, I decided to start [the next session] by saying, 'Now … you want *me* to start the session'—because the point about that would be that you'd hear my voice, and it would give you something to 'tune into'. What I felt was that there was a lot about you needing to hear my voice—to estimate how I was—to estimate whether you'd done any damage—to estimate what had been going on inside me since the last session. And at this point I was getting a huge sense of a 'you' that was really needing to adapt yourself to me in a kind-of 'looking after mother' way—and I was trying to work with that, and to see what would happen if you didn't have a 'me' to tune into. It was about trying to give you a sense of a 'me' being able to be a container for you—the 'mother' that can contain the 'baby'—even a yelling baby, a screaming baby, a pooey baby—whatever it is. But at that point, you didn't feel at all safe enough, because you didn't feel your stuff could be contained really. So it was as if you were trying to kind-of 'be like me' in a very tuned-in way—and this gives us something to work with, doesn't it?"

"And so, by opening the session in that way …" I invited Anna to elaborate.

"… You would know that I'd remembered what had been said. You could hear my voice, and you could work out whether it felt cross, or 'damaged', or whether it felt facilitative—whether I was 'okay' for you … it was a way of resolving the fight, of not having 'winners' or 'losers'," Anna explained.

"Did it work?" I heard myself ask her.

"Yes—it relieved it, I think."

In terms of my personal history, Anna's perception of this need and the difficulties it presented made perfect sense. My need to "protect" Anna from my own pain reflected my response to my real mother, and the way in which this need had been reinforced by my father's "messages" about my mother's emotional vulnerability. The image I had described in the poem of "sinking into a big black hole" struck Anna as having particular significance in terms of the mother–child relationship:

"If we think 'mothers and babies', and if we think in terms of the very early developing psyche, 'the big black hole' is a place where there's 'no mother'—where you're totally isolated. It's almost as if there's no human being there for you."

Though deeply disturbing, this was a place and a feeling with which I could identify. I recognised it as a "nowhere" place, suffused with unspeakable pre-verbal pain and terror.

"No," I replied. "… There's nothing and nobody there—just dark …"

"… And you can get there if you feel I'm furious with you at this point—or when you feel you've said something that's so damaged me that I'm not there anymore," Anna suggested.

I experienced a deep resonance with Anna's interpretation of what "the black hole" might signify for me. Anna now offered me a theoretical explanation, based on the ideas of the Kleinian child analyst, Donald Meltzer, as described in his book *The Claustrum* (2008). Meltzer begins with Klein's theory of projective identification, which *The New Dictionary of Kleinian Thought* describes as:

> ... an unconscious phantasy in which aspects of the self or of an internal object are split off and attributed to an external object. The projected aspects may be felt by the projector to be either good or bad. Projective phantasies may or may not be accompanied by evocative behaviour unconsciously intended to induce the recipient of the projection to feel and act in accordance with the projective phantasy. Phantasies of projective identification are sometimes felt to have 'acquisitive' as well as 'attributive' properties, meaning that the phantasy involves not only getting rid of aspects of one's own psyche but also of entering the mind of the other in order to acquire desired aspects of his psyche.[1]

Meltzer considered psychoanalysis to be a form of parenting, and being a child analyst he empathised with the immature infant brain, where the world is experienced in terms of the body. Hence he imagines the infant's internal world in terms of bodily regions. In extending Melanie Klein's concept of projective identification, Meltzer proposed the idea of the infant's "intrusive" projective identification into certain hidden bodily spaces of the internalised mother figure. As Anna explained:

> "If you have the idea of the mother as a psychological 'container', then the infant is 'contained' inside the mother. And that's very helpful, if and when it works mutually well. But there will be times when it doesn't work well, or when something goes wrong. Well, Meltzer's idea was that if the baby can't be contained, for whatever reason, the opposite happens. Then the baby might need to 'get itself inside the mother' in what he calls 'a claustrum'. So instead of it being something mutually beneficial, there's the feeling that there isn't a container, and the baby needs to 'get in' because it's got to be there. And because Meltzer was a child analyst, he's very much into 'the body'. So he has 'body regions', and he describes how the infant might need to 'dwell inside the feelings in the heart'. And, I think, sometimes it could feel like that for you—an overwhelming need to be in the feelings ... And empathising with the feelings when it's mutually beneficial feels really good and close. But it can easily

---

[1] Bott Spillius, E., Milton, J., Garvey, P., Couve, C., & Steiner, D. (2011). *The New Dictionary of Kleinian Thought*, p. 126. Sussex: Routledge.

tip—and then it can feel like you're *trying* to 'get into the feelings' but you're not wanted—and then you can be worried that's it's an intrusion … It's really the 'shadow side' of containment."

This explanation did indeed make sense of my early desperate need to be "contained" by Anna, and the way in which this need would then "tip over" into huge anxiety concerning the fear of "damage" resulting from these phantasies of invasion and control. Meltzer describes how:

> … the most primitive form of relief of psychic pain is accomplished by the evacuation into the external object [i.e., the analyst] of parts of the self in distress and the persecutory debris of attacked internal objects, receiving back through the introjective aspect the restored objects and relieved parts of the self.[2]

Thus, when the urgency for "internal containment" becomes paramount to survival, the infantile phantasy will become a drive to find another way "in to" the mother by means of such intrusive projective identification. In line with Bion's "contained/container" model of thinking, Meltzer tells us that: "the contained must be allowed to enter the container".[3] Meltzer's extension of this idea concluded that, if containment can't be found in a "feeling place" inside the mother, or if the mother is non-receptive, then the desperate need will be to get "inside" the mother in a very darkly secret place, which he termed "the claustrum". According to Meltzer's theory, the claustrum dweller will psychologically inhabit one or more of "the compartments of the internal mother"—namely, "the mother head/breast",[4] "the genital compartment" including the womb (p. 88), and/or "the maternal rectum".[5] And as Anna, explained:

> "Then you're in a *really* 'black hole' place … because once we get into this feeling that you have to be 'inside', and you're really worried about 'intrusion', then ideas about the body, and infantile

---

[2] Meltzer, D. (1992). *The Claustrum: An Investigation of Claustrophobic Phenomena*, p. 39. London: Karnac, 2008.
[3] Ibid., p. 58.
[4] Ibid., p. 72.
[5] Ibid., p. 91.

phantasies, begin to make sense even though they can be very disturbing."

Though she found Meltzer's ideas thought-provoking, Anna had already made it clear that she also experienced them as personally disturbing, explaining that she had always had "a very ambivalent relationship to Meltzer." I think her concern was that I might experience something similar; and so, by sharing these feelings with me, I could feel free to express my own discomfort. At that time, I did not experience a particular sense of discomfort. In fact, I was able to tell Anna:

"Funnily enough, I don't find his idea particularly disturbing … And for me, because my conflict about 'wanting to get inside you' was also about my fear of doing damage, I can understand that there could be something very murky about the place where I would end up …"

"Yes …. And Meltzer would say you'd be really scared about being 'shat out'!" Anna speculated. "Well, yes … if we're *really* going into the realm of the 'body' …"

"… And if I'm feeling very bad about myself, maybe I need to be in that really black, nasty place?" I reflected.

"Yes," Anna agreed. "So I think there was something around at this time which made me question whether we were in that place. I saw that I'd made a note: 'Are we into claustrums here?'… And I think this tussle about which of us would speak first meant that we were getting into a struggle about 'power and control', and about 'who is pushing stuff into whom'. Then I do think Meltzer's thinking begins to make some sense of something which otherwise is so anxiety-provoking."

"It's fascinating … but certainly not something I would have wanted you to tell me at the time …" I heard myself say.

"Absolutely not!" Anna responded emphatically. "But it was something that helped *me* to make some sense of it … And I also needed to think about how, if you did feel you'd got yourself into a 'secret place' inside me, then you were going to be hugely vulnerable—because you don't want to be discovered. And all sorts of worries were coming out then, which is why I felt that it was really vital for me to keep my integrity, and not to feel that I was getting cornered into accepting things that I felt uncomfortable doing—because otherwise I thought I would be with you in that place … And the important thing was, that the more I let you give me things without bringing them into the open, the more I'm encouraging, or allowing your phantasy that you're 'pushing things inside me' that we can't really know about together. So the more I'm colluding with that."

Meltzer's theories derived from his clinical work with seriously disturbed patients who were psychotic or had a borderline personality disorder. However, Anna made it clear that she was not inviting me to perceive my own mental distress as a similarly extreme example. I fully understood that her intention was for me to appreciate that, as with any mental health condition, all human beings occupy a place somewhere on the mental health spectrum with regard to these ubiquitous capacities. Bion certainly regarded the phantasy of projective identification as ubiquitous, since he distinguished between normal and pathological projective identification. In the case of a traumatic event occurring in our lives, we may find ourselves moving some way along this spectrum, perhaps crossing the invisible (and questionable) border which divides "normal" from "pathological". If the impact of the trauma is felt by the psyche as too painful or damaging to be contained safely by the ego, it is likely to be split off and "disowned" as a psychic defence mechanism. The projection of these disowned aspects of the psyche into the external figure of the analyst represent a pathological need for "a container", into which it becomes possible to defensively "evacuate" all the "bad" and threatening internal objects safely.

Regarding the question of what might be considered ubiquitous, (i.e., normal), or pathological, (i.e., abnormal), Meltzer points out that:

> Knowledge of the phenomenology of the claustrophobic world comes largely from analytic work with a certain category of psychotic children, from psychotic breakdown in adolescence … but also, surprisingly, from the early stages of the analysis of the so-called normal and well-adjusted people who come to analysis for professional development of one sort or another … From these experiences it has been concluded that the entry into projective identification is an ubiquitous phenomenon in early childhood …[6]

---

[6] Meltzer, D. (1992). *The Claustrum: An Investigation of Claustrophobic Phenomena*, p. 118. London: Karnac, 2008.

Meltzer further suggests:

> In the neurotic patient, and perhaps in most people generally, the existence of an infantile part still inhabiting the claustrum casts its shadow on the person's "picture of his world" ...[7]

Though I would not have had the remotest knowledge of Anna's theoretical thinking during that period, my training had begun to alert me to differences between "counselling" and "analysis" in basic theoretical terms. However, since this was primarily humanistic, I was frequently driven to question Anna about aspects of the analytic model that could feel harsh and punitive when her approach seemed to conflict with what I thought I wanted and needed from her. In finally reading Meltzer two years after my analysis ended, I could comprehend how my early psychotic fears sometimes resonated with his theoretical perspective. It was deeply disturbing at times, to find myself experiencing a sense of re-visiting ominously familiar territory in his description of the claustrum dweller's habitation in the rectal compartment of the internal mother. Despite the pain of having to acknowledge it, I could recognise this truly dark, joyless, and forbidden place, devoid of genuine comfort and a breeding ground for suicidal feelings of hopelessness. I understood why Meltzer talked of the analyst needing to "maintain the working-level of hopefulness" while bearing "the full burden of the hopelessness",[8] which constantly recurs as an intolerable burden for the patient. And yet, while the "black hole" claustrum of this compartment is suffused with all the danger of discovery, Meltzer describes how "exit" from it produces another, even greater fear: this is the fear of "expulsion to the 'nowhere' of the delusional system".[9] In the rectal compartment, all that matters is survival, since "Survival has the meaning of evading expulsion which seems to constitute the most nameless dread of mental life".[10]

This "nameless dread", according to Meltzer, "consists in being 'thrown away' ... [it] is exponentially worse even than exile ... it is absolute loneliness in a world of bizarre objects".[11] It is now evident to me

---

[7] Ibid., p. 120.
[8] Ibid., p. 79.
[9] Ibid., p. 119.
[10] Ibid., p. 119.
[11] Ibid., p. 91.

the many ways in which this "nameless dread of expulsion" manifested itself in my relationship with Anna in those early years—a dread undoubtedly aggravated by the trauma of "expulsion" induced earlier by the relationship counsellor; though the origins of the original trauma must surely have emanated from some deeply unconscious pre-verbal birth or infantile experience of expulsion about which it is now impossible to "know". But I was struck by the way in which the intense infantile aspect of my transference towards Anna, which regularly manifested itself in my strong need to tune in to her "internal being", bore a striking resemblance to Meltzer's case study of an adult patient, in which he describes:

> A strong desire to look at the analyst, minute monitoring of his noises, smells and appearance as well as those of the rest of the house, all accompanied by intense oceanic emotionality at times ...[12]

In Meltzer's view, "acting in the transference" begins an important development in the analytic process—not just at times of separation, "in the absence of the object", but in each other's presence in the sessions:

> Lightning attacks ... demands for information and emotional directness spark the sessions. The patient's curiosity begins to monitor what is observable and scavengeable about the analyst's history and way of life. We are in business at last, on familiar territory of the transference–countertransference. The real life of the mind has entered the consulting room.[13]

I have no difficulty now in understanding what lay behind Anna's challenge to open up and share my material in the space and moment of the sessions. What I was bringing her, in my silences about the writing and the talking, was some very split off, often psychotic material. Anna saw her role as trying to get hold of these "split off bits" of my psyche. At the same time she fully understood how fearful this felt for me, because of the reasons I had split it off in the first place. But while she understood the many ways in which this fear led to angry resistance to her

---

[12] Ibid., p. 79.
[13] Ibid., p. 106.

challenges, her decision was not to reinforce one system in my psyche at the expense of another. It therefore became a vital aspect of the therapy that we continue to find ways to confront and manage these significant conflicts. In an earlier reference in which he quotes Bion's *Memoir of the Future*, Meltzer reflects on "catastrophic change, and recovery therefrom" as significant junctures in the analytic relationship, seeing them as "the moments which hold in suspense the possibilities of both 'break-down and break-through'".[14] As Anna would later reflect:

> "It's going to be like that, isn't it? Because you came to therapy with lots of very difficult, confused, and conflicting feelings. And if you've got a therapist who doesn't reassure you, but who makes a space and waits to see what comes up, you're automatically going to feel that you're getting those feelings back from me … But if I reassure you, I'm never going to get a feeling of what it is that we're dealing with—because we're trying to deal with things which are 'below words' … I'm sure you thought I was all sorts of things—but the important thing for me was not to be scared of you thinking that I was those things—because you were very scared of thinking those things for yourself …. It wasn't an easy therapy … and I wasn't an easy therapist."

In a later chapter, Meltzer describes the consulting room as a place where "two highly unique mentalities are met in love and battle".[15] His continuing picture of its essentially paradoxical nature strikes me as a beautifully apt description of so much of my own experience of the analytic relationship:

> … But they are also met in interest, both in themselves and in one another, and certainly there are moments in which the intensity of this interest holds together the love-making and the battling to initiate a truly passionate conjunction. It may not, does not last very long each time but its growth-promoting quality, for both, is unmistakeable.[16]

---

[14] Ibid., p. 53.
[15] Ibid., p. 111.
[16] Ibid., p. 111.

CHAPTER TEN

Quite abruptly, between May and September 2002, the poems ceased. After such an intense period of darkly creative output, it seemed important to reflect on this written silence and its significance in terms of our therapeutic relationship. My resistance to opening the sessions had gradually resolved into something which suggested more safety and trust in the process, and this seemed to offer some relief from the need for written expression:

> "Looking back at what I wrote, the work became much more 'between you and me', and so not so many poems were necessary at that point," Anna reflected. "I think writing became the way in which you and I worked with the tension of opposites, so that if one side was very strongly felt—but the other side was also important—then this other side came out in the poems ... When the poems stopped, I think it was a period of less ambivalence; it wasn't a period of 'opposites', but a period of relocating with what was going on. In the beginning it *was* about the tension of opposites: things were very black then, and it was about you needing us

both to find a really 'tuned in, being-together place' to make you feel safe. The images in your poetry kept coming back to that. And then, as I see it, it stopped oscillating so much, and we managed to feel really engaged in what went on between us. But then at other periods, when we returned to the tension of opposites, the poems would appear again."

Anna's interpretation was certainly borne out by the evidence. The poems continued to re-emerge periodically, indicating the re-emergence of our struggles. But as the tensions were resolved by our repeated working through of these difficulties, the poetry would emerge in bursts, rather than the ceaseless outpouring from my tortured psyche. Though troubled waters still lay ahead, the lack of poems during these five months suggests my growing belief that tensions could ultimately be reconciled between us.

By now I was nearing the end of my Certificate Course. Though not an easy year, it had not been unduly challenging. We had been introduced to theoretical ideas, and were gradually and gently assisted to explore our personal process within the context of our relationship with the group. As the academic year was ending we received a "warning", lest we assume a natural progression onto the two-year Diploma Course. In May, our tutor announced a visit the following week from one of the tutors on the Diploma Course, who would explain what would be involved in committing to the next stage. Nothing about this announcement troubled us. Indeed, it seemed entirely appropriate that we understand fully the nature of the commitment involved in further training.

But the reality proved formidable. Within minutes of starting our session the following week, the "visiting tutor" walked into the room. As she seated herself in front of our small group and gazed searchingly into each of our faces, we instinctively fell into apprehensive silence. Her expression unchanged, she announced her role as co-facilitator on the Diploma Course. Assuming that we had satisfactorily completed our portfolio and experiential work for the Certificate Year—which, she sternly reminded us, had yet to be decided—we would have the option of continuing for a further two years, leading potentially to a professional qualification as counsellors.

"How many of you are contemplating this progression?" she asked.

Her tone was grim. Looking anxiously around the group in search of moral support, we each raised a hand in slow and fearful response. This was accompanied by one or two faint murmurings of indecision:

"I haven't *quite* made up my mind yet ..."

She peremptorily silenced the murmurings:

"Then you all need to listen *extremely* carefully to what I am about to say ..."

A dramatic pause followed, as she glared purposefully around to assure herself that we had absorbed her serious objective. As I recall, "frightened rabbits caught in the headlights" aptly describes the mood which had by then overtaken us. We continued to listen submissively to her warning:

"If you have any ideas that this year has prepared you for what to expect from the Diploma training, I am here to disillusion you. There is no comparison between what you have experienced this year, and what you will experience if you choose to continue onto the Diploma Course—and I think I can promise you that it will prove to be the toughest and most demanding training any of you might previously have undertaken."

Uncompromisingly tough, she certainly generated the desired effect of terrifying us into unquestioning attention to what followed. Nothing she said was designed to alleviate our worries as we were given "chapter and verse", not only on the obligatory academic requirements, but also of the importance of furthering our "personal development". It was clear that this vital aspect of the course was the most rigorous and demanding—since how we "grew" in terms of our personal development would be more influential on our ability to become successful practitioners than the mere application of theoretical knowledge. And so we were left in no doubt of the significance of compulsory "personal therapy" hours, of finding a trainee placement to fulfil 100 hours of client work, of various compulsory supervision arrangements during which we would learn to reflect on ourselves, our client work, and application of theory into practice. It was what it was intended to be: a salutary warning to any of us with even the slightest doubt about our willingness or ability to commit physically, intellectually, emotionally or financially to this two-year undertaking.

The talk over, our visitor left us to carry on with our class as usual. But the intense impact continued to reverberate amongst the group long after she had gone. Too frightened to raise any questions in her presence—for fear that these would be interpreted as doubts about our readiness to make a total commitment, our poor tutor, a gentle, empathic man, was left to pick up the emotional debris. Following her departure, fear quickly turned to defensive resentment as we attempted to repair our demoralised egos. Confronted with this onslaught, our tutor strove valiantly to maintain an empathic balance between the views expressed by the visiting tutor and our own dispirited responses. Yes, he tentatively agreed, perhaps she had been rather heavy-handed in her "warning messages". Personally, he reassured us, he had no doubts about the way in which we had consistently shown our commitment to the course and to the group in this first year. But finally he felt bound to agree with everything we had been told about the demanding nature of on-going training, giving us sensitive but compelling evidence from his own experience. The repercussion of this episode proved to be that from our group of five, only two of us chose to continue onto the Diploma Course.

* * *

However, this was not an unequivocal decision on my part, and events which transpired between May and September were destined to produce another tense episode in my analysis. Though I had no doubt that I wished to continue with counselling training, I had begun to consider whether there were other routes into the profession—and to recognise that I had choices about which route to follow. Certainly fears had been raised in my mind about my ability to cope with the academic and emotional demands of the course. And yet the inner voice of questioning and self-doubt was familiar; it had made itself heard at every significant crossroad in my life as I faced a new and unknown challenge. It was the voice of fear anticipating failure as a likely outcome, originating from my childhood experience of "failure". But as an adult I had proved that I could overcome this fear. And so, while I heard the voice, I do not believe it was this which made me equivocate.

As I stood at this particular crossroad, at this particular period in my analysis, my mind flooded once more with thoughts of Gemma, our relationship counsellor. Though by this second year of analysis my transference attachment to Anna was unquestionable, there remained "unfinished business" which prevented closure to the painful feelings of rejection which had accompanied the ending of that earlier counselling relationship. My love for Anna had helped subdue these feelings, as I felt myself contained in a deeply therapeutic relationship. But now, as the idea of "choice" took root, what emerged was the thought that I could choose instead to train as a relationship counsellor. I recognise now that this stemmed from an unconscious drive. But at that period it was perhaps inevitable that I would rationalise my decision—as an "intellectual urge" to find a theoretical explanation for what had happened between Gemma and me. And my decision also suggested an opportunity to understand the relationship difficulties in my marriage … or at least, this was how I reasoned it to myself at that time. It would take many more years of analysis before I could fully acknowledge the unconscious process which had compelled me towards a resolution to the painful feelings of rejection.

And so, I informed Anna in May of my decision to apply for interview to train as a relationship counsellor. Not surprisingly, this led to conflicts similar to those which had arisen at the time of my original decision to begin a counselling training. But an important difference lay in several added layers of emotional complexity which would rumble disturbingly beneath the surface during the months ahead. Firstly, I knew before meeting Anna that she had spent many years working as a relationship counsellor for the same organisation, prior to her training as a Jungian Analyst. My need to talk about the trauma of my ending with Gemma left me wanting to know more about Anna's own experience of this work. Though she answered some of my questions, she was understandably very careful not to express a professional view on what had happened to me. Her role was to find an empathic way to understand my pain—not to pass professional judgement on Gemma. But I discovered that Anna's position had been an important one within the organisation. For me, this meant that she had "inside information" concerning many things which I was desperate to understand. Thus, I came to see her reticence as depriving me of information which might have helped me come to terms with the outcome of that earlier relationship. I argued to myself that if anyone was in a position to understand what had happened to me, surely it was Anna, who could now view this event from various theoretical perspectives.

Perhaps it was Anna's necessary guardedness which fortified my belief that I needed to "go in there and find out for myself"—to quote Anna's earlier recognition of my capacity for determination. But professionally, ethically and therapeutically, I now understand that there was every reason for Anna to remain silent on this subject—though unsurprisingly, many of the same doubts and fears around my sense of her covert disapproval resulted from this silence. Reflecting on this situation later, Anna explained:

> "Between us, it was very difficult, because I'd been part of the selection process for years, and knowing what I knew about where you were psychologically and what you were struggling with, I didn't really think that they would select you at that point—the time was wrong. But it was very tricky to know how to deal with that therapeutically. You were hugely wanting to know what I thought—but I wasn't sure that what I thought would feel particularly helpful."

Despite my desperate desire to "know" what Anna could tell me, it is interesting to reflect on the fact that I chose not to ask for her view on my decision directly,

> "... Because I think you were terrified that I might say something like, 'What! You *must* be joking!'" Anna speculated, "And that would have totally demolished you."
>
> "Yes, you're right," I concurred. "I'd already had to face a lot of disapproval from friends about my counselling training. I didn't want to hear any more disapproving stuff ..."

But my decision also revealed the continuing need to "get close" to Gemma, and my explanation of a desire for "theoretical understanding" did not deter Anna from making this connection:

> "The question of whether you were really wanting to 'get near' to Gemma felt to me like the obvious interpretation—because you were still missing her awfully. And where we got to with that, according to my notes, was that my wanting us to think about that possibility became too difficult for you to think about. Your defences got up, and several times we got into a battle. And I was writing notes to myself saying, 'Why do I get drawn into these battles? How else could I manage it?'"

"Was I getting angry with you?" I questioned Anna.

"Well, you were getting very defensive, because I was saying something you couldn't bear to hear … Later on, we thought about how you felt compelled to find out where Gemma was coming from in order to make sense of what she'd done to you. But that did suggest that you were needing to 'get into her mind', to work out why she'd done what she'd done … and then, of course, that brings up the fear of 'intrusion'—because if you do get into her mind, you're going to worry about what you might be doing to her."

In time, events would prove Anna to be correct: that this re-emergence of my urge to make sense of what had happened to me was not just an intellectual need, but also a deeply emotional one, in which the urge to "connect" with Gemma was most certainly the unconscious motivating force.

But for now, my determination led me to plough on in the face of all these unacknowledged doubts. Finally I received a letter inviting me to attend a "Selection Process Day". From a choice of dates, I chose a date in August.

When Anna and I reflected on this decision, another unconscious process was clearly being "acted out" by my choice of this date. I knew that Anna would be taking her summer break, so we would not be meeting during August. This meant that there would be no opportunity to reflect on the interview either immediately before or after it had taken place. Effectively, my unconscious wish was to "shut Anna out" in order to "punish" her for what I perceived to be her disapproval. I seemed resolved to prove that I could, and would, manage without her support. This also allowed me the illusion of believing that I had resolved the question of my own ambivalence about this interview. In fact, it was merely another example of my projection onto Anna of the unconscious disapproval which I felt towards myself.

The truth was that I was also punishing myself by choosing an interview date which would deprive me of Anna's much-needed support. I already sensed that attending the interview was likely to be a demanding experience. To begin with, it involved a journey of more than a hundred miles, and the early morning start meant travelling on the previous day and staying overnight. With his usual gallantry, Patrick came to the rescue. From the very beginning, he had keenly supported me in training for a new profession. I imagine that my re-engagement with life must have come as a huge relief after so many dark months of withdrawal from the world, and I was grateful for his unquestioning and supportive presence. It was a welcome escape from my own self-questioning, to know that there was one person so close to me who appeared to entertain no doubts about what I was choosing to do. And so, when Patrick offered to book a hotel, drive me to my interview, and spend the next day sightseeing on his own until the time came to collect me, I felt deeply grateful for his unspoken acknowledgement of my need for his supportive presence on that day.

When the morning arrived, Patrick was firm in his insistence that I eat "a proper breakfast", knowing that this was regularly something I chose not to do. "You need to build up your strength for the day ahead," he announced firmly. I didn't argue. Instead I was touched by this further evidence of his care and concern. Though it wasn't easy to make a pretence of having any appetite, I did my best—noticing how Patrick watched me eating with anxious approval, all the time endeavouring to keep the conversation light and relaxed. In his determination to avoid unnecessary additional stress, Patrick had already thoroughly researched the journey we would need to make that morning. I recognised that he was making a supreme effort to convey *his* strength, in order to reinforce my own self-belief—and it was immensely reassuring to feel his determined encouragement. As we embarked on the final leg of the journey, Patrick continued to maintain this strong presence—but all too soon we arrived. As I kissed him goodbye and watched him turn the car around and disappear from view, my heart was filled with deep love, tenderness, and gratitude. I felt suddenly bereft, and at that moment I wished he could be by my side throughout the day's proceedings, feeding my deep uncertainty with his unquestioning belief in me.

I had not over-estimated the challenge I was about to face. The interview process proved arduous and demanding, beginning at the Reception Desk where a coldly officious woman pushed a form at me, demanding a signature as proof of my arrival. She avoided looking up from her paperwork, making it clear that my presence merely constituted an administrative task to be accomplished without delay. As I signed my name and listened to her impassive and well-rehearsed directions about "how to find the room", I became aware of the arrival of other candidates. I hung about, noting how they went through the same impersonal process. A small voice inside my head had begun to question whether this experience set the tone for the day's proceedings.

I could feel my anxiety level rising to a familiar and disabling crescendo, and was eager to make contact with similarly anxious others who were about to undergo this long and demanding day with me. There was some consolation in observing the shared sense of discomfort at this unpromising welcome, as a small group of us found our way to the room, chatting briefly as we went. This offered some temporary relief. But as we entered the room, we found it already occupied by candidates who had arrived earlier. And so, as we took our seats in the pre-arranged circle of chairs, a nervous silence descended as we awaited the arrival of the remainder of the group.

At some point a woman entered the room, announcing herself as the person responsible for overseeing the day's selection process. Her welcoming manner was encouraging after our brusque reception. Though my memory of that day is sketchy, I believe that finally we were a group of twelve candidates. We were given a schedule of the day's events, and told that these activities involved group and individual exercises during which we would be continuously watched and assessed. Some of the exercises required written responses, which we would have to submit as an additional aspect of the assessment process. Nevertheless, the hope was that we would "enjoy our day together" and regard it as "an enlightening and valuable experience", regardless of what the final outcome might be.

These efforts to be reassuring did little to subdue my already heightened misgivings. Since I had not the faintest idea of what "answers" the selectors would be looking for, it was clear that my whole day was destined to be fraught with uncertainty. But the concern provoked by this information was as nothing compared to the misgivings aroused by one further event we were told to expect—not listed in the schedule. We learnt that we would each have to attend an "interview" with a psychotherapist. These interviews would take place throughout the day, and we were each allotted a time when we would need to leave whatever we were doing to attend this meeting. Already filled with dread, I waited to hear my name and time. Finally my name was read out as the last interview of the day. If I had been asked to predict a worst scenario for myself this would undoubtedly have been it, since I now knew that that I would have to contain my anticipated dread throughout the entire day.

I think I knew from that moment on that I was destined to fail the interview process. My psychological breakdown had already left me with a discomforting sense of "transparency", making me believe that my innermost soul was visible to others. This belief had translated into a conviction that all psychotherapists were trained to possess this "power" … and so I presumed it would be with this unknown psychotherapist. Nevertheless I tried hard to contain my anxiety, and to engage as fully as possible in all the challenging exercises of the day. I watched as candidates disappeared and reappeared from their interviews, trying to read their faces for any illuminating signs which might fortify me to manage when my time came—but its only effect was to constantly remind me of what was still to come. Feelings of dread preoccupied my mind, steadily eroding what remained of my self-confidence and determination.

And so, by the time my interview finally arrived, the outcome had effectively become a self-fulfilling prophecy. As I faced the man who I had already imbued with such huge and fearful power, the last vestiges of my emotional stability disintegrated in his presence, leaving me exposed and vulnerable in the face of his gentle but incisive questioning. I have no recollection what he asked, or what we spoke about. But I know that I found myself close to tears—and that he could do no other than sense my extreme fragility.

When Patrick came to collect me I put on a brave face, desperately searching for hopeful and positive experiences to recount about my day. I felt huge guilt about the time, effort, and expense with which he had so lovingly encouraged me. It was as though I had deceived him by my determination to pursue an objective which I now saw as doomed before it had even begun. Somehow, contained within her eloquent silence, I also knew that Anna had correctly anticipated it all—and now she would be away for several more weeks, so there was no-one and nowhere to turn for support. It was a horribly painful period which I was now obliged to confront alone. And when the letter arrived, less than a week later, even my anticipation of this event had not really prepared me for the devastating effect of this second rejection.

CHAPTER ELEVEN

What did you come back to
After your holiday?
A whirlwind of pain and anxiety

Which had swept me up
And left me stranded on a beach somewhere,
Waiting for warm hands to lift me up again.

But this anxiety was deep inside.
On the surface was bravery and renewed hope.
But you delved below the surface

And found what was lying in the mud—
Something trampled and forlorn
That was waiting for resurrection.

"…. And so you came back from the summer break with the news that you hadn't got through the interview—and then there was a series of poems …"

—*Anna*, recorded on 27th November 2008

Entitled *Return*, I presented this poem to Anna in our first session following her summer break, in 2002. The weeks following the fiasco of my interview were a dismal period of self-questioning and decision-making, during which I longed for Anna's supportive presence. But I knew I had only myself to blame as I confronted the pain of failure and rejection alone.

In the event my determination took over, as my resolve to continue with counselling training surfaced in the face of defeat. A choice was still available—to pursue the Diploma Course—and so I made the decision to commit to two further years of training. But the anxiety that had been stirred up was now intensified by rejection. As my childhood fears of failure reignited, I also had to confront the reality of my psychological frailty as a serious consideration to continuing with such an emotionally demanding course—Anna's unspoken words assuming a voice which echoed insistently troubling questioning inside my head.

And so, while I longed to feel Anna's strong presence again, I also dreaded having to regale her with news that I was certain she had anticipated. Having confessed to my failure, I informed her of my subsequent decision to continue with the Diploma. A series of four poems then emerged in-between our first two sessions, written on the same day. As Anna commented in her recorded reflections, after a five-month interval, this was evidence that I was trying to resolve something profoundly disturbing.

Neither of us had a clear memory of how Anna had responded to my news. But we both agreed that she must have made some reference to "the timing not being right". However on this occasion I was not moved to defensiveness. The evidence was there, and I could no longer avoid confronting the painful reality. Now I was ready to openly acknowledge that Anna was right to have doubts with which I must also question myself. In spite of my earlier defensiveness, I had absorbed something significant with which my unconscious had continued to wrestle while we were apart—this was my difficulty in allowing Anna to have "different thoughts" to me without feeling threatened. Now we were able to explore this openly, and what I came to understand was the way in which this dynamic also paralleled my relationship with Patrick. Anna later expanded on her interpretation of the situation:

"I think that's something that you and Patrick have been struggling with too … because you're telling me that he can find it hard to let himself have different ideas to someone else. So he will say 'yes' when he actually means 'no', or when he doesn't really want to."

"… Because it took me a long time to realise that he was saying 'yes' when he meant 'no' …" I added.

"… And he was saying 'yes' because he thought he had to agree, because he's not supposed to think differently—And certainly we've talked about that an awful lot … I think certain aspects of one's personality get reinforced in a marriage. So you marry somebody who's got things that fit in common with you and then they get strengthened. So that becomes more and more 'the way it is' between you. And then that part of your psyche gets reinforced at the expense of something else. And that seems to be something that had really got 'woven in' to the way you were together."

"Yes … absolutely … But I can see that it's also got to be about appreciating the differences … Because we often choose a partner that fits the bits of us that we're not good at … So it's important to appreciate those differences, and to see them as strengths, not weaknesses."

"Oh yes, definitely …"

"… So we're really back to what you were saying to me just now—about our battle around allowing you to have a different view to mine without feeling threatened by that."

"Yes—because that doesn't then have to 'globalise' everything—and it doesn't have to be about 'right and wrong'. It's a different possibility—a different set of ideas—and it's a question of whether it's possible to play with those ideas. But the answer is that it's usually very hard to play with them if you're feeling defensive and threatened."

In terms of the history of my relationship difficulties with Patrick, I could now clearly understand how I had used Patrick's reluctance to allow himself to "think differently" as a vehicle with which to exert control over him, following the traumatic breakdown of our marriage relationship all those years ago. And inevitably, as issues of "control" surfaced in the therapeutic relationship, I would be driven to respond with similar resistance. But now this series of poems suggested that I was arriving at an understanding of what lay behind this response.

Another poem entitled "Travelling" records similar expressions of doubt, but in combination with a new and unusual spirit of optimism:

> Tonight I feel full of words.
> They are bursting inside my head
> Demanding to be released.
>
> You started something tonight.
> Despite the heaviness, the fog lifted
> And suddenly I could see again.
>
> You let me know that the struggle isn't over.
> 'More work to do,' you said.
> But still things fell into place
>
> And everything began to make sense—
> About me and that day,
> And why things hadn't worked out.
>
> But in spite of everything I feel hopeful.
> This is not the end but the beginning—
> Another road to travel; a new journey to make.

"… As indeed it turned out to be," Anna reflected six years later. But optimism had never been my strong point, and I am left to consider why it surfaced at this point in my analysis, in the face of so many future challenges. My belief is that this spirit of optimism marked the growth of a new dimension in my transference towards Anna. As we worked through our difficulty concerning "difference", the feelings of defensiveness transformed themselves into a deeper understanding of Anna's objective to "hold me safely" as we embarked on this next stage of my precarious journey. Whatever her private thoughts and concerns might be about this undertaking, I finally appreciated that her intention was *not* to withhold her support, but to decide how best to provide it. But this time we both understood the potential dangers of the "uncharted territory" into which we would be venturing. As I experienced Anna's willingness to face this huge therapeutic challenge, I no longer feared that she would abandon me—and it was from this belief that my spirit of optimism sprang. With Anna by my side, I believed that, somehow I would reach my destination safely, supported by her love and strength.

As we discussed this whole episode together six years later, I recorded the following dialogue, which begins with my own reflections:

> "I think your reservations were absolutely valid at that time. But I also think that my intuition was valid too ... but at that point I couldn't really explain it. It was more just a feeling—it wasn't a rational process."
>
> "Yes, of course. So what you had to do—and you really managed to do it—was to go on with it in the face of my deafening silence. And that's what you did," Anna concluded.
>
> "Well yes ... I did ... But I also know that there were times when I nearly did fall down a 'black hole' again—or even when I did actually fall into it—and you were always there for me, however much you might have disapproved, or had doubts."
>
> "Well it wasn't a question of disapproving. It's not up to me to disapprove ... No, it was 'fasten your safety belts' time ... because I really wasn't sure what you were going to be doing to yourself ..."
>
> "... No ... Neither was I," I was forced to admit.

I felt moved by such clear evidence of the strength of Anna's concern. It was a stark reminder of how little I could comprehend the therapeutic difficulties with which I had confronted her at that time.

> "Yes ... So interesting times ..." Anna continued after some silent reflection. "... And that sense you've always had, that if you learnt to understand what had happened to you it would help—of course that's what we're doing now, through these recordings. You actually said that this is the way you need to do it—and you knew that ... always. So again, I think our route has been very much about 'feeling our way', and needing to find out what was going to work."

*   *   *

It would be seventeen months before any more poems surfaced. In September, my training began in earnest with the first term of the Diploma Course. As if to underline the significance of this transition, the venue was markedly different. In contrast to the small, intimate setting of the Certificate Course, I now found myself in a large, gaunt building whose floors and corridors, flanked on either side by shabby, impersonal classrooms, seemed to wander on forever into some anonymous hinterland. The classroom in which our training took place was particularly horrible, perhaps because its large size emphasised its most unattractive features—added to which was a larger than life-size model of a skeleton suspended from a stand in one corner of the room, whose ghastly stare it would prove difficult to ignore during the two years in which he silently shared the demands of our training. We never did discover the reason for his presence. Perhaps it rested in some previous and long-forgotten anatomy course. But certainly, for one or two members of the group, he proved a decidedly unwelcome guest—an unavoidable trigger to thoughts of death and loss, which we were inevitably encouraged to confront as an aspect of our "personal development". And so, eventually (and perhaps existentially), we learnt to accept this archetypal image of death as a continuing and "living" presence amongst us for the entire period of our training.

But this is to anticipate events. Back then, as I entered this room for the first time, its starkness was somewhat softened by the circle of chairs arranged in readiness for our first meeting. This was only a temporary relief, however. The circle was large, and the room was filling up with people obliged to look discomfortingly across at each other, since there was nowhere else to look once you had taken your seat. It was a daunting initiation, and I began to doubt whether I would manage to survive two years, subjected to such a forbidding environment.

In fact, things were not destined to remain the same—as time would reveal. When I began my training, we were a group of twenty-three students. By the end of the first year the group had shrunk, until ultimately, only eight of us completed the course. This is a measure, not only of our powers of endurance, but also of the truth contained in the visiting tutor's warning. From now on, she would play a significant role in my life, together with the other tutors responsible for different aspects of the programme. The seriousness of our undertaking quickly became apparent, as we were each handed an intimidatingly thick "Course Handbook", containing information on every aspect of our training over the next two years. But as we stood on the threshold of this new endeavour, we were instructed to pay particular attention to the extensive reading list, which was divided into two parts: "essential" and "recommended" reading. As I devoured the titles on the list, I felt my spirit soar in anticipation of my imminent entry into this hugely exciting profession. For now, my anxiety was quietened by the conviction that I was exactly where I wanted to be.

As the first term got underway, and I became increasingly engaged in this new learning experience, it inevitably produced changes in my relationship with Anna. Her understanding of why the poems stopped at this point became the subject of one of our recorded sessions, as she explained:

> "Once you started the Diploma Course, I think you were able to bring much more of yourself into the room ... because you had begun to learn and to understand what the transference meant, and what it meant to work with the feelings in the room. So you were gradually learning to appreciate what I was talking about, when I was trying to get us to think about what was going on between us. And I think that the poetry—or the images of the poetry—became experienced by you as 'between us' in the room ... So that's my thinking about why the poems may have stopped."

It became clear from Anna's notes that I was trying hard to engage more openly with her, as my knowledge and understanding of the process of therapy was deepening. I started to describe what was going on in my inner world, and in place of the poems, a number of dreams surfaced about which I was able to talk—sometimes without having written them down at all. This is not to imply that I found it easy—as events would subsequently reveal. And an added difficulty arose from my expectation that Anna would "explain" the meaning of my dreams to me, since I found them at best totally baffling, and at worst, deeply disturbing. I sensed that Anna was interested in dreams from her responses, when I would say something to her like, "I've got a dream for you ..."

But Anna's way of working was to resist giving me her interpretation—with the result that I often felt convinced that she was "keeping something from me". Unfortunately, this feeling was aggravated by my reading of a book entitled *The Lady of the Hare: A Study in the Healing Power of Dreams*. The book by John Layard was originally published in 1944.[1] Layard was one of the first Jungians to be trained at the newly formed C. G. Jung Institute in Zurich. Consequently he

---

[1] Layard, J. (1944). *The Lady of the Hare: A Study in the Healing Power of Dreams*. Boston, MA: Shambhala Publications.

worked in the classical tradition, in which the analyst assumed an authoritative expertise in his interpretation of his patients' material. This is definitely not the position taken by modern Jungians, but my ignorance at that early stage of training increased my frustration. While Anna was aware of these feelings, and would offer tentative thoughts about a dream, I was not generally able to move forward very effectively in my own thinking. In Anna's words:

> "That was something we had to negotiate—because in a way, at this stage, you were being 'a good girl', and bringing me dreams because 'I liked dreams'. And if I liked dreams, then my part of the deal was supposed to be to tell you something interesting about them. Then you'd know that 'mummy was pleased with you'. There was that dynamic going on ... But, once again, we were working with 'difference', and I was trying to give you a sense of me and how I work, so that we could find a way to work together ... For me, it would be really vital for you to be able to associate with a dream, and to tell me what the images brought up for you—because, after all, it's your dream—rather than me 'feed' something into you ... But what you wouldn't really have understood at that point was that, what happens between you and me *after* you've told me a dream is also extra information—about the feeling in the room around it, and how we can use it or not. These are also important things to think about. It's not just the substance of the dream ... And we did get there in the end."

Despite the inevitable difficulties, those few months since September had been a period of relative calm. As this first term drew to a close, I found myself experiencing an unfamiliar sense of pleasurable anticipation at the approach of the Christmas break. Patrick and I planned to spend Christmas and New Year in Australia, with my sister and her husband. Added to this pleasure was the anticipation of being joined by our son and his girlfriend, currently engaged in a "round the world trip". For the first time, I found myself able to say goodbye to Anna without fearing my emotional ability to survive our separation ... And it did indeed prove to be a joyous time.

CHAPTER TWELVE

I remember New Year as a magical celebration. We welcomed in 2003 from the balcony of my sister's home, while the fireworks erupted in majestic illumination of Sydney Harbour Bridge. My sister had organised a party of friends in honour of our visit. As I stood there revelling in this unique occasion on the other side of the world, it was impossible not to reflect on the change to my emotional and psychological health, in comparison with other New Year's Eve celebrations.

By the time my sessions with Anna began in January, a dramatic disruption had occurred. This set in motion a train of events whose outcome it would only be possible to comprehend fully many years later. It had been an extremely wet winter in the south-east of England, with rainfall well above average for several months leading up to January. The threat of flooding was a serious possibility in certain areas, and since Anna's home faced directly onto the river, her home and its surrounding area were inevitably at risk.

This would not be the first time flooding had occurred since Anna and I had begun working together. During a previous winter, I clearly remember receiving a phone call from Anna on the day I was due to see her for a session. To begin with, the conversation between us left me feeling quite bewildered:

> "Naomi …" Anna's voice began, "… I'm phoning to ask if you possess a proper pair of wellies?"

Unaware of what had occurred, my immediate thought was that this was an unusual kind of conversation to have with my analyst. I struggled to understand why Anna would phone to ask me such a question.

> "Yes … I have got a pair of wellies," I replied, keeping my perplexity to myself.
> "…. But are they a *serious* pair? Do they come up to your knees?"

Puzzled by her insistence and why she was suddenly taking such an interest in the height of my Wellington boots, I racked my brain in an effort to remember precisely where they might be. I hadn't worn them for years—probably not since my children were very small, and we used to go on occasional muddy walks at weekends and on holidays. But as a native Londoner who only rarely ventured into the countryside, I abhorred mud. And so my Wellington boots, wherever they were now, had long since become a relic of a bygone era. Nevertheless, I knew that they were still somewhere—and that they reached to my knees.

> "Yes …" I assured Anna, "… They do reach my knees."

Anna sounded relieved—and then her strange questioning became clear.

> "Well, I'm afraid you're going to need them. Our lane is flooded and the water is quite high. You can't bring the car down here—but it is possible to walk to the house if you've got a suitable pair of boots."

Eventually I found my wellies, lurking in a dusty and long-neglected plastic bag in the cellar. It felt quite surreal to be wearing them again in order to wade through water to visit my analyst. But something about this whole adventure had begun to feel exciting—a sense which stayed with me as I embarked on my journey. Parking the car nearby, according to Anna's suggestion, I began the unusual process of walking to her house. Uncertain of what to expect, I turned into her lane. A little further on, I could see what looked like a large puddle. It was clear that I would have to negotiate my way through it in order to reach Anna's house—but at a distance, it hardly seemed to present much of a challenge. Perhaps she had over-estimated its depth? But as I began to wade into the centre of the "puddle", the water became ever deeper, finally threatening to reach over the top of my boots. I slowed my pace, taking each step carefully so that the water didn't wash over into the inside of my wellies. Suddenly I found myself totally engrossed in this "game", as if re-visiting some delightful childhood experience. It was strangely pleasurable, to notice how the force of the water struggled so purposefully against my efforts to keep it under control and away from total invasion. It proved to be a close-run battle—but finally I arrived, with dry feet, on Anna's doorstep.

I remember that Anna was concerned and keen to explore the effect of this untoward occurrence, and the extent to which I might have been disturbed by it. And yet I remember my spirits being lifted by this reconnection with innocent childhood enjoyment. At the end of the session I looked forward to a second opportunity to "do battle" with the water, as I waded back down the lane.

I phoned Anna before my second session that week, to ask if I should wear my wellies again.

"No ... the water has gone down. You won't need your wellies today," Anna told me.

I recall a sense of sadness and loss at the transient nature of this all-too-brief childish interlude.

But this time events had taken a much more serious turn. As the heavy rainfall continued into January, a cold arctic air stream descended on the Thames Catchment area. The river levels rose while temperatures fell to below freezing. By the 4th January, ice began to cause an additional hazard to the whole region.

Having returned from an Australian summer to these arctic conditions, I suspect that I had not taken in the significance of this situation when I received a phone call from Anna a few days before we were due to meet. Her easy tone of voice did not prepare me for the news that followed. She had phoned to tell me that the steadily rising waters had finally entered her home shortly after New Year, and large parts of the ground floor were now flooded. She and her husband had been forced to move out, and were in the process of finding somewhere else to live. Inevitably this crisis would delay her return to work, though Anna's hope was that the delay would be short-term. She would phone me as soon as this problem had been resolved.

Anna's effort to avoid any hint of drama in her voice was probably an attempt to protect me from the full impact of this catastrophe. And so it wasn't until I had put the phone down that I began to imagine the situation now confronting her. A nightmare image grew in my mind, of how familiar parts of her home might look, submerged under water. Perhaps precious objects had been damaged beyond recovery, such as the piano? And as if this wasn't worrying enough, Anna and her husband now had to find temporary accommodation, and somehow, essential items which she required to live and continue her work needed to be rescued from the floodwaters. I was overcome with anxiety and distress for Anna and her family, who would all suffer the inevitable impact of this catastrophe.

But within a few days I received another phone call from Anna—to tell me that they had found a temporary home not too far from where she lived. She gave me the address, commenting light-heartedly that my journey would be shorter than previously. I saw this as another attempt—for my benefit—to play down the drama of what was happening to her. Our sessions could begin the following week, and so our start had only been delayed by one week.

Though it was necessary for us to work through the impact of this unfortunate interruption to my process, Anna's strength and courage in the face of this adversity proved to be powerful evidence of her unwavering support, through her determination to continue her work regardless of what was happening in her personal world. In the disruptive outcome of what was to follow, I believe it was this strength that enabled us to survive the many challenges that would arise over the next two years of our work together.

* * *

At that period, my first session of the week was on Monday evening that, during winter, inevitably meant that it was dark by the time I arrived. From Anna's directions, I recognised the name of the road in which she was now living. She had warned me that I would need to drive some distance before reaching her house … and so I kept going.

It wasn't difficult to find, since I had been told that it stood on its own, set well back from the other houses, and at the end of a rather long driveway. "You will be able to park right outside," Anna had cheerfully informed me. Stopping the car at the end of the driveway I sat staring for several minutes at Anna's "new home". I could see her car parked outside, so there was no doubt that this was the correct address. As I stared at the scene in front of me, I was struck by something slightly absurd about the whole setting. From a distance, the tiny little house at the end of such an impressively long driveway seemed incongruous. With so much space in front of it, I found myself reflecting, why was the house itself not larger and more impressive? And the driveway, flanked by exceptionally tall hedges, seemed deliberately designed to block out any intrusion of light. Anna had turned on the porch light in an effort to brighten the surrounding darkness. But this merely exaggerated the impression of isolation, which seemed to envelop the strange little house and its bizarre setting.

Although there was space, I decided not to park directly in front of the house. What caught my attention was the shingle driveway. Were I to drive down it, Anna would be sure to hear the noise and be alerted to my arrival. Normally this would not have mattered, but my obsession with being late meant that I regularly arrived twenty minutes early, and the space to sit and reflect quietly had become an important addition to my "therapy hour". If Anna was aware of my arrival, I did not think I could sit comfortably for twenty minutes outside her house—and perhaps visible to her—before ringing the doorbell. I finally resolved this problem by parking my car a few minutes' away—in a road with brightly lit modern houses, in front of which I could sit comfortably in the glow of their warmth, quietly and unobtrusively contemplating my forthcoming session.

Having parked my car in the space that would become my regular spot, I proceeded to walk the short distance to Anna's house. Although it only took a few minutes, on those dark winter evenings it was a walk I came to hate. On the second occasion, coming for my daytime session, I could see two horses grazing peacefully in the field opposite. But at night they were invisible—and contemplating their close presence offered me little comfort. I came to anticipate those few hundred yards as a fearful "emptiness", which seemed to mirror my internal world … a feeling which never left me during Anna's residence in her temporary home. I clearly remember her readiness to explore my responses to her new environment, and though I did express some of these feelings, my overriding concern for her situation mostly led me to keep silent. Inevitably deep feelings of insecurity eventually surfaced from this, and other disruptions resulting from this episode of flooding.

As I struggled with the influences of physical and symbolic darkness on that first visit, I knew that the sound of my footsteps crunching over the shingle on the long walk down the drive was bound to alert Anna to my presence. With or without the car, there was no way of arriving quietly.

I rang the doorbell. Anna opened the door, and I imagine we must have exchanged some kind of peremptory greeting. And yet so much of what passed between us during that time is lost to memory, even though we continued to meet twice a week between January and April 2003. Much later, in our recorded sessions, Anna would remind me of my profound discomfort and anxiety at a situation in which I perceived us both to be "trapped" by forces beyond our control.

As Anna opened the door to me on that first occasion, I found myself in a narrow hallway with stairs immediately ahead. Anna invited me to follow her up the stairs, as her consulting room was now on the first floor. I can remember feeling some awkwardness, and deliberately avoiding looking at her legs as she led the way. This was not a view of her I was accustomed to. In the few seconds it took us to reach her new consulting room, I had already begun to feel uncomfortable about this seeming break with a former boundary.

It soon became clear that Anna had done her best to maintain the therapeutic environment within the confines of this new space. But the room was smaller, and the stairway narrow. As we sat down together, it wasn't long before I became aware of significant differences to the surroundings. The chair in which Anna sat was not her usual chair—and in time, I noticed her discomfort. During our later recordings, she acknowledged that her usual chair had been too big to negotiate up the narrow staircase, and that the chair she had used during this period resulted in her suffering backache. Anna's openness on this subject would have an interesting outcome. When I bought my own "first chair" on setting up in private practice, I confessed to Anna my guilt at having spent so much money on a beautiful leather chair, which I suspected to harbour "delusions of grandeur" about my new role as a therapist. But as I described my sense of being "safely contained" within the security of its generous and comfortable arms, Anna's response was to tell me, "Your chair is one of the most important tools necessary for the work you will be doing," explaining her view that "containing arms" would help me to stay grounded at challenging times in my work. This allowed me to let go of my guilt … and as a result, I have never regretted the extravagance of my supremely comfortable "therapist's chair".

The second significant change I noticed was that the couch on which I sat was different. It was definitely the same couch … but it appeared to have something missing. Previously it had seemed huge, but now one of the ends (presumably detachable) appeared to have been removed, and Anna had endeavoured to make up this deficiency by filling the gap with various unfamiliar cushions. In fact, so much of what was happening at that time felt "different and unfamiliar". Ultimately my hope was that this nightmare period of destabilisation would come to an end, and I would finally return to Anna's refurbished home. I think I held onto this thought of returning normality as a sustaining image. I remember questioning Anna about "what was happening to her home", and her telling me cheerfully that "the bonus" of this horrible experience was that she would have "a new kitchen floor and new carpets." By now I had learnt to admire Anna's positive hold on life as an energy that I longed to share with her. Though I couldn't experience this for myself, it was a comfort to witness Anna's ability to believe in this energy as a force for survival.

* * *

With no written material being produced during this period, it would be easy to assume that my distress at these disruptive events was resolved and that I had accepted the situation. This was deceptively intensified by Anna's notes, which revealed that I finally agreed to "use the couch" for the first time. So instead of sitting directly facing her, I now agreed to put my feet up and look away while talking. Though I rarely chose to lie down, this change was nevertheless significant, as Anna later explained:

> "For me, it was a relief when you agreed to use the couch. It made it more possible for me to find thinking space … because often you would sit looking at me, and you were still very quiet. You used to do a lot of just staring at me and not saying anything—trying to 'read' me … So wanting you to use the couch was partly for me, because then I could look away and think … There was something

about it which felt as if you really needed to know what was going on inside my mind, or my feelings … in quite a desperate way, it often felt. And that made it quite hard for me to think …"

It is true that my new position—curled up in one corner of the couch with my feet tucked under a cushion—felt much more comfortable. But I also wonder whether my motivation for agreeing to this was to make Anna feel "more comfortable". My perception was that everything in her life at that time was about "discomfort"—including her therapist's chair. So if putting my feet up on the couch would make life easier for her, then I was prepared to do it—in spite of my previously expressed anxieties about "absorbing the pain of others", which still troubled me. Anna's recorded reflections have enabled me to piece together what was really going on during those deceptively quiet months.

In reality, it was a profoundly disturbing period. Soon after her temporary move, Anna prepared me for the news that things would soon be changing yet again. As a result of increasingly regular episodes of flooding to her area, she had finally decided to find new consulting premises. Though we would return to her home between June and July, Anna informed me that her practice would be moving permanently after her summer break. During our recordings, Anna explained that those few weeks of our return were because, "I wanted everybody to have a chance to say goodbye before moving permanently." At the time, Anna conveyed this news with great sensitivity, knowing the impact it would have on me. My huge need to hold onto an internal image of her as "safely contained in her home" had been a vital element in creating my own sense of safety, which now felt suddenly threatened.

By June 2003, we returned to say goodbye to Anna's home. It was a relief to be back in a familiar environment, and to know that this drama was over—at least for Anna. And I was grateful for her humane insight in allowing this brief interlude in which I could confirm the image of her restored safely and comfortably back into her accustomed surroundings. But for me there was no comfort—and though I struggled to contain my anxiety, we both knew it was simmering below the surface.

And more unpleasant news was to come. My insistent questions about the move to a new consulting room led Anna to reveal another piece of information which came as a substantial blow. She explained that we could never return permanently to her home because her future plans now included demolishing her house—to rebuild it on "stilts" to avoid any danger from future flooding. Though these plans were only at an early stage, I still questioned why we could not return once her house had been rebuilt in the future. For a number of reasons this was clearly not an option. Bereft of any future hope of being allowed back, I was now confronted with an image of Anna as effectively "destroying" the therapeutic environment. I knew that her children had grown up in this house, and as Anna's 'child' in the transference, it now felt as though it was "my home" that she was planning to destroy. This news severely challenged the sense of security which it had taken Anna so many years of painstaking work to convey to me through her therapeutic containment.

Despite the intense emotional upheaval, it astonished me to discover that I had not recorded these feelings in any written form. Not a single poem, letter or dream exists as written evidence of the powerful emotional battle which was raging in my internal world between January and June of that year. Since this was in such contrast to my previous need to record every shade of feeling in writing as it emerged from therapy, something had clearly occurred to block this process. Finally, I must assume that my continuing need for Anna's support made it essential that she remain as "the good enough mother/therapist" in my internalised image of her. And the only way my unconscious mind could achieve this was by repressing any expression of my distress at these events.

But inevitably my distress did surface, leading me to project a jumble of confused and conflicted feelings onto Anna. As I wrestled to contain the rejection I felt in the face of her future plans, I recognised this as the expression of my "hurt child". Once again, it aroused the response of wanting to "protect my vulnerable mother" from my own hurt, as I had learnt to do in childhood. My rational "adult" mind had no difficulty in understanding the reasoning behind Anna's future decisions, nor of appreciating that they were not intended to hurt or reject me. On the contrary, Anna's intention was to protect the emotional well-being of her patients and herself—by ensuring that we would all be spared any future distressing episodes of flooding. Nevertheless, with my sense of security now under serious threat, some unconscious challenge to our relationship would clearly emerge before too long.

And so it proved to be. In our recorded recollections, Anna reminded me of an episode about which I had completely forgotten. Before leaving her temporary home—and by now fully aware of her future plans—I had apparently informed Anna that I wished to return to once-weekly sessions after Easter. It was easy for me to justify this decision in order to disguise its unconscious process—but this did not deceive Anna. By now, I was into the second term of training. The "personal development" aspect allowed me to feel part of an increasingly close-knit group who were learning both to give and to receive the core conditions of congruence and unconditional positive regard, and this was proving to be a unique relational experience.

As I listened again to our recorded discussions about that period, I think it was my sense of Anna as vulnerable—and also as destructive—that left me questioning whether I could, or should, continue to rely on her strength and support in the face of all the challenging events occurring in her own life. And so I unconsciously began to turn to the support of my fellow trainees in the face of these doubts. Referring back to her notes, Anna reminded me:

> "You were scared of becoming too dependent. Most people on your course were only doing once-a-week therapy, and you were thinking with them about their problems. So it seemed to me that the course became like your extra session, and if your colleagues were only doing once-a-week therapy, you didn't think you needed more than this."

"I imagine that must have been quite frustrating for you?" I queried.

"Well … it felt like it was 'decision time'. It was a question of whether we were really going to try to work at deep issues, or whether we were going to treat it as 'a therapy for counselling'. And at that point, it seemed that this was what you wanted to do. So I thought, 'Okay. We'll change the way we're working here, if that's what Naomi wants to do'—because I *had* been thinking, for the therapy to work as I'd imagined it would, we would need three times a week—and you certainly weren't going to do that. So I agreed to do once a week … because sometimes there's that choice to be made."

Anna's words led me to consider the way in which our work had moved from serious analysis to an increasing focus on my struggle to manage the demands of my training. But in reality, I believe my choice to use our sessions as "a therapy for counselling" was a defensive resistance arising out of my need to protect us both during this period of mutual vulnerability. It was an effort to hide my emotional insecurity behind a show of strength, in the face of doubts about the ability of the "therapeutic container" to continue to hold me safely. Confronted by my resistance, it is clear that Anna decided to maintain her support in the only way possible at that time—by agreeing to once weekly sessions. Fully aware of my inner struggle to manage these hugely disruptive events, Anna's empathic response reflects this understanding:

> "Well of course, it was really awful—because we were re-enacting 'being refugees', a bit like what had happened to your mother. I was a 'refugee'—and so you were a refugee with me … And the problem of how to hold the therapeutic container so that we could continue to work with these feelings was really very difficult."
> "Yes … it did feel very uncomfortable …. But it was as much about my feeling uncomfortable for you as it was for me."
> "Oh yes … indeed … It's very hard when you're pretty sure that your therapist is in a vulnerable place. That's hard for you as well as for me, to know how to manage that appropriately … Yes … So it's interesting that then there's nothing in our records about that period—nothing at all actually …"

And interesting to consider whether the dearth of written material for each of us during those months reflects a parallel process of inner disquiet. There is no doubt in my mind that we were both conscious of what that brief return to Anna's home would signify for me. The reality of being "shut out" from the place in which I had formerly been welcomed inevitably surfaced, often in dreams in which I would imagine myself "invited" into her home. From the time when I had first stood outside Anna's door on the occasion of our first meeting, this—and the intervening years—had offered me opportunities for insights into her existence outside the consulting room. I still treasure these memories, and feel convinced of their significance in enabling me to connect in a way which would not have been easy, or perhaps even possible, had I first encountered her in a less personal "consulting room" which did not form part of her home.

It was a time of intense change and uncertainty—not only as a result of what was happening in Anna's world, but also due to events in my own life quite distinct from the demands of personal analysis.

By January 2003, having left my part-time job as an administrative assistant at the adult education college, I had returned to teaching—the profession from which I had retired from full-time work two years earlier. I took up a new position as Supervisor, with responsibility for a team of assistants at a nursery school. Though it was a demanding job, it allowed time to continue my training and personal therapy. A condition of my course was that I now find myself a "placement" and complete the 100 hours of client work that were a course requirement. By February, I had been accepted onto a three-month training programme to become a volunteer counsellor at a local bereavement agency. Having successfully completed this training, I met with my first client in June of that year.

Despite this period of intense instability, the growth of activity in my external world provides remarkable evidence of emotional recovery in my desire to re-engage with life so determinedly. Nevertheless, it is impossible to ignore how this conflict between my internal and external worlds became paralleled in the therapeutic relationship. Inevitably, it is the way in which such threatening predicaments are dealt with by the analyst that embraces the potential to deepen the therapeutic relationship. Anna's training and experience would undoubtedly have prepared her for such challenges—though this is not intended to diminish the huge demands she was now required to make on my behalf. And so, in the face of my subversive and unconscious resistance, Anna continued to support me by her efforts to maintain a safe therapeutic container, in spite of my many doubts and insecurities.

And then, between July and August, several dreams emerged which symbolised this period of inner turmoil. By the end of that year, Anna's ability to work creatively and empathically with these symbolic challenges had brought about a deeply reparative process of reconciliation.

CHAPTER THIRTEEN

Surprisingly, I had lost all recollection of the dreams that emerged during these summer months. But as we both sifted through our copies of my writing for that year, Anna produced them from her session notes. I was mystified—and though I searched my computer in the belief that I had saved everything I had given to Anna over the years, I could find no record of them. Finally I concluded that I must have considered the dreams as intended solely for Anna:

> "My feeling about the fact that I didn't keep a copy of these dreams for myself was that I was dreaming them for you … And because we'd had the battle about me not wanting to read the poems aloud, the poems became dreams—but somehow they were only for you, not for me."
>
> "Yes … and you were able to talk about them."
>
> "But it's interesting that I didn't feel a need to keep a copy—as if they weren't actually mine to keep."
>
> "Well, a lot of what we talked about at that time was about you really wanting us to be ever so 'together'. And because you'd *told* me the dreams, there was a sense that you were 'putting them into me', and so they were kind-of 'parked'—and that felt okay."

> "Well, it must have been evidence that I did believe you could hold them ... all that 'messy stuff' ..."

So it would appear that my deep trust in Anna had not deserted me, though it was clearly being seriously challenged by events in her life which were having such a disturbing impact. Listening again to our recordings, Anna fully recognised how my focus had moved from "internal reflectiveness" to a concern about events in my external world. But at this difficult period, our focus necessarily shifted back to my troubled internal world, now increasingly reflected in the analytic relationship itself. At the time when these dreams emerged, as Anna pointed out in our recorded reflections, I was "already very caught up with the destructiveness of what was going to happen." Because of my insistent questioning about the possibility of returning to her home, Anna faced a difficult decision about how much personal information to reveal—once again raising the question of therapist disclosure.

What I didn't know at that time was that Anna anticipated that her elderly mother would move in with her once her home had been rebuilt—occupying the room which might otherwise have been Anna's consulting room. As she explained:

> "... That wasn't for sure then, but we'd got that in mind, and it looked likely ... But from where you were, I didn't think it would help you to know all the details at that point ... But it made you terribly concerned for me, and it then got into a lot of stuff about me—and really I wanted to try to hold it, so that we could work with what it brought up for you."

I could certainly appreciate the therapeutic dilemma provoked by my insistent questions. Even so, I felt bound to discuss Anna's decision not to clarify the details to me earlier, since the "not knowing" appeared to heighten the difficulties we were already confronting:

> "... Of course," Anna agreed, "... we can never really know whether I'm protecting myself, because I don't want my sessions with my patients full of stuff stirring up me ... There is a degree of self-protection about it, I know that ... But you have to 'toss it up' ... It's very difficult ..."

Since all that either of us had at the time of our recordings was the benefit of hindsight, I remain grateful for the honesty of Anna's reflections, which clearly highlight the painful predicament which we both faced at that time.

One of the dreams contained the familiarly recurring theme of "babies", and became a detailed subject for discussion in our later recordings:

> My son was a baby. I was with him in a very strange place. Maybe a hotel, but with lots of different staircases—some of them spiral. I felt very lost and had trouble finding my room. My daughter was with me. She was grown-up and had my grandson with her. She helped me to find my way back to the room. It was small, untidy, and not very clean. I was trying to change my son and put clean clothes on him. I realised that I hadn't changed or fed him for a long time—maybe days. I was in a state of panic about this. My daughter was watching me, but I didn't seem to know what I was doing so she offered to help. I remember feeling confused and embarrassed by my incompetence.

In discussing the frequent re-emergence of the "baby" theme in my dreams, Anna explained that:

> "Babies often come up as dreams in therapy, and one tends to think of it as a symbol for your 'infant self'—and at this point in your therapy, you don't know how to look after her ... And you weren't too sure about me as 'a mummy' in the transference either, with me pulling my house down, and all the moving around. So you weren't at all sure that I was 'a mummy who was going to look after you' at this time."

Anna's thoughts certainly seem an accurate reflection of the insecurity troubling me. The dream's reference to "a hotel" suggests a place of temporary accommodation which is not "my home", and which appears to resonate with these feelings. But time has given me a deeper insight into the psychological significance of my "vulnerable baby son", and my "competent adult daughter"—who regularly appeared in these roles in my dreams involving babies. Reflecting on the histories of my real children, and the very different circumstances affecting me at the time of their birth, I begin to understand the metaphoric and symbolic roles which they both came to occupy in my dream imagery. In relation to my analysis, these "baby dreams" were emerging at a time when both my children were adults. But time is of no consequence in terms of the unconscious process reflected in dreams. Here, all the logical boundaries of time and space are available for transgression, in order to illuminate what the unconscious dream imagery seeks to bring to conscious attention. And so, despite the reality that my son was now grown-up, his appearance as "a baby" in my dreams contained important information which alerted my consciousness to the significant events surrounding the period of his birth.

In terms of my own psyche, my son's "vulnerability" suggests aspects of my own shadow. But since he always appears as a baby or young child in these dreams, this image also contains the potential for future growth and creativity. Now in the middle passage of his life in Jungian terms, this creativity is finding increased expression in numerous ways.

In contrast, my daughter's role in my dreams suggests the strong, "adult" part of my psyche. This aspect suggests the adult strength I must find within myself, to withstand the threatening self-doubt of my own "vulnerable child" at times of crisis. I am conscious of the many ways in which my daughter continues to provide evidence of this quality for survival, through her ability to confront her own challenges in the external world.

Because of the traumatic events occurring in my marriage relationship both before and after the birth of my son, I came to perceive him as "vulnerable" from earliest infancy … and perhaps even anticipated it as a pre-birth expectation. As his mother, I wanted to protect him. And this instinct was compounded from birth and throughout his early years by episodes of asthma, eczema, impaired hearing, and various childhood "accidents" which necessitated frequent visits to hospital. In contrast, my daughter's birth and early childhood contained almost no medical history of note, other than a few typical childhood illnesses which had not aroused undue concern.

As I watched both my children mature into early adolescence, and subsequently into adulthood, it was impossible not to notice significant differences in their personalities which emerged in spite of our best attempts to "love them both equally". While my daughter inevitably encountered many difficulties and disappointments on her journey to adulthood, I was conscious of how her strong sense of self gave her the confidence to overcome these obstacles. Now, as I watch my daughter's patient, loving, and deeply intuitive nurturing of her own children, I find myself forced to reflect on how the circumstances surrounding her birth were in such sharp contrast to those of my second pregnancy, which reached their climax during the year following my son's birth. By comparison with his sister, my son's less secure sense of self became apparent in early childhood. It would seem that the battle to maintain his self-belief in the face of life's challenges has been a much tougher one for him than it appears to have been for his sister.

Nevertheless, I cannot ignore the question which arises for me when I reflect on this perspective: the question of how far my son's "vulnerability" was a projection onto him of my own vulnerability during his infancy. In this case, it would clearly be arguable that we unconsciously co-created a relationship dynamic which effectively became a self-fulfilling prophecy. This is the familiar "nature or nurture" debate, and though it continues to trouble me, I accept that I can never finally "know" the answer. More recently, the latest findings in neuro-scientific research have helped me to govern my feelings of maternal guilt more appropriately—though I accept the likely element of self-defence contained here. This research is increasingly throwing new light on how the complex interaction between early attachment styles and the development of the brain will have consequences for future relationships and emotional well-being. In her wonderfully accessible book on this subject, Sue Gerhardt comments that, "There is remarkably little recognition that the adult's brain is itself formed by experiences starting in the womb …".[1] Elaborating further, Gerhardt writes:

> During the period of development in the womb and in early post-natal life, various internal systems that are central to emotional regulation are being set up. The stress response is "set" by the age of 6 months, and the various neurotransmitter and neuropeptide systems are also strongly influenced by both pre-natal and post-natal experience.[2]

---

[1] Gerhardt, S. (2004). *Why Love Matters: How Affection Shapes A Baby's Brain*, p. 116. Sussex: Routledge.
[2] Ibid., p. 173.

If the trauma of my circumstances during and after pregnancy did indeed result in my own vulnerability becoming an emotional legacy which I passed on to my son—both in the womb and continuing into infancy—it certainly originated in an unconscious process over which I could have had no control. And perhaps, ultimately, the guilt for this legacy need not rest entirely with me …

* * *

The purpose of this digression is to link this earlier personal history with Jungian theory. In his volume on *The Archetypes and the Collective Unconscious*, Jung wrote extensively on the subject of "The psychology of the child archetype". In this complex analysis of the imagery, certain passages stand out as resonating with the "vulnerable baby" image of this dream. As Jung explains, the emergence of the child archetype in dreams may have less to do with regression than with notions of "futurity":

> One of the essential features of the child motif is its futurity. The child is potential future. Hence the occurrence of the child motif in the psychology of the individual signifies as a rule an anticipation of future developments, even though at first sight it may seem like a retrospective configuration. Life is a flux, a flowing into the future, and not a stoppage or a backwash … Our experience of the psychology of the individual … shows that the 'child' paves the way for a future change of personality. In the individuation process, it anticipates … the synthesis of conscious and unconscious elements in the personality. It is therefore a symbol which unites the opposites; a mediator, bringer of healing, that is, one who makes whole.[3]

In the same chapter, Jung discusses the psychological significance of the archetypal image of "the abandoned child". Again, this struck me as relevant to the subject matter of my dream:

> Abandonment, exposure, danger … are all elaborations of the child's insignificant beginnings and of its mysterious and

---

[3] Jung, C. G. (1959). The archetypes and the collective unconscious. In: A. Stevens (1982), *The Archetypes and the Collective Unconscious*, p. 164. London: Routledge, 2002.

miraculous birth. This statement describes a certain psychic experience of a creative nature, whose object is the emergence of a new and as yet unknown content. In the psychology of the individual there is always at such moments, an agonizing situation of conflict from which there seems to be no way out ...[4]

And Jung continues:

'Child' means something evolving towards independence. This it cannot do without detaching itself from its origins: abandonment is therefore a necessary condition, not just a concomitant symptom ... Because the symbol of the 'child' fascinates and grips the conscious mind, its redemptive effect passes over into consciousness and brings about that separation from the conflict-situation which the conscious mind by itself was unable to achieve. The symbol anticipates a nascent state of consciousness.[5]

Jung writes of the "agonizing situation of conflict" arising from the child's need to detach itself from its origins in order to move towards independence. This seems uncannily to describe the conflict which had arisen in my analysis at the time, exemplified both in the dream of my "abandoned baby", and in my rationale to Anna of dropping to once-weekly sessions. Seen as the "nascent state of consciousness" to which Jung refers, it explains my attempt to strike out for independence in the face of this necessary conflict. But in the words of the Jungian Analyst Anthony Stevens,[6] the "secure base" from which to pass from one stage of the life-cycle to the next had been threatened by the disruptive events occurring in my analysis. And so, my unfortunately timed bid for independence merely added another layer to the conflict through which Anna and I had to negotiate our way in the months ahead.

Reflecting further on this dream, another important image that invites consideration is its reference to a number of "spiral staircases". Though this held no special meaning for me at the time, my recent

---

[4] Ibid., p. 167.
[5] Ibid., p. 168.
[6] Stevens, A. (1982). *Archetype Revisited. An Updated Natural History of the Self*, p. 196. London: Brunner-Routledge, 2002.

reading of Stevens' work has illuminated the potential significance of this symbol. In fact, the front cover of Steven's book depicts a spiral staircase—a symbol containing personal significance for the author, which he subsequently understood to be a symbolic representation of his life. As Steven's explains:

> … the unfolding life cycle is well conceived of as a spiral staircase, each stage of the cycle being a landing or 'secure base' which, once reached, provides a temporary resting place before yet another rite of passage moves one onwards and upwards to the next.[7]

Although my dream included several spiral staircases, at this point they do not appear to invite a way forward—I simply "notice" them as significant, but continue to feel lost. With my thinking illuminated by Steven's ideas, this prediction by my unconscious of the potential for future movement suggests Jung's "Transcendent Function".[8] As a vital process in the drive towards individuation (i.e., psychic wholeness), Jung sees the transcendent function as requiring a "symbol" (e.g., the spiral), which denotes "the bringing together of opposites for the production of a third".[9] This is the intended outcome of the alchemical processes as defined by Jung in "The Psychology of the Transference"[10]—previously referred to in Chapter Eight, in relation to my earlier "Wedding Dream". In his use of alchemy as a metaphor for the developing transference in the analytic relationship, Jung saw the wedding of the king and queen (the *coniunctionis*) as symbolizing the uniting of opposites to create the birth of a new "third". In relating this directly to the image of the spiral, Stevens explains:

> The inherent affinity between opposites, drawing them together into a union to yield a new form that was more than its parts, became the central inspiration of [Jung's] life and work: the *thesis* of the unconscious statement, the *antithesis* of the ego response,

---

[7] Ibid., p. 196.
[8] Ibid., p. 196.
[9] Ibid., p. 87.
[10] Jung, C. G. (1954). The psychology of the transference. In: G. Adler & R. F. C. Hull (Eds.), *Collected Works of C. G. Jung, Volume 16: The Practice of Psychotherapy*. Princeton: Princeton University Press, 1985.

synthesis through the transcendent symbolic function, with the birth of new consciousness—repeated and repeated, round and round, up and down, circumambulating the goal of the *opus* [i.e., the work of analysis].[11]

Perhaps it might help the reader to picture in their mind the image of a spiral staircase, "circumambulating" around a pole of central axis which signifies the psyche's connection with both the "heaven and hell" of existence. It is the spiral surrounding this axis which holds the potential for upward (though also downward) movement and which, in Jungian terms, symbolises the transcendent function.

According to Jung,[12] it is the ego, not the unconscious, which must take the lead in enabling the psyche to manage the upward movement required of the transcendent function. So while my dream image of "spirals" seemed to indicate my ego's readiness for this process, the dangerous turmoil raging in my inner world was a threat to my ego's capacity to unite the opposites of *thesis* and *antithesis* into their final *synthesis*. Since this threat inevitably impacts on the transference, and consequently on the analytic relationship itself, Jung's own words seem an apt description of the challenges which Anna and I were negotiating:

> [The ego] is confronted with a psychic product that owes its existence mainly to an unconscious process and is therefore in some degree opposed to the ego and its tendencies … This standpoint is essential in coming to terms with the unconscious. The position of the ego must be maintained as being of equal value to the counterposition of the unconscious, and vice versa. This amounts to a very necessary warning: for just as the conscious mind … has a restrictive effect on the unconscious, so the rediscovered unconscious often has a really dangerous effect on the ego. In the same way that the ego suppressed the unconscious before, a liberated unconscious can thrust the ego aside and overwhelm it. There is a danger of the ego losing its head, so to speak, that it will not be able to defend

---

[11] Stevens, A. (1990). *On Jung*, p. 238. London: Penguin, 1991.
[12] Stevens, A. (1982). *Archetype Revisited: An Updated Natural History of the Self*. London: Brunner-Routledge, 2002.

> itself against the pressure of affective factors—a situation often encountered at the beginning of schizophrenia. (pp. 87–88)[13]

It is only now, reflecting from a position of greater knowledge and insight, that I can truly appreciate the dangerously delicate analytic situation that Anna faced. With the security of my transference attachment so deeply threatened and clearly evident in this dream, the symbols of "a baby" and the "spiral staircases" nevertheless suggested a future possibility, which now strikes me as a remarkable prediction of hopefulness amidst all the images of despair contained in the other dreams.

---

[13] Ibid., pp. 87–88.

CHAPTER FOURTEEN

I found myself alone in a car in a strange part of London. The car was hired and I was very worried about damaging it. I had been driving for hours, getting increasingly lost. Suddenly I saw a small hotel down a side street. I decided to stop and ask for help. A man and a woman were at the reception desk. I could smell soup and suddenly realised how hungry and thirsty I was. When I started to speak I had almost lost my voice. I told them I was lost, and trying to get home across London. They were very helpful and said they would get a map. I commented on how nice the soup smelled, and asked if I could have some because I was so hungry. The woman brought me a bowl of soup. Sitting in the hotel with two other people made me less frightened. The man then produced a map, but neither of them knew how to direct me home because they didn't know my part of London. I looked at the map and saw a road which I thought would lead me home. I left the hotel, and by now it was dark. When I returned to the car, I saw that someone had driven into it and damaged it. I tried not to worry about it, as I was more concerned to find my way home. I drove off and thought I had found the road which would lead me home, but after a long drive I found myself in a dead end—by some sort of marina. It was very dark and the open space scared me. I saw a small office which was brightly lit, and decided to ask for help. As I left the car, two young boys appeared and started to follow me into the office. There was no-one else around. I ignored them and decided to phone Patrick. The boys came over to me. I suddenly thought that they might help me find my way, and decided to ask for their help ... but then I woke up.

28th August 2003

This unsettling dream emerged a few days before Anna and I were due to begin meeting in her new consulting room following her summer break. It appears to be the culmination of the theme of "losing my way", which had been building up as an anxious undercurrent in the other dreams that summer. Though the process of analysis is often symbolised in dreams as "a journey", my sense of "feeling lost" has finally burst out as a glaring and unmistakable anxiety.

My interpretation of the dream suggests that I am desperately searching for "the way home" and need a map to help me. Though the "hired car" holds the promise of my continued journey with Anna, my anxiety about her new consulting room and the loss of my therapeutic "home", which no longer "belonged to me", seems evident. My fear of damaging the car, and its subsequent damage, contains both my fear of damaging Anna and that *she* has become "damaging and unsafe", leaving me uncertain of her ability of help me "find my way". The "temporary shelter" of the hotel offers an illusion of comfort, but my "hunger and thirst" express a need for emotional nourishment. The loss of a safe, therapeutic space and my awareness of Anna's vulnerability are suggested by the fact that I have "almost lost my voice", which makes it difficult to talk openly about my own anxieties.

Since I no longer remember our discussion following this dream, I now wonder whether what I brought to that first session effectively blocked this process. During the summer break, I had struggled to balance my ambivalent feelings towards Anna, and subsequently an idea had begun to take shape in my mind—that if Anna no longer represented "safety", perhaps I should consider looking for another therapist to provide this.

Although this thought offered a solution, it was by no means a comforting one. The prospect of ending a three year journey with Anna was no less terrifying than the prospect of continuing. If I were to do this, I knew that I would be walking away from something immeasurably valuable, and I also understood that leaving our journey unfinished would only compound the feelings of loss which I was already experiencing. But try as I might, I could not imagine how Anna might do or say anything to repair this damage for me.

As my feelings veered from one extreme to the other during these months, I sought refuge once more in "rational" thinking. My counselling course had introduced me to the philosophical ideas underpinning existential psychotherapy, and I found myself deeply drawn to the writings of American existential psychotherapist, Irvin Yalom. Quite mistakenly, I assumed that Yalom typified the existential model of practice … and I fell in love with everything I read about his therapeutic philosophy. If I could find an existential psychotherapist to work with me in this way, I talked myself into believing that this presented a possible solution.

This desperate attempt to resolve my ambivalence allowed me some small degree of intellectual satisfaction. But it was not a rationale that addressed my deep emotional need—which was for Anna to find a way to repair this damage. Even as I determined to explain my thinking to Anna, I hoped she would not allow me to win this battle. From the subsequent interaction between us, it was clear that what I needed was "evidence" that Anna would fight to prevent my desperation from adding to the destruction by terminating my analysis.

Anna painted a powerful picture of my profound distress, clearly evident in that first session in her new consulting room:

> "You came here for the first session after the break terribly nervous and scared. It was a new place, and you had 'lost' my house. You were shaking, and saying, 'There's something really awful— I don't know what to say and I don't know how to say it.' And finally, three-quarters of the way through the session, you told me about wanting to end in December. So certainly a way of thinking about this dream is of having 'lost your way'—and we did talk about how you didn't feel you could work with someone who could be so destructive, and that it had made you feel so unsafe …"

It was clear that all my fears and insecurities were now being acted out in the agony of my ostensible decision to end our work. There is no doubt that learning of Anna's plans to demolish her home had emotionally been "a step too far" for me, on top of all the unsettling events resulting from the flooding, which had inevitably coloured every aspect of our relationship since the resumption of our work in January. Now eight months on, my sense of Anna's "destructiveness" created a crisis of trust from which there was no escape for either of us—because, as Anna pointed out:

> "… You needed to know because you couldn't understand why we couldn't return to my home. We had gone back there once it had

been repaired, so it didn't make sense that I would want to move my consulting room somewhere else."

"Yes, I remember that you gave me the reason of 'not being able to risk upsetting patients' if it flooded again."

"Well, that was one reason, certainly … and I think I probably also said, 'I can't bear the stress'. Because once it had flooded, you could never say it wouldn't happen again. It changed everything … But of course, those were my decisions—but from where you were, you really became taken up with concerns that I could do something so destructive."

Remembering my distress at this crisis, I needed Anna to remind me of how we had managed this threatening situation:

"Well, we tried to 'stay with it'. Your rationale for wanting to end was your training—that it would be helpful for you to try a different kind of therapy. And you'd already gone down to once a week and felt that you'd 'lost' me, and you were really struggling with a powerful ambivalence. This was the shadow … the negative had come into the work with me. The flooding, and the messiness around changing venues felt hugely unsafe—and it's absolutely understandable really. No surprises there … And I think it 'pushed' the part of you that really didn't think you could stand it—because you felt I had become 'destructive' not 'constructive' … Then, I don't know exactly what it was, but there was definitely something which suggested that you felt I'd given in too easily—that I hadn't really 'fought' for you, and that it didn't matter too much to me."

"Yes … I remember longing to hear you tell me that I was trying hard and that I was going to be okay. And I suppose not hearing it made me wonder whether you thought any of this was working—because I couldn't be sure myself. It was such a roller coaster ride so much of the time … And I suppose I was hearing about other people's therapies. Not that I always liked what I heard, but I could see that there were different ways of working, and I began to wonder whether maybe I'd like some of that …"

"Yes, of course … indeed …"

"… But if I had ended, then we wouldn't have achieved anything like the work we have done."

"Absolutely not ... no ... But from my perspective, it felt vital that I find a way to make space for either eventuality. So I wasn't going to talk you out of it—because I don't think that's ethical ... So I took into consideration the way you delivered this 'message' to me ... because it wasn't that you came in an ego-state, saying, 'I've been thinking about this very seriously, and because of my training, this is what I've decided to do ...' That's not how it came out ... So I would be thinking about what that meant, before we got to what the message was. So we stayed with all the feelings around it before you actually got to the 'ego place' where you said you wanted to end. And we talked it over for a long time, and I think I said, 'Well, it's an option' ... But then we got into your feeling that I'd given in too easily—so then it was quite clear that there was much more to it than that."

Listening again to Anna, I am aware of how her somewhat reticent recollection of what produced the dramatic catalyst for change is considerably underplayed by her words. What stays in my memory is the way in which she rose to the challenge of affirming what I needed to hear at that crucial time. In Anna's view, I had "thrown down the gauntlet" by my decision to end—and she took this very seriously, appreciating that the symbolic message of my dream was now being acted out by my decision. What I wanted was Anna's acknowledgement of my desperate sense of loss. This would be the evidence that her "guiding hand" was still available to me. It was the desperate cry of "the child who has lost her mother"—and I needed Anna to demonstrate her willingness to "find me" again. In rising to this challenge, something significant was opened up between us. In Anna's words:

"... Gradually the therapy turned around then ... and at that point I think I said some very validating things—because it did feel that you were working very hard and struggling with some very difficult things about the course ... And then the feeling changed, and it seemed like you really understood that I cared—that it did matter to me. And so you decided that you weren't going to end your therapy—that you didn't think you could possibly do that ... Yes ... So then we had a period of hugely powerful, loving and positive feelings ..."

This was the creative culmination of an extremely painful process. In reality, as I reminded Anna, I would regularly return from the long summer break saying that I wanted to end. It was a pattern resulting from angry feelings of abandonment. But on this occasion, I recognise that it was vital for Anna not to rush to rescue my "insecure child", without also considering where the "adult" aspect of my psyche stood in relation to my decision to end. As Anna's reflection suggests, this situation signified a complex crisis which was operating on both these psychic levels:

> "Sure, you had a million and one reasons to feel angry after this break—because we were here, in this new place ... But it often seems to me, in this kind of work—or perhaps in life—that if you can face the reality and the possibility of one pole—and we were really facing the possibility of your ending at Christmas—that this can then lead to a shift in perspective. And it seemed to be this shift which made you realise that this was not what you wanted."
>
> "So it was important for me to actually have to confront that reality?"
>
> "Well, I thought so ..."
>
> "... Because, if you talked me out of it, then ..."
>
> "... It has become my responsibility ..."
>
> "Yes ... I can understand that ..."
>
> "... And then we haven't really faced the possibility of something else—of another option ... Yes ... So it was at that point that the powerful, loving and positive feelings emerged ..."

In describing this critical period, it is difficult to place events in a way that adequately reflects their development to the reader. In reality, it was not until December that "the powerful, loving, and positive feelings" to which Anna refers actually emerged. Months of difficult and demanding work followed, during which, ostensibly, we had begun to plan an ending. In the event, neither of us clearly recalled what provoked these loving feelings to surface. Anna's recollection was that I had been "talking about the needs of five-year old children"—perhaps in connection with my work at the nursery. Something I told Anna must have triggered a connection with an unconscious memory of being a five-year old child who suddenly felt "lost and alone". In a moment of uncontained distress, this feeling completely overwhelmed me, so that I can remember turning away and burying my tears in the cushions of her couch.

We stayed with this spectre of deep-seated childhood pain, and then, in the midst of my tears, I heard Anna gently ask me:

"What does the five-year-old Naomi need from me?"

I was in no doubt of what I needed:

"I need you to hold my hand."

By now, I had turned to face Anna. I watched as she moved her chair closer, finally holding out both her hands to me in a loving gesture of containment.

"You can hold my hands for as long as you need to," she assured me.

In that magically transforming moment of connection we held hands, occasionally looking into each other's eyes. It was a powerful expression of love, the memory of which will always remain with me.

Though I did not recognise it at the time, my request to Anna denoted the physical evidence I needed—that her hand was still there to hold me, and that she would not leave me lost and alone in my despair. But I am also acutely aware of how Anna's courage in allowing me to record this episode in writing may provoke criticism concerning the much-disputed question of "touch" in the therapeutic relationship. Finally I must leave this question to the reader's individual judgement. In my own mind—since I am now able to view this episode from both "patient" and "psychotherapist" perspectives—I have no doubt that Anna's creative break with an accepted boundary came from a genuinely loving and empathic response to my emotional needs at that moment. And it proved deeply reparative in healing the crisis in our relationship.

Reflecting as a professional on this contentious question, I am reminded of Irvin Yalom's writing on this subject, which remains a guiding light for my own philosophy of practice. In *The Gift of Therapy*, in a chapter entitled "Don't Be Afraid of Touching Your Patient", Yalom movingly writes from his own psychiatric and psychoanalytic training, as well as from his wealth of experience as a clinician:

> If a patient is in great despair ... and asks during the session to hold my hand or for a hug, I would no sooner refuse than to decline to help an old woman facing a snowstorm put on her overcoat. If I can find no way to ease the pain, I may ask what he/she would like from me that day ... To move my chair closer? To hold hands? To the best of my ability, I try to respond in a loving, human way, but later, as always, I debrief: I talk about what feelings my actions produced, and I share my feelings as well.[1]

Ultimately, Yalom's advice to therapists is:

> Do touch. But make sure the touch becomes grist for the interpersonal mill.[2]

I would not wish the reader to assume that this example of therapeutic practice represents Anna's view on the matter. Apart from a moving and memorable "goodbye hug" when we did finally end our work together, this incident of "touch" was the only occasion in the course of our eight and a half years together, when Anna and I made physical contact. Though I remember other occasions when I expressed my desire for her to physically hold me, Anna would encourage me to focus on her words—urging me to experience them as a "verbal hug". I learnt to do this—and eventually also learnt to adopt it into my own clinical practice.

But this dramatic crisis required more than a "verbal hug"—and Anna clearly sensed this need. It is at such times that a therapist's ability to respond creatively requires them to "shift the boundaries", in order to meet the overwhelming needs of their patient at a critical moment. In my own case, I believe this example of Anna's loving and creative response requires no further justification. I must hope to carry the reader with me in this belief, since its reparative outcome seems to speak for itself.

---

[1] Yalom, I. D. (2002). *The Gift of Therapy: Reflections on Being a Therapist*, pp. 188–189. London: Piatkus.
[2] Ibid., p. 188.

Anna's notes revealed that I had written her a "loving poem" around the time of this episode—but I didn't give it to her or keep a copy of it. Once again, I found this break with my former pattern of "putting everything into writing" strangely incomprehensible. In our recorded recollections, Anna shared her thoughts about this with me:

> "Well, my thought about it at the time—and I do still think this—was that it was almost too precious to write down … Because we talked about when two people are in that very special place, and how it's so vulnerable—because you're really opening yourself right out … So it's very dark … and how we both are with it is just, oh, immensely important! It really feels to me like it's right down to 'the Self' … the place where you're totally open and totally vulnerable, and can be hugely wounded. And so we talked about the real preciousness and sensitivity of it … and I think that perhaps you just didn't want to write that down. And the session where we held hands was as if you needed a real physical expression of what we'd said—to make it more real … to really forge a link."

In the face of all my former doubts that Anna could possibly find a way to repair this dramatic rift in our relationship, she had managed to achieve it. I ended that year in a deep spirit of love and trust, which never left me throughout our remaining years of work, despite the inevitable challenges which arose from time to time. What had occurred proved to be a timely process of healing and reparation. By February 2004, the requirements of my counselling training took on a new and demanding dimension which made it vital for me to depend on this place of safety and containment for my emotional survival. In Anna's words:

> "Thank God we got there! Because by then we'd got a safe place to hold it all."

CHAPTER FIFTEEN

By January 2004 the end of my counselling training was in sight. A requirement was that we attend two residential weekends, designed to enhance our personal development through an exposure that would deepen our relational experience. As the new term got underway, we were informed that our final residential, at the end of January, would be a "Jungian Weekend". We were each asked to prepare a presentation to be delivered to the group, which should reflect the "theme" for the weekend. With significant emphasis, our tutors announced that the theme was, "From my Soul to my Being".

In the weeks that followed, this theme provoked much anxious discussion, since we were initially very uncertain about the expected content of our presentations. It emerged that having now spent almost three years developing self-knowledge and reflectiveness in personal therapy and within the group, it was now time to reveal something of the depth and significance of what we had learned about ourselves. Our tutors encouraged us to approach the theme as imaginatively as possible, by including any creative medium which would help express our self-awareness. In contrast to our usual circle of chairs, a different environment would be devised—one which would enhance the relational quality of the encounter. However, there was a reluctance to give too much away beforehand. We were simply promised "an inspirational weekend", which would profoundly deepen our self-growth and empathic rapport with each other. The subject of the Jungian weekend was to become a constantly recurring topic of conversation—and as January drew to a close, a mood of excited anticipation was evident.

But this was not my response to the news. From the moment that it was explained to us, I was seized by terror at the possibility of so much public self-revelation. It only added to my suffering to discover that I was alone with these feelings. Despite the expression of some understandable nervousness from my fellow trainees, it became obvious that they were actually relishing the prospect of an excitingly different experience.

Unable to share my sense of dread with anyone—with the exception of Anna, of course, it saddened me to confess how much the Jungian Weekend filled me with anything but pleasurable anticipation. I couldn't even precisely express what it was that I "dreaded" so much. I simply could not ignore a powerful inner voice warning me of impending danger ... in some guise which I couldn't yet foresee or understand.

My sessions with Anna now focused on these feelings of dread and danger, and of finding a way to manage the experience safely. It was clear that Anna not only understood my fear, but also concurred with my sense that I would be putting myself at emotional and psychological risk by participating in the weekend. Her session notes described my anxious resentment at being expected to participate in such a public revelation of "my Soul and my Being":

> "You really didn't want to share so much," Anna recollected, "because there was a feeling that we'd been somewhere very intimate ourselves, which wasn't shareable ... And in my notes I wrote, 'She doesn't want to give them any of that—and I must say, I agree with her!' That's what I wrote ..."
>
> "... And the nearer it got, the more I panicked ... until I remember phoning you up the night before. Your advice to me ... well, not 'advice' exactly ..."
>
> "Probably! It was 'Don't go there', I think!"

Some of my resistance undoubtedly stemmed from the fact that I was the only member of the group to be working with an analyst—and certainly the only one engaged in long-term work or to have attended twice-weekly sessions. Furthermore, my relationship with Anna had not begun as "a therapy for counselling training", but as the result of a life-threatening crisis. I recognised a relational and psychological depth to our work, which I rarely sensed from the experiences of personal therapy recounted by my fellow trainees. Was it wrong to want to guard so jealously the sacred "specialness" of my relationship with Anna? Was I being dishonest, deceitful, or elitist, by trying to avoid sharing "the depths of my soul" as it had emerged in this unique relationship? I was plagued with self-doubt. But Anna made it clear that she did not entertain these doubts. Nevertheless, she recognised that I now found myself caught in a painful dilemma.

In spite of my fears, I knew that, realistically, I had little choice but to attend the residential. It was an essential requirement of the course, and somehow I must find a way to survive this process. And so, Anna and I began to think about what I might safely share with the group, which would not be experienced as the "tearing out of my soul from my body" for public scrutiny—but which nevertheless contained enough personal honesty to qualify as a contribution worth sharing.

Not surprisingly, my thoughts turned to the growing collection of poems which I now recognised as containing a record of my journey through analysis. I searched for some words which might reveal something about this journey ... but not too much: something that was both sufficiently "safe" and sufficiently "self-disclosing" to adequately meet the requirements. As I struggled with this task, every shred of my being rose in angry and resistant protest. Ploughing painfully through the dark outpouring of words, I was forced to face the reality that almost everything I had written during my analysis signified a confrontation with my shadow. And I knew that I did not possess the psychological or emotional resilience to expose this confrontation safely to public gaze.

I found myself in torment over this decision, right up to the Friday night when I was due to leave for the residential. My panic-stricken phone call to Anna that night indicated my despair. Despite other desperate episodes, I had never before broken the boundary by phoning her between sessions. Aware of this, Anna understood this transgression as evidence of my anguish. I don't remember our conversation. Mainly I think I just needed to hear her voice—reassuring me that she was there for me, and conveying her strength to hold me through her words. By now my torment had led me to construct a "rationale" to explain why I was putting myself through this ordeal. In the face of

Anna's decisive words "not to go there", I regaled her with the "script" I had mentally written for myself. In an effort to quieten the inner voice of doubt, which continued to warn me of danger, I argued that if I could find the courage to share something of my shadow with the group—and still be accepted and "forgiven" by them—then I might also find a way to truly forgive myself. Finally, my inner debate continued, this might relieve me of the enormous weight of guilt that I still carried, and consequently of the need for further self-punishment.

* * *

This carefully constructed rationale gratified my cognitive mind with its notion of maintaining control over my ego, in the face of the danger with which it was once again threatened. Although the hope expressed in this thinking was ultimately to remove my need to self-punish, the benefit of hindsight has helped me understand the deeper unconscious motives being enacted here. As Anna was implying, it was open to me to "play it safe" in my presentation, by the careful choice of what I elected to share with the group. But emotional triggers had now been activated which "demanded" that I participate in this exercise of self-revelation with total honesty and openness. Finally, my belief that I had no alternative but to suffer the pain of exposure was, in itself, a regressive return to the need to self-punish. The whole concept of the Jungian Weekend had taken on the image of a "crusade", becoming a challenge to my courage and integrity which I felt obliged to confront. It is clear to me now that putting my emotional well-being so deliberately in danger was a symbolic and ritualistic act of "self-cleansing", which promised the possibility of "washing clean" the darkness of my soul if I was brave enough to face this threatening encounter.

Donald Kalsched has written of "the malevolent figure in the self-care system" which offers "a compelling image of what Jung called *the dark side of the ambivalent Self*".[1] According to Kalsched, this is "a 'duplex' figure, a protector and persecutor in one".[2] The primitive and ferocious intensity of this archaic figure represents something much more than Jung's original conception of the "shadow". Its "unfeeling

---

[1] Kalsched, D. (1996). *The Inner World of Trauma: Archetypal Defenses of the Personal Spirit*, p. 4. Sussex: Routledge, 2010.
[2] Ibid., p. 3.

murderous acts assure psychic disintegration", according to Kalsched, and originate from "a more primitive level of ego development".[3] In summarising this "duplex" figure, Kalsched describes its system of attacking the ego:

> When the Protector/Persecutor is present in the inner world, aggression that would normally be available to the ego for separation/differentiation is cut off from consciousness and appears in daimonic form, attacking from within.[4]

I would not wish to parallel my own life experiences with those of Kalsched's deeply traumatised patients whose personal histories he draws on for his clinical illustrations. Nevertheless, somewhere on this spectrum of archetypal defences of the self-care system, I recognise a similarity with my own psychological struggle and the way this could manifest in self-destructive behaviour. With particular intensity, I recognise Kalsched's description of the inner conflict created by the ambivalence of the "Protector/Persecutor" figure as it operates within this defence system:

> Like the immune system of the body, the self-care system carries out its functions by actively attacking what it takes to be "foreign" or "dangerous" elements. Vulnerable parts of the self's experience in reality are seen as just such "dangerous" elements and are attacked accordingly ... And just as the immune-system can be tricked into attacking the very life it is trying to protect (auto-immune disease), so the self-care system can turn into a "self-destruct system" which turns the inner world into a nightmare of persecution and self-attack.[5]

As I contemplate the self-punishing nature of my insistence that "suffering" needed to form an integral aspect of my participation in the Jungian Weekend, I cannot ignore the powerful resonance of Kalsched's words, which offer such an enlightening exposition of the nature of my own inner conflict:

> Designed to protect the personal spirit from annihilation by reality, the self-care system provides a fantasy that "makes sense" out of

---

[3] Ibid., p. 28.
[4] Ibid., p. 184.
[5] Ibid., p. 24.

> suffering but splits the unity of mind and body, spirit and instinct, thought and feeling. The "mind" becomes a tyrannical perfectionist, persecuting its weaker feeling-self ... until finally, with all contact lost between the ego and this victim-self, a dreaded triggering word is mentioned ... The ego is now totally displaced by the loathsome weakling inside, who now becomes the only self and the whole world turns tyrannical, persecutory, perfectionist. The ego has now been "possessed" by the split-off victim-self.[6]

On the eve of this weekend, Anna wisely chose not to engage in a discussion about my distorted and self-punishing perception of what I now considered myself involved in. Instead, she firmly reminded me that she would be there for me as usual for our session next Thursday ... implying her hope that, somehow, we would both find a way to "hang on" until then.

* * *

Later that evening, thanks to the generous offer of a fellow student willing to drive, three of us travelled to the weekend venue together. However, her offer contained a proviso—that we make allowance for the age and condition of her car. Nevertheless I was grateful, and relieved not to be adding to my anxiety by having to find my own way to some unknown destination. I remember it as an absurdly "happy" journey. To our unrestrained humour, my friend's idiosyncratic old car lurched and jolted its way uncertainly across the countryside. In the darkness of winter, and with unlit country roads, we managed to get lost several times despite having a map. It was as though we were engaged in some oddly entertaining "orienteering exercise", and our laughter offered me a brief but very welcome distraction from the inner tumult that I was battling to contain. Such a differently charged emotional atmosphere almost convinced me that "things would be okay"—that I would find the emotional strength to survive whatever lay ahead—and perhaps maybe ... just maybe ... my fears would not be realised as the threatening experience which I so dreaded.

I managed to sustain my relative optimism for that evening. Waiting and watching as members of the group drifted in with stories of their

---

[6] Ibid., p. 95.

journey, I remember a lot of laughter, and our effusively affectionate welcoming of each new arrival. It was comforting to be surrounded by close colleagues, whose warmth temporarily obscured our nervousness. But beneath the light-heartedness was a tense anticipation that lay barely hidden.

Eventually, once the group had all arrived, our tutors called us together for a meeting to outline the next day's agenda. We were told that we had the use of a large and beautifully renovated old "barn". We were reassured that it was warm and comfortable, and would provide us with a spacious and informal environment that would enhance an atmosphere of intimacy between us. As if to quell any remaining scepticism, we were told to bring with us the duvets and pillows from our beds. Not surprisingly, this last instruction provoked bewildered amusement at the incongruous image it aroused. And so, beguiled by thoughts of what tomorrow might bring, we finally wandered off to find our respective rooms for the night.

Saturday dawned dull, grey, and cold. As I anticipated what lay ahead, not a trace of the previous evening's optimism remained. But I was not alone in my dispirited feelings. As the group gradually emerged for breakfast, it was clear that last night's elated exuberance had been replaced by subdued reality. Breakfast over, we returned to our rooms to collect duvets and pillows as instructed, and to prepare ourselves to finally confront the purpose which had brought us all there.

The "barn" proved an unexpected delight. Its large, lofty roof exposed a panorama of beautiful old wooden beams, suggestive of strength and stability. It was, as promised, both warm and comfortable, with the surprisingly welcome addition of a carpeted floor. We learnt that the barn was our tutors' home for the weekend, in a bedroom created high up amongst the rafters. Now, as we created our own comfortable space around the walls, wrapped up in duvets and propped up with pillows, a glimmer of light-heartedness could be felt to ripple gently around the room. And so, having organised ourselves in such stark contrast to our usual environment, the day finally began in earnest.

There was to be no prepared "order" to the day: it was up to each of us to decide when we felt ready to present to the group. We could also choose how we wished to do this—by standing or sitting at the front, or by remaining where we were lying, amongst the "circle of duvets". Some of us had brought music to accompany our presentations, and one group member thoughtfully offered to operate the CD player. The two tutors also assured us that they intended to participate in this shared experience, by offering something of their own journeys of self-discovery. Now all that remained was for someone to volunteer to go first …

This was not—and is never likely to be—a choice that I would willingly make for myself. Although I now know what to expect when I find myself surrounded by a familiar "circle" of colleagues, I still prefer to gently feel my way, assessing how and where I might stand in relation to other's contributions—and needing to assimilate the atmosphere and dynamic uniquely created by each group which gathers for a specific purpose. But it was my initial training that drew my attention to the many fascinating and complex ways in which we construct defences to help us overcome vulnerability in the face of threatened exposure.

What I had noticed was that certain colleagues would almost invariably choose to "go first" in any new undertaking. My initial judgement—admittedly stemming from envy—suggested an over-inflated ego, and perhaps narcissistic tendencies. However, I came to appreciate that "choosing to go first" might be another defensive strategy requiring no less bravery. Perhaps "biting the bullet", or "getting it over and done with" as quickly as possible, helped to contain an overwhelming anxiety, and was simply another way of trying to maintain the ego's emotional balance.

It was one such colleague who volunteered to present first—choosing to stand at the front of the group. I remember it as a wonderful combination of seriously reflective self-analysis, tempered with self-perceptive humour. She undoubtedly provided an inspiring start to the day's proceedings. Others then found the courage to volunteer their contributions. The day had begun to develop its own momentum, and a focused energy suffused us all with its vitality. Occasional glimpses of humour would surface now and again, but what lingers in my memory are the stories of the struggle for survival in the face of painful and often tragic life events. At times, it became impossible to hide our tears at the history of so much affliction. Gradually I became aware that I was absorbing it all—every expression of pain seeping its way in, where I could feel it building deeper layers to my personal anguish. So totally consumed by this invasion of intense feeling, I couldn't identify it as the "danger" that I had intuitively feared would overwhelm me. My fragile defences had begun to crumble—just as Anna had sensed they would—and with their destruction, my capacity to separate emotionally from this formidable material effectively evaporated. It was as if each story of personal tragedy became my own … and though

I didn't recognise it then, the weight of this burden would ultimately become a grief that threatened to crush me.

But for now, I still had my presentation to deliver. As the day wore on into the afternoon I knew I would have to force my way in. The fever pitch of excitement meant that people were now almost competing for the next available space ... and while I hadn't wanted to be the first, I certainly didn't want to be the last. When we returned from lunch, a friend noticed my heightened anxiety and expressed his concern. He took me into a corner for a private talk. It was at this point that I began to recognise how close I had come to emotional disintegration. Despite his loving solicitude, I couldn't risk expressing the depth of despair now oppressing me.

But somehow, I did finally find the strength to force my way in. I read a poem. The most innocuous poem I could find amongst my collection. It was called *New Beginnings*, and was an attempt to describe my feelings at learning that my daughter was expecting the birth of our first grandchild. I wish I could say that it was a poem full of optimism and hope ... but even then I knew that it merely hid all my fears for the future of this unborn child, triggered by painful recollections surrounding the birth of my own son. The resulting trauma, which I still struggled to contain so many years later, refused to be forgotten. As I delivered my presentation, I fought to keep my voice from trembling under the influence of so many invasive memories.

But finally the ordeal was over. I sank back for a while, believing that my "rational explanation" for confronting this challenge had actually met my hopes and expectations. The empathic response of my colleagues seemed evidence that I was not "beyond forgiveness" for my human frailties ... and perhaps this was the need which so many of us were expressing in our courageous exposure of our souls' deepest darkness.

By Sunday afternoon it was all over. After many affectionate "goodbyes", the three of us embarked on our homeward journey in our friend's eccentric old car. This was not without further incident, as the car threatened to break down totally at one point ... perhaps mirroring my own emotional fragility. But finally, and well behind schedule, we arrived at the destination where Patrick was patiently waiting to collect me.

I was back home at last—and I suspect Patrick must have sensed my barely contained distress. I remember attempting to join him later, to watch a television programme. Time to relax and unwind I thought ... But I found it impossible to concentrate on the voices and images which bombarded me from the screen with irrelevant trivia. Instead my mind "switched off", desperate to find a space for silent reflection. Suddenly, and quite unexpectedly, the tears began to flow—not just for myself, but as an outpouring of grief for what I now felt to be the deeply universal pain of existence. These were tears expressing the agony of trauma. Finally my despairing spirit had collapsed under the weight of a weekend of harrowing self-revelation.

I am left with a memory of having cried ceaselessly for hours … a more frighteningly uncontrolled out-pouring than I could ever remember experiencing. I actually felt my ego disintegrating under the weight of so much grief, and I recognised a parallel with the emotional breakdown that I had first brought to Anna at the time of my original crisis. Without doubt, Anna's worst fears were being catastrophically realised.

An anguished night of sleeplessness followed, despite my emotional exhaustion. Unable to calm my restlessness, I eventually gave up all attempts at sleep and went downstairs to the kitchen. The dark hours of wakefulness drew me once more to seductive images of "the knife". Lost in my nightmare reverie of universal suffering, I took my "favourite" knife from the drawer. In a pretence of wounding, I superficially drew the blade across my wrist. But now my imaginings were not merely confined to ideas of self-harming, but to the enticing image of death itself. The sharp, shining blade spoke to me of the relief promised to my tortured soul, which now felt as if it was carrying the unbearable weight of the world's grief.

But on this occasion something stopped me. As the enticing sting of the blade against my flesh promised its bloody resolution, Anna's image entered my mind. Disturbingly, an inner voice reminded me that my pain would also be her pain. It was enough to persuade me that I couldn't repay her love by a destructive act that threatened such damaging consequences for us both.

I phoned Anna the next morning and she immediately grasped the depth of my despair. In response to my confession that I was on the point of wanting to end my life, Anna's firm instruction was, *"Don't* do it … And I will see you on Thursday." Though uncertain that I could survive until then, Anna finally added the words which still resonate in my memory: "Anything is possible with a live patient—but with a dead one, nothing is." It was enough to convince me to hang onto life … at least until Thursday.

CHAPTER SIXTEEN

I am holding onto your hands,
Soft, gentle, strong,
Powerful enough to grasp my pain
And hold it as your own.

Now I need to feel your hands
Taking hold of my life—
Keeping it safe for me,
Showing me another way.

I feel myself
Sliding downwards
Into black despair.
Hold me, hold me

From this second descent
Into madness.
Give me your hands
And pull me free.

19th February 2004

I wish that, at the time of our recordings, I had thought to ask Anna what feelings had emerged for *her* during this extremely grim period. Now I wonder what it must have been like to see so many months of painstaking work sabotaged by one weekend of dangerously mishandled "containment". I do remember her saying at the time, "Nobody was taking responsibility for holding the group safely,"—since our tutors had joined in the process, rather than maintaining safe boundaries by emotionally separating themselves from the experience. Now viewing this whole episode from a professional perspective, I find it hard not to imagine that Anna would have been angry at having her work so devastatingly undermined by these events. In her place, I would probably have been driven to make some explicit reference to such feelings.

But if Anna *was* angry, she offered no overt evidence of this, other than the merest hint contained in her comment. Instead, she seemed patiently to resign herself to the lengthy period of reparative work, which had dramatically become the pressing priority. Reflecting on this, I am struck once again by Anna's loving patience, exemplifying unconditional maternal love for a despairing child. In the troubled weeks that followed I returned to twice-weekly, and sometimes three-times-weekly sessions, never doubting Anna's ability or willingness to safely contain the dark destructive turmoil which had returned to plague my internal world.

The poem *Falling* which opens this chapter was part of what Anna would later describe as "a haemorrhage of poems" which, as she correctly surmised, expressed my need for safe containment following the residential weekend. It was this need which had led me to phone Anna a second time, to regale her with the return to thoughts of death and wanting to self-harm:

> "The poem makes sense of what you were feeling, because I *know* you wouldn't lightly have chosen to phone me. So it's showing the desperate state that you were in when you returned from the residential, and how you needed to let me know that … And just to phone me up and say, 'It was awful. I've been really disturbed, and can I have an extra session?' didn't feel like it would do it. You actually felt that I *had* to be part of some 'enactment'—it was the only way to reach it."

What I described experiencing during that harrowing weekend was my sense of "unity" with the group. It was my use of this word which particularly alerted Anna:

"... Because it's as if your ego boundaries went—and so you're totally exposed to the flow, and the conscious and unconscious of *everybody* ... And you don't have any place in which to hold or manage it, because you've lost that place."

"Yes ... I could feel myself falling apart when I got home. And that's why I phoned you again ... because there just wasn't anywhere else to take it."

"And then your thinking about cutting," Anna considered. "... That would make sense too. Because the huge desire to cut would be to try to take control of something. You'd had an experience of all this really soul-searing material, and a feeling of having lost your ego-boundaries ... and Patrick didn't know what to do with you. And so it makes absolute sense that the person you'd need to contact was me. The knife would be your way of trying to get control of it for yourself if there wasn't anybody there to help you ... And I imagine that you had the confidence to phone me because of the previous sessions that we'd had ... It was so lucky that we'd got that firm foundation in place—because you were then able, inside that relationship, to see a possibility that we could manage it together ... which indeed we did, at that time."

In this heightened state of emotional fragility, the weekend following the residential unexpectedly provoked another painful encounter with my shadow. Two old friends came to stay, and the wife was the friend who had cared for me so devotedly when my marriage was threatening to fall apart. Our weekend included an excursion to London involving a train journey to Waterloo. As we left the station, there was the inevitable encounter with homeless people, whose tragic presence suddenly resonated with so many of my early dreams, in which I dreamt of sharing their homelessness beneath dark and dismal railway arches. I took this deeply disturbing encounter to my next session with Anna—our last before her break. According to her notes, she recognised that:

"... This image is always connected with the shadow when it comes up for you. And so, I said to you, "When you become unwell, you identify with the shadow. It takes over ... and in that place, you dismantle your 'grounded' place in the world and you make yourself 'homeless'". That was my interpretation ... And then you take yourself to the extreme end of the pole, so that you become one of the 'homeless people', and you release the opposites ... And in that session you wrapped yourself up in the blanket, as a way to ground yourself, and give yourself a sensation of something to hold onto for the break."

As I re-read the poems of that period, I am struck by the accuracy of Anna's interpretation—that they represented another way of trying to maintain control over my destructive impulses. Like the cutting, it was a less harmful attempt to "get something out". But if a lengthy break occurred during a period of crisis, I could still find myself needing to resort to both methods of "release and control" in Anna's absence. Anna's description of this flood of writing as "a haemorrhage of poems" appealed to me:

"I think that's a very good description," I reflected. "... I needed you to *know* what I had done ... especially over a holiday break ..."

"Yes ... It was a way of trying to 'capture the moment' wasn't it?" Anna agreed. "So that you would be able to let me know about it, when you were hopefully in a different place ..."

"... And when it had healed and there was nothing left to see—although it generally left a scar. But I didn't have the wound anymore, and I think part of this was about wanting *you* to suffer my pain as well ... because if I just sat here and told you what I'd done ..."

"Yes, absolutely ... It wouldn't have had the same powerful impact," Anna reflected.

The poems clearly signify the powerful urge to end my life, in conflict with the loving and containing messages of "safe holding" from Anna, as my strong mother/therapist. As Anna reminded me, I did finally resort to another episode of self-harming in early March, following her break and a horrible argument with Patrick—which was hardly the unfortunately timed coincidence it might appear to be. In Anna's words:

"... Patrick went to bed, and you 'went to town' ... And you cut yourself round the front of your wrist as well, trying to cut your veins. But you told me 'It didn't work.' I asked, 'What does *work* mean?' You said, 'It means *kill myself.*' You wanted to know why it hadn't worked. I said, 'I don't know why it didn't work—unless it wasn't meant to.'"

It will be apparent from this brief extract how much our work over these months involved Anna having to manage my return to obsessional thoughts of death. Effectively, I had regressed to where we had been at the beginning of analysis, and in Anna's words:

> "I thought you did some 'mental gymnastics'—because you told me that to let people know about your thoughts and distress was *extremely* damaging—but to kill yourself *wasn't* … because they would get over it. My response was, 'What a reversal!' Because my thought was that death must be the most damaging, because it can't be undone … And I reminded you of my words to you— that 'anything is possible with a live patient—but with a dead one, nothing is' … and I think you got the point."

According to Anna's notes, we then had a session in which I talked about the way in which I used music to calm me down. I described how hearing my mother play the piano had a calming influence on me in childhood, and since I knew that Anna also played the piano this emotional connection was important at this pivotal point in our work. In Anna's view, it was this connection which produced "a poem in which you really voiced your recognition of how you were reversing things in your mind":

> Today,
> My mother held me
> In her arms.
>
> Frightened,
> I felt her fear.
> She fought for me,
>
> Denying
> Death unflinchingly,
> Challenging the life in me.
>
> Words
> Assault my head
> Like knife wounds.

Blood
Swims in front
Of my eyes.

I watch,
As my death
Causes others to die.

Hold me
Tight. In your arms
We will all survive.

What
Is your love,
That can resist all my attempts at destruction?

Contemplating this period, I heard myself attempting to describe the distorted thinking which is recognisable as a familiar pattern in suicidal ideation:

> "I think it's terribly hard for anybody that hasn't been to that dark place, to understand how it *does* feel as though everybody would be better off without you ... And I know it's not just me, because I've heard clients tell me the same thing ... But I've also worked with clients who've been on the other side—coping with the aftermath of a suicide, and trying to help them understand this distorted perspective ... It's about a 'perverse caring' ... and I've found myself trying to explain that it's *because* they care, that the person wants to take themselves out of the picture ..."

Anna's response was to explain to me:

> "It's not about wanting to hurt—but it's about being in a place where it isn't possible to appreciate how much it *will* hurt ... Because you're so de-valuing yourself at that point that you can't imagine how much your loss *will* matter to other people ... And I think this thought is what you consider in the last verse of the poem—'*What is your love, that can resist all my attempts at destruction?*' ... Because I had to risk saying all kinds of things when you were in that self-destructive place, that a part of you could scoff at ... But what I was able to do, because of the relationship that we'd established, was to say, 'Well, I don't

know about anybody else—but I *can* speak for myself' … which is why I talked about wanting you to remain as a 'live' patient."

"Because by then I knew that it *did* matter to you whether I lived or died … that you weren't just 'saying the words' …"

"That's right. That's why it was so vital that we had got our relationship to the point where it was really working … so that I *could* speak for myself, and hope that you would believe in what I said."

In March, a number of synchronistic events occurred which appeared to have meaningful connections with my efforts to control these self-destructive impulses. I learnt that one of my fellow students was due to give a presentation to the group on the subject of "self-harming". I was tempted to avoid attending that day, but feared that my absence would only draw attention to myself. My Learning Statement for that week described how "I listened quietly to all the guesswork around what was going on in the minds of people who self-harm … some of it way off-track from my perspective." Then one group member told us she had talked in depth to an acquaintance who described her own experience of self-harming. "It was as though she was talking about me," I wrote at the time, "because it so exactly described my feelings." And my reflections continued:

> I re-experienced the sense of shame which follows the relief, and now it is like a vicious circle that I am caught up in again. I want to punish myself for the shame, and then the shame of that will need further punishment. I am really struggling with black feelings after today.

From her session notes of that time, Anna reminded me of another synchronistic event:

> "You told me that your college supervisor had a client who took her own life. Her experience put you in touch with what an awful thing that was—and what you had been threatening *me* with. And I wrote that you made yourself a promise that you wouldn't do it."

"I made *you* a promise …"

"Well, you made a promise in front of me …"

"I made it because, when I saw how it had affected her, I couldn't do it to you. I mean, it was still a case of it not really mattering to *me*, but I began to realise that it would matter to other people …"

"Yes … yes … So that was synchronistic as well …"

This was a reiteration of the promise I had made to Anna early in my analysis. But witnessing the effect which this suicide had on my supervisor, an experienced psychotherapist, truly brought home to me the full cruelty of this tragedy. And so I think I needed Anna to hear me reaffirm my promise to her, as a result of this painful confrontation.

Anna's notes also contained her record of a dream which I brought to her at this time. Our recordings indicate my attempt to dismiss this dream as unimportant—but Anna resisted this because, in her view, she considered that the dream contained significant evidence of many aspects of my internal conflict:

> I am counselling my client, a man in his mid-seventies. We are in a large room in a very grand Victorian house. Our session is nearly over and my client tells me that he would like to take me out and show me around London. There is something suggestive in his manner and I feel unnerved. I tell him that a counselling relationship is not about friendship, and that agency policy forbids socialising with clients. I can see that he is angry. He gets up and grabs hold of my hands. I ask him to let go. I tell him that I will have to report him to my supervisor, and that I no longer feel able to counsel him. He leaves, threatening: "Don't worry. I'll find you again." I feel very shaken. Then another counsellor comes into the room with his client. They are waiting to use the room. I hurriedly collect my belongings, but I seem to have so many and they are scattered around the room. One is a portable radio which is playing music. For some reason I can't switch it off. I quickly push it into my large bag, and hurry out of the room. I feel very upset, and suddenly realise that I am descending a strange staircase. When I get to the bottom, there is no exit. I feel lost and frightened. Then I see a room on the left with its door open. I walk into a vast room filled with grand pianos, like a showroom. A woman is standing there, so I ask her the way out of the building. Without speaking, she points coldly to a large door. I leave through the door, but it does not lead to the street. Instead, I find myself in a garden with a path appearing to wind around the house. It is bordered by a metal fence with spikes. Frightened at not being able to find a way out, I follow the path—but there is no exit anywhere. Then I see a small café and decide to ask for help. I walk in and see five women behind the counter. At first they seem helpful, but then they ignore

me and continue talking amongst themselves. I beg them to give me directions, but they all find excuses not to help me. I leave the café feeling full of fear. I continue to follow the path, feeling lost, frightened and claustrophobic, as though I am imprisoned.

As I consider this dream now, it is not difficult to recognise the allusions to many painful episodes in our analytic work. Beginning with "my client" in the dream, whose "inappropriate behaviour meant that I couldn't continue working with him", Anna reminded me that this was what our relationship counsellor had expressed to me. So there were elements of my affectionate feelings towards this counsellor and of our difficult ending. By extension, and recognisable in the "dream client", were those elements of myself that wanted to be close to Anna. The "supervisor" might then signify my unconscious self-judgement on the "inappropriateness" of this desire for closeness.

When I first brought the dream to Anna, I had been disturbed by the fact that the client in my dream had appeared in the form of an actual client, with whom I was working at that time. Anna had made a note of my reluctance to consider the possible sexual implications that it might contain:

> "I talked about sexuality," Anna reminded me, "which you refused to look at, and you got cross with me. So I said, 'You don't want to think about your client's sexuality', and you told me that you would take that to supervision. And then you identified the man with your father because of his age ... so of course that made any thoughts about his sexuality feel very uncomfortable."
>
> "Yes ... I remember the client. He did treat me like a daughter, and always seemed concerned about me ..."
>
> "... And he told you that he was leaving to live abroad ... So in terms of your dream, he was leaving you with all that 'junk' which you couldn't clear up ... and you were cross about this, and I think it left you feeling 'stuck in a parental couple' ..."

In the second-half of the dream, the feelings of being "lost and claustrophobic" suggested to Anna:

> "... Something about being stuck in a complex—of feeling trapped, and not really being able to find a way out yet ... because that's a dilemma which we can recognise as a place where *we* have been together. And you're not at all sure yet that you've found the exit,

and the people around can't help you—so somehow, you've got to find it for yourself."

Although we didn't discuss it at the time of our recording, a number of other images now strike me as significant indicators of the transference, and the way in which this could often produce feelings of anguish as well as solace. Firstly there is the "strange staircase", leading me down to a place that deepens my sense of claustrophobia. The "vast room filled with beautiful grand pianos" suggests the comforting emotional connection with Anna, as my mother/therapist ... And yet, the "woman" guarding this room in my dream is cold and uncommunicative. Another musical connection would seem to be "the portable radio" playing music. In reality, music was a vital source of consolation for me during this turbulent period. But a radio that refuses to be switched off has now become an intrusive assault in the dream. The "garden" implies a place of beauty and tranquillity ... but this proves to be nothing more than a frightening illusion, since the "winding path" apparently leads nowhere—except endlessly back to my own inner confusion. The metal fence which borders the garden appears to promise safety and containment ... but it has "spikes", and is therefore more suggestive of "imprisonment".

I can now appreciate that Anna was right to insist on the importance of this dream: condensed within its many images lie the evidence of unconscious conflicts which had, and would continue to be, played out within the transference. Nevertheless, by the middle of March I was able to write the following words in my Learning Statement:

> I have been in a very angry place: angry with myself at the power of my Shadow to control my thoughts and feelings. I really can't bear to live in that black place anymore. Inside that black void it is too difficult to hold onto life. I am really struggling to break free and move into the light.

Indications were emerging of a resolution to this grim period of depressive self-destructiveness. In Anna's words:

> "Yes ... lots of synchronous events *did* come up at this time ... And on the 18th March, I wrote in my notes: 'The tide is turning ... She is beginning to harness her anger to fight the destroyer, rather than to destroy'."

CHAPTER SEVENTEEN

Five years later, when we discussed this difficult episode, Anna speculated on a perspective which, with hindsight, I felt bound to agree:

> "... What we don't know is, if you hadn't had that experience at the residential, whether something else—between you and me, or in life—would have taken you back to that place. We could hypothesise that something like that *needed* to happen, so we could work on it here."

I couldn't deny responsibility for the choice I made at that time, nor my reasons for making it. Reflecting back on the event from a theoretical perspective seems to confirm Anna's thinking that "something like this needed to happen." A long period of calm was to follow—the longest so far in my analysis. In May I wrote "Mother Love"—a poem for Anna. It was the last piece of writing I would produce for almost two years:

> I love you.
> You are my mother and father
> Merged into one.

You believe in me—
Like my father.
You care about me—
Like my mother.

But something is holding me
Stronger than the first time.
This time, the child in me
Is allowed to be weak.

My mother is strong enough
To hold me.
My father feels no shame
In recognising that weakness.

Now my child can grow
In her own time,
Learn to trust in her own strength,
Learn to support herself.

Your love is teaching me
To be strong for myself.
For now you are holding me …
But one day you will help me to fly free.

This poem, and the lack of any other written records over the next two years, is an unmistakeable indication of greater emotional stability and inner resourcefulness which had grown from our deepening analytic relationship through this painful episode. Out of the trauma arose an even more profound trust in Anna. But the poem also signifies a deepening trust in myself. As Anna would later explain to me, the writing stopped because there was no longer a need for it. Now able to express my thoughts and feelings openly in our sessions, we could process them together. Through the evidence of her "safe containing" of my damaging destructiveness, I was at last able to recognise the strength of the "analytic container" within which Anna held the material I found too terrible to hold for myself. This regressive need, unconsciously expressed in the above poem, appears to equate with Wilfred Bion's theory of containment, as interpreted in *The New Dictionary of Kleinian Thought*:

Bion's theory assumes that one of the most important elements of the early environment is the mother's mind. Through his realistic, or communicative, projective identifications the infant arouses in the mother feelings that he cannot as yet bear or make sense of. The mother, with her more mature mind and her love for her child ... "contains" and gives meaning to the unbearable mental content, which can then be returned to the infant in a more manageable form. In time, the infant introjects not only processed mental content but also the containing capacity itself.[1]

* * *

Events in the two years following this episode indicate that this improvement in psychological stability enabled me to cope with a great deal of loss and change during a period of significant endings. In July 2004 the Diploma Course ended. Out of the original twenty three students, only eight of us survived to qualify as "counsellors". We celebrated our achievement at a party in my home on the final day of term. Surrounded by the tutors and fellow students who had shared this life-changing journey, it stands out as a moving memory recalled by our many photographs. By now fully aware of my difficulty in coping with endings, I knew that the loss of this regularly shared, closely knit group experience would be profound, and that it would involve the need to manage the intra-psychic isolation certain to emerge from the gap left by the loss of this supportive emotional environment.

On another, more personal level, I was also facing the departure of my son, who had made a decision to emigrate permanently to Spain with his partner. I battled to celebrate their courage in starting this precarious new life abroad. But I could not hide from myself my ambivalent feelings, as I contemplated the loss that this distance would inevitably create.

Lastly I needed to manage the substantial changes happening for Anna at that time, which felt as though they were a disturbing aspect

---

[1] Bion, W. R. (1962). A theory of thinking. *International Journal of Psycho-Analysis*, 43: pp. 331–332. Reprinted in *Second Thoughts* (1967). Cited in Bott Spillius, E., Milton J., Garvey, P., Couve, C., & Steiner, D. (2011). *The New Dictionary of Kleinian Thought*, pp. 331–332. Sussex: Routledge.

of my own experience. My reflections concerning that period clearly reveal the pathological aspects of my projective identification.

Following delays and difficulties, the re-building of Anna's new home was scheduled to begin in June 2004 ... starting with the demolishing of her existing home. I dreaded the impact of this, even though our strengthened relationship enabled me to manage the prospect with more equanimity than when I had first learned of this event a year earlier. Nevertheless, it was a reality which was to become a serious emotional challenge until August 2005, when Anna was once again safely established in her home.

What strikes me about this memory is how impossible I found it to ignore what was happening in Anna's life at that time. There was nothing obviously occurring between us to provoke my concern, and a year had passed since our move to Anna's new consulting room. So the demolition in no way mirrored the environment in which our analytic work was taking place. In truth, I can remember nothing in Anna's demeanour to arouse my apprehension about her well being. I am therefore forced to recognise that the concern I felt was entirely a projection onto Anna of my own inability to cope with this situation. Though now possessing sufficient psychological stability to avoid being totally overwhelmed, the event nevertheless took on a "nightmare" quality. And I believed that Anna must have similarly been experiencing this nightmare, despite any overt evidence to confirm this.

When I reflect on my reactions, it seems that I needed Anna to experience my nightmare imaginings in order to help me contain them; and my unconscious desire to "enter into Anna's mind" would enable me to feel and understand her strength to contain these imagined anxieties. But a potential for destruction lay in the fact that I also needed to "blame" Anna—since my deep identification with her through the transference led me to assume that she had "caused" the distress I was experiencing.

Initially the destructive element of this energy threatened to take precedence, as I became intent on turning the "nightmare" into a reality. Once the demolition work had begun, I felt forced to witness the action with intuitively well-timed precision, when my visit to the site would coincide with some significant new development in the destruction process. Often I would leave sufficiently early for my session to allow time to drive to Anna's "old home" first, so as to review the building work. But it was my initial visit which confronted me with the reality of what was happening.

As I turned into Anna's lane on that first occasion for almost a year, the space created by her half-demolished home had dramatically transformed the skyline, suddenly allowing for the effect of unaccustomed light to alter the whole configuration of the lane. This invasion of light had a ghostly quality—something that transfused the scene with a hollow emptiness.

I parked my car at a discreet distance. The house was now surrounded by metal fencing intended to exclude uninvited entry, though it did nothing to obscure the view. I got out of the car for a closer look. The scene appeared to me as a grotesquely surreal vision. Still only partly demolished, parts of the ground floor were discernible evidence of its previous existence. I recognised the ravaged remains of Anna's former "consulting room"—the room in which she and I had first met, and in which we had shared the first two and a half years of our relationship. As I contemplated it now, the "safety" previously contained within this room had evaporated.

Similarly disturbing was the experience of suddenly finding myself "invited" to share in the desolated remnants of other rooms, to which I had never previously been allowed access. In particular, I remember the half-demolished kitchen that extended to the back of the house. And beyond this, I could also see through its destruction into the garden beyond, from which a prospect of the river was clearly visible. With no roof, the untoward intrusion of daylight suffusing these ruined remains created a macabre evocation of their former life. A scene of destruction assailed me, dramatically compounded by the sight of the wallpaper—now hanging from the walls in a tragic-comic parody, which, in that moment, suddenly symbolised the ephemeral nature of life itself. As I thought about the "solidity" that Anna had come to represent for me in those early days, this scene was a stark reminder of the fragility and transience of human existence. So much of the stability and security which I had invested in Anna had been symbolically embodied in her home, and her history as a wife and mother had, in my mind, become securely embedded within the bricks and mortar in which I had imagined this family life taking place. I had trusted in this symbolic representation as something "secure for all time". Now I was witnessing its destruction taking place before my eyes … and as something which Anna had chosen to do.

Though I felt an unsettling sense of "intrusion" into Anna's private space, I couldn't resist the opportunity for encounter which it offered, despite its eerie painfulness. This had also been *my* "home", my place of safety during those first turbulent years. I couldn't avoid the feeling that I was entitled to this intrusion … as a last memory of that space to which I would never again be allowed entry, and which was now disappearing forever. As I surveyed this scene of desolation, I recognised that a grieving process had begun for me …

Lost in reverie, I became aware that the builders were now watching me suspiciously. I felt obliged to explain, telling them, "I'm a 'friend' of the owners. I'm just interested in seeing how the work is progressing." Though it was a deception, it seemed enough to put their minds at rest.

But the deception did not quieten my mind, and Anna and I spent many analytic hours exploring my need to engage myself so closely in this destruction. Since I was no longer putting anything into writing, I have no record of precisely what took place between us. For the purposes of this history, if not in terms of my analysis, the lack of written evidence of this period feels like another loss—particularly since Anna and I did not return in depth to this episode in our recorded reflections in January 2009. Perhaps we both feared that time was running out, with little more than two months until Anna's retirement and our final ending—a disturbing parallel which had definitely begun to resonate as a subliminal process during that final period.

With only my memory as a guide, I am nevertheless convinced that Anna was able to contain my distress safely. What persuades me of this is the thought that another distressing episode of anxiety would have overwhelmed me had she not been able to do so … with all too predictable results. However, in the deceptively quiet period between 2005 and 2006, it seems that this "resolution" became the impetus for another unconscious energy to emerge. A past episode of "destructiveness" still remained disquietingly unresolved, concerning the events that had precipitated my psychological breakdown in the period before my analysis. Now a very peculiar process began which would lead me, through an extremely convoluted series of happenings, to a final resolution of this earlier trauma. Gradually, over an eighteen-month period which began half-way through my final year of training, the time was right for these events to develop their own momentum.

* * *

With the end of my Counselling Diploma in sight, I began to consider my future plans once qualified in this new profession. At fifty-eight years old I did not seriously consider myself to be employable, and the thought of establishing a private practice hardly occurred to me as a possible option. Although I would be qualified to practice, it became apparent that my training was simply "the beginning" of a process of learning—and did not signify "the end" of anything very much. I had come to appreciate that the more I learned about the theory of psychotherapy, the less I actually knew, and the initial experience of training had merely whetted my appetite for more. And so I decided to embark on further training, while continuing as a voluntary bereavement counsellor.

In a process that Anna was later to describe as "very perverse", I found myself drawn again to the idea of training as a relationship counsellor—with the organisation which had rejected me in 2002. I did have some conscious awareness of this perversity—but my deeper, unconscious need only became clear by the end of this lengthy undertaking. What I did recognise at the time was the desire to now prove myself "good enough" to be accepted, after the previous experience of "failure"—and I *was* willing to admit, if only to myself, that some kind of reparative, narcissistic need lay behind this thinking. Investigating further, I was gratified to discover that a new course had been developed, intended to attract qualified practitioners. This was much shorter, comprising four weekend residential modules. By September 2004 I had received confirmation of an interview.

This time the interview process proved to be a very different experience. Now convinced that, as a "qualified counsellor", I would be able to present myself with reasonable confidence, no trace remained of the anxiety and fragility so unmistakeably evident on the first occasion. I did not even need to fear an interview with a psychotherapist, since the only personal interview was conducted by one of the organisation's tutors, whose main role was to identify which theoretical models had formed the basis of our previous training.

Once again, the interview day involved an overnight stay. For a second time Patrick came to my rescue by offering to drive—though he confessed to being perplexed by my admission that I was not particularly drawn to working therapeutically with couples. Patrick's questioning of my motives was similarly mirrored by Anna's eloquent silence on learning of my decision to put myself through this process for a second time. I could only insist that it was "the training" which primarily interested me. This explanation was clearly inadequate, and as Anna would later reveal, she saw my decision as "something which worked for the hidden agenda", signifying her recognition of the powerful unconscious forces driving my motivation. And though she made no specific reference to it, I wonder if she recognised the influence of the "shadow" behind my determination to pursue a training for which I could offer no convincing explanation.

Even before the training began, a development occurred which made it impossible for me to ignore this possibility. Before being accepted onto the course, I first needed to establish a placement with one of the organisation's agencies—to ensure completion of the required clinical practice element. I subsequently learnt that I had been accepted as a "trainee counsellor" at the local agency closest to my home. I knew exactly where this was ... It was the place where Patrick and I had first met Gemma, our former relationship counsellor, now nearly five years ago.

I certainly recollect experiencing some anxiety about the placement—but more formidable was a deep sense of gratification. On the assumption that Gemma was still working at this agency, I now contemplated the prospect of working alongside her—as her equal, professionally if not in terms of experience. Finally I was qualified to enter into the previously "forbidden territory" of Gemma's world. Though I had no concept of what I planned to "do" with this connection, the opportunities it promised were enough to leave me with a sense of having achieved something potentially powerful. As I began to absorb the powerful possibilities I had now unlocked, a disturbing combination of excitement and alarm became a warning undercurrent to the feeling of gratification. I knew I had placed myself in the grip of a dilemma, from which emotional, moral, and ethical questions were likely to emerge to which I didn't yet have the answers.

At this point, I could have openly confessed my previous connection with the local agency. Instead I chose to say nothing. I had begun to sail into dangerously shadowy waters—though without fully understanding my need to do this. Nevertheless, despite the underlying anxiety, I was enjoying the sense of danger. I resolved to bide my time—to wait and see what emerged. I was willing to trust that events would eventually point me in the direction of an appropriate resolution to my dilemma.

Mostly I found the training enjoyable and stimulating. For the first time since qualifying, I was surrounded by experienced practitioners.

I felt inspired by the frequently strong expression of their views, many of them opposed to the theories and philosophy of practice proposed by the training organisation. I learned as much, if not more, from close engagement with these practitioners than from the training itself. Whether in private practice or employed by the NHS, some were already working with clients from within the organisation's agencies. And so I regularly found myself regaled with their problematic experiences of working from inside the organisation. It was something of a revelation, and as the training progressed, I became increasingly convinced that the organisation's ethos did not sit comfortably with my developing philosophy of practice.

Despite these considerable reservations, I completed the training modules in July 2005. Earlier that year I had set up in private practice, having been encouraged by a number of well-respected colleagues. To my surprise my practice built up quite quickly, and I became increasingly preoccupied with this aspect of my work. Nevertheless, I resolved to maintain my commitment to continue with my placement as a trainee Relationship Counsellor.

But first I had to be interviewed by the person allocated to be my supervisor. I recognised that the time had arrived to make an important decision: would I stay silent about my previous connection with Gemma, or would I risk exposing my personal life by revealing myself as her former client? Finally, the need to be ethical and honest prevailed. I knew that, morally, I would feel unable to begin working for the agency while harbouring a secret which meant maintaining a deceptive silence.

It was not a comfortable revelation to have to make on meeting with a new supervisor, and her response to my news only added to the discomfort. While acknowledging "appreciation of my openness", she expressed "surprise" at my revelation. "It's not a situation we have ever encountered before," she confessed. Clarifying that Gemma was still working as a counsellor for this local agency and that she knew her well, she resolved to speak with Gemma on how best to manage this unprecedented situation. She would let me know her decision in due course.

Shortly afterwards, I received confirmation of my re-allocation to another local agency in a different borough. Since my supervisor worked between both boroughs, this move would allow continuation of our supervisory arrangement. My reaction combined worry with relief.

My "revelation" had left me feeling exposed, particularly since the discussion between Gemma and my supervisor might have revealed details concerning Gemma's challenging experience of working with me at that time—details which might still be held on the agency's records.

In recognising the part I had played in creating this uncomfortable scenario, all my earlier sense of "empowerment" evaporated. I had now effectively relinquished all possibility of a connection with Gemma—and inadvertently might even have given her the power to thwart my intention of achieving this. And yet this thought also contributed to the sense of relief. I was now absolved from having to make a decision about what to do, since there was no longer a risk of meeting Gemma in the course of our work. I had reluctantly begun to acknowledge the lurking presence of my shadow behind the circumstances which I had precipitated, and though the "hidden agenda" to which Anna later referred still remained unclear, I was grateful that no serious question concerning my moral integrity remained unresolved as I began my new placement in September 2005.

And so, in addition to the increasing demands of private practice, I began work each week as a relationship counsellor, while also attending numerous group and individual supervisory meetings. It was a challenge, and I struggled to adjust on a number of levels. While my skill and experience in working with individual clients had begun to grow, I became aware that this did not easily translate into working with couples. Often finding myself confronted with angry and antagonistic clients meant having to manage a very different dynamic in order to create a therapeutic environment. My embryonic skills left me feeling far from confident about my ability to manage this successfully, and though I considered her to be supportive, my supervisor was unsentimentally tough in her expectations of her supervisees.

I also continued to have other professional reservations concerning the organisation. Frequent organisational "Memos" were relayed to us in meetings, immediately demanding that we change our practice to incorporate some new approach—without allowing us any voice to question implementation of these practices. Some practices I considered antithetical to the ethos of the profession in general—and certainly they often conflicted with my own philosophy of practice. Nevertheless, I persevered with this undertaking for several months, silently questioning my obstinate need to continue challenging myself in this way. By now, with all thoughts of Gemma pushed from conscious awareness, I could recognise the accuracy of my original instinct: I was not temperamentally suited to this work. Furthermore, the organisation's ethos was increasingly presenting me with ethical and philosophical conflicts, and I was frequently full of resentment at the lack of democratic consultation around the changes which we, as counsellors, were obliged to implement without question.

Despite these doubts, my supervisor had grown quite encouraging of my client work during these uncomfortable months. As I recounted the difficulties and self-questioning confronting me in this work, she would respond with reassuring confidence about my growing skill. Since by now I trusted her integrity and experience, I found myself disturbingly obliged to accept what she was telling me.

However, by December of that year, my situation had become untenable. My private practice had now grown sufficiently to make the agency's demands impossible to incorporate into my busy week. Effectively, I felt forced to make a choice … and by now it was not a choice which presented me with a problem. But a new situation had arisen which *did* present me with a serious dilemma, and reignited my urge to resolve the trauma of my former ending with Gemma.

As counsellors for the organisation, we were all notified of an AGM to take place in early December, and informed that all counsellors were expected to attend. Following my "revelation" prior to beginning my placement, I had effectively banished all thoughts of meeting Gemma again. But now, as I anticipated the prospect of the AGM, I was convinced that Gemma would be attending. Suddenly, with this renewed opportunity for "connection", I imagined a scenario in which I sought her out and introduced myself—fantasizing that my physical presence would cause her acute embarrassment.

I re-experienced a thrill of excitement in anticipating this flirtation with danger. This was my opportunity for revenge—at least to some degree—for all the suffering which I believed had resulted from the traumatic ending of that first counselling experience. As the days passed, I became increasingly immersed in these dark vengeful thoughts. Without the courage to reveal them to Anna, I assume she was already aware of this as "the hidden agenda" emerging from my shadow. Lying dormant for so many years, it seemed I had finally constructed this perversely convoluted chain of events in order to create an outlet for my revenge.

But another extraordinary chain of events would finally remove the need for such a vengeful outcome. Though I resolved to attend the AGM, I had also decided to end my association with the organisation, to coincide with the Christmas break. Anticipating this, I wrote a detailed letter to my supervisor, explaining that my decision was based on the increasing demands of my practice, but also elaborating on the conflict between my philosophy of practice and the ethos of the organisation. It was this conflict, I emphasised, which had finally settled my decision to discontinue my placement.

My supervisor contacted me to arrange a special meeting to discuss my decision. I sensed her concern. Writing the letter had proved cathartic, and it was a welcome relief to allow myself this opening for honest expression—though I was careful to word this thoughtfully and professionally. I could not risk being accused of having given vent to a "hysterical outburst" of irrational feeling.

Unexpectedly, I found myself moved by our meeting. With disarming openness, my supervisor acknowledged her empathy with my conflict around certain aspects of the organisation. She expressed sincere regret that the previous training of "qualified practitioners" like myself was not more highly valued. "We need people like you," she told me, "so that we can learn and grow from the different training and experience you bring." She told me she valued my work and the depth of insight into my clients' issues, finally adding, "I am *very* sorry to lose you." Her look of regret was sufficient to convince me that her words expressed genuine feeling.

As I walked away, the colossal weight of something indescribably painful was suddenly released from somewhere deep inside me. I felt it as the shifting of an "historic" pain. I couldn't name it then, but in the days that followed, I recognised it as the start of an intense process of healing. My peculiarly perverse association with this organisation had been my way of "getting inside it", in an unconscious attempt to find reparation for wounds I considered to have been inflicted years ago. In a state of profound vulnerability, I had been "rejected"—first by Gemma, and then by the organisation itself. Now, from a position of relative strength, I had found a way to reject them. This was the "hidden agenda" Anna recognised. Revenge indeed! But ultimately it was a revenge which did not cause serious harm to anyone. My unconscious motivation had been to restore my sense of self through this perversely convoluted exercise—and events were to prove that I managed to achieve this.

On the morning of the AGM, as the prospect of meeting Gemma loomed nearer, it dawned on me that this no longer mattered. The importance it had previously occupied in my mind had shrunk to insignificance—because Gemma herself had now ceased to hold a place of significance for me. And so, in the final hour left to me for decision-making, I chose *not* to attend the AGM. A week later my association with the organisation ended. I had found a way to heal the painful wounds, and the relief of this healing process was profound and lasting. The wheel had come full circle. To commemorate this consummation I paid one final visit to Carl, in his strange little tattoo parlour. Around the top of my left arm, I asked him to execute a complete circle of thorns containing one red rose. It was to be the last tattoo I would ever need to show Anna.

In her recorded reflections on this episode, Anna was inclined to the view that this acting out of the perversity of my motive for revenge "hadn't worked." Since the intervening years have allowed me a more objective perspective, I am inclined to disagree on this occasion. I am convinced that it *did* work, in spite of its "perversity"—and not just for the "hidden agenda." In struggling to balance the conflict between self-gratification and moral questioning, an extract by Samuels et al. caught my attention by its resonance with this inner conflict:

> Jung suggested that it was an innate principle of individuality which compels each person to make moral judgments in accord with himself. This principle, compounded of a primary responsibility to the ego on the one hand and, on the other, in relationship to the supraordinate demands of the Self ... is capable of making the most arbitrary and trying demands ... The result of making a conscious decision to surrender or to renounce (to sacrifice) an ego position may bring apparently little personal or immediate outward satisfaction but it sets things right psychologically, i.e. it "works", to use Jung's word. It restores a balance between conscious and unconscious forces.[2]

---

[2] Samuels, A. (1986). *Jung and the Post-Jungians*, p. 94. London: Routledge & Kegan Paul, 1997 Edition.

Nevertheless it is a difficult question, and finally I must leave it to more astute minds to decide on whether the outcome constituted an "acting out" of the "hidden agenda", according to Anna's view—or whether, in the final denouement, it represented a sacrifice of the ego position through the difficult moral decisions which ultimately led me to forego my opportunity for revenge through a personal confrontation with Gemma. Whichever is "the truth", the end result finally laid the ghost of Gemma to rest in my internal world—thankfully forever.

CHAPTER EIGHTEEN

Although it would take until the end of that year for events surrounding my training as a relationship counsellor to reach their final conclusion, the summer of 2005 marked a period of continuing psychological and emotional stability. As Anna and I looked back, I was reminded of how often my analysis would lead us to speculate on whether I might learn to view endings not as a "death", but as containing the potential for change and more akin to "re-birth and renewal".

While not naturally drawn to this perspective, I now recognise this as an aspect of my pathology—so that I no longer regard my affinity with death as containing a "philosophical truth" demanding unquestioning acceptance. During this particularly strengthening period, Anna helped me develop a deeper appreciation of an alternative outlook … though a more definitive resolution had yet to be achieved.

Unsurprisingly, the process of re-visiting this issue provoked a dream that emerged three months before my analysis ended, at a time when Patrick and I were re-decorating:

> I am missing my mother and wanting to see her. I am at home. The place is in a mess because we are decorating. It is early morning and I hear a knock at the door. Looking from the bedroom window, I see my mother there. We wave to each other and have a conversation from the window. She says she has come to help with the decorating. I feel delighted to see her so unexpectedly, and grateful for her offer to help. I go downstairs to open the door. Then she tells me, "I've brought somebody else with me," and my adult son suddenly appears at her side. They both look pleased and happy … and I notice that my mother is wearing a cape which I had knitted for her years ago, when I had sat with my son, then a very young child recovering from an operation.

My first words to Anna concerning this dream were:

> "It was really lovely—until I woke up … And then I found myself thinking about how my mother *would* have happily helped with the painting, and to sort out all the mess."

Since my mother had died many years earlier, such a powerful evocation of her "living" presence provoked an intensely emotional response, clearly evident in my voice as I reflected on the dream in that recording.

> "Do you think it's just about that?" Anna enquired gently.
>
> "No … no … I know it isn't," I acknowledged, despite the tears evoked by the dream's association. "That's just the obvious connection … It's got to be about you as well, hasn't it?"
>
> "Well, we're 'sorting out', aren't we?" Anna suggested. "It's a mess, but we're going through a process of 're-sorting' … and we're sorting out some very difficult bits …"

With the final ending of our work so imminent, it was inevitable that a parallel process of grief was emerging as we considered my past and present conflict in coming to terms with "loss and endings". And so I responded to Anna with thoughts in acknowledgement of this bitter struggle:

> "Yes, we *are* sorting through some messy, difficult stuff … And I'm also losing you, so I think the dream suggests that I'm wanting my

> 'other Mum' back if I can't have you … But I can't actually have either of you …"

This was a poignant confrontation with the depth of sadness concerning both a real and an anticipated loss. But Anna was not prepared to leave me floundering in that painful place:

> "But I wonder … when you have a dream like that, does it give you any kind of a feeling that you've still got Mum there inside you somewhere?" Anna questioned.

Yes, I was sure that I had—and the dream suddenly enabled me to appreciate how much I had previously focused on my mother's "vulnerable aspects"—and similarly, those of my son. But now Anna had prompted me to a different perspective:

> "In the dream, they were *both* there … *both* there for me," I conceded.
>
> "Yes … they *were* both there," Anna agreed. "… And being inside you, you have much stronger feelings about the 'awfulness' than about the good feeling—that you *could* have a dream like that … And that's your take on it, always!" she emphasised with a hint of irony.

Her thoughts about the dream continued to reinforce this different perspective:

> "I think it's a dream that people will often have about a year after they've lost somebody—when they've done quite a bit of mourning … which is why I'm thinking more about 'regaining' somebody after a mourning process."

And as Anna reminded me, my memory was of "a Mum who did find a way to get through her grieving" following the death of my father. Inevitably we were led to consider the many losses I had experienced during 2004, and the way my Learning Statement had recorded my determined efforts to see them as "not about death—but about 'change'". While Anna saw her role as one of helping to keep my attachment to death more balanced, she could also empathise with the strong connection that it held for me:

> "Well, 'change' *is* about a death … If something changes, something *does* die … Sure it does. But the whole idea of 'change' is that

something *new* arrives as well—whereas death doesn't have that idea about it …"

This consideration was one we would often return to during the next few months. As far as our recorded sessions were concerned, only three months were left to us until Anna's retirement in April. And so, by January 2009, it seemed timely to reflect on an earlier, parallel process, between the summer of 2005 and the spring of 2006, to which Anna and I would subsequently refer as "our *first* ending."

* * *

Something of this shift in perspective had evidently begun to take place in my internal world, since I remember the summer of 2005 as suffused with the feelings of hope and renewal to which Anna had opened my mind. After the darkly challenging years of depression, I felt my spirit rising again—to encounter a sensation I hardly dared name as "happiness", but which nevertheless flourished and gathered strength during this summer of significant inner growth.

Anticipating the long summer break, and with our son now living in Andalucía, Patrick suggested a journey of exploration, beginning with this province in Southern Spain about which we knew almost nothing. Imbued with a spirit of adventure and his love of geography, he spent many weeks planning our trip with mounting excitement. Firstly, we would fly to Seville, the capital of Andalucía, spending several days in the city before collecting a hired car. Patrick then proposed visiting the city of Cordova, driving on from there to Ronda, a beautiful old Moorish town above a spectacular gorge. After two weeks of exploratory travel we would journey on, for a further ten days at the home of our son and his partner, now living 3,000 feet up in the Alpujarras, a mountainous region to the south of the Sierra Nevada.

But while Patrick was preoccupied with arranging this exciting adventure, I had been busily engaged in organising another "adventure" of my own. On our first visit to their spectacular mountain home the previous summer, I had learnt that my son's partner had returned to her first professional training as a chef. With her talent and expertise, she had succeeded in gaining employment at a place offering "alternative holidays in Spain", on the outskirts of a nearby town.

On our previous visit, I had found a booklet lying around giving details of the "alternative holidays" on offer at this resort. The booklet described "a holiday centre like no other, nestled among spectacular mountains in enclosed gardens", offering holidays "entirely devoted to personal development" in an environment suffused with "harmony and beauty." I had no knowledge of the existence of such holidays … but its resonance with the experiential aspects of my counselling training struck a deep chord. Since my training had ended, this offered the possibility of "filling the gap"—and perhaps also of repairing the consequent feelings of loss. Our son's partner had offered to show us around the resort to satisfy my growing interest, and I was not disappointed. The beautiful setting and facilities confirmed my resolve to experience a week of "personal development" within this magnificent setting.

And so, whilst Patrick was bringing his dream of a Spanish adventure to fruition I began to do the same. I had begun to play with the idea of inviting a close friend to share my dream of an "alternative" holiday experience—and a particular friend came naturally to mind in this connection. She had been a fellow trainee with whom I had grown increasingly close during our counselling training. Although we had stayed in regular contact, the geographical distance between us had made it impossible to meet up since the previous summer. As our course was ending, my friend had suddenly announced her decision to return home to Ireland with her husband. Her obvious happiness had left me uncomfortably deprived of a suitable space to adequately express the grief which her loss would cause. In rapid succession, events transpired which resulted in her move taking place on the last day of term—the final day of our training.

I remember it as a day of profound mourning for me. As my friend's husband pulled up outside the college—the car loaded up for their journey back to Ireland—there was barely time to express our mutual sadness at this hurried ending to our close connection. With no opportunity for privacy, we shared a final and very tearful "goodbye" in full view of the administrative staff sitting in the Reception area. Watching them drive away I was left to manage my tears alone … then obliged to return to the classroom, where the rest of my fellow trainees were confronting their own loss at the ending of our group. No privacy for this personal aspect of my grief was possible in the circumstances … but finally this hardly seemed to matter, since so much personal pain and so many tears had already been shared between us all during our training. In fact, I think the spectacularly "public" nature of my grief became a symbol of the mutual grief of the group on that poignant final day.

But almost a year on from this experience, I now anticipated an opportunity of softening the blow we both felt to have been caused by my friend's rapid departure. If she would agree to join me for a week of personal development at this resort, we might recapture something of our former closeness within a familiar and containing group environment.

I sent my friend details of the resort, and we spent much time on the phone discussing the course options—while I eulogised on the beauty of the location, the facilities available … and the wonderful food which would be prepared by my son's partner. Eventually, to my great delight, my friend agreed to join me. A considerable logistical exercise then followed, involving integrating this arrangement with Patrick's plans, and our visit to the home of our son and his partner.

I am willing to risk ridicule by making the clichéd pronouncement that it was "the holiday of a lifetime"—while refuting this as an idealised memory due to the passing of time. Since the start of my analysis, the long summer break had proved difficult in various predictable ways, arousing regressive feelings of anger, resentment, and abandonment. Emerging before the break in anticipation of its impact, these feelings would become a self-fulfilling prophecy, so I tended to regard summer breaks as bitter-sweet experiences, resonating more with pain than with pleasure.

But the summer of 2005 is evidence of the emotional shift in my internal world. For the first time in years, my spirit was free to enjoy the pleasures that this holiday offered. As I recollect them now, they form a picture which confirms that my memory is not an "idealised" one—because finally this was not a time of undiluted happiness. In spite of its many delights, some painful aspects still remained to be confronted.

After two weeks of hectic travel with Patrick, the reunion with my dear friend was a welcome opportunity to reflect on both our lives over past months. Our feelings would often run high with the excitement of being back in each other's company after such a prolonged absence. And the resort's beautifully calm atmosphere also provided the perfect setting for some deeper reflection on our internal worlds, further enhanced by the personal development course which we attended daily. But as with all such experiential encounters, there were inevitable moments of deep sadness as I found myself confronting again some recognisable struggles which were the on-going subject of my analysis.

In the absence of Anna's support, I feel bound to pay tribute to the skill of the course facilitators, for the way in which they safely and empathically contained several such episodes as they arose amongst the group.

This inspirational week was perfect in terms of my psychological and emotional recovery process. And the knowledge that I had created the means by which to share this experience with my friend, added to the significance which it continues to hold for me. I believe I can say with confidence that, for both of us, the holiday added another precious dimension to the closeness of our relationship.

As we packed our bags on the final morning, the room seemed to echo with the myriad emotions shared in the intimacy of so many hours. But finally it was over, and I recognised that I was already mourning the loss of this closeness. As I watched my friend board the bus to the airport, a tumult of feelings flooded through me. Most prominent was the painfulness of our goodbye, which held no comforting certainty of when we would meet again. But I was also conscious of the fact that this ending marked the start of something new—since I could now look forward to joining Patrick, our son, and his partner for a further ten day's in this glorious environment.

It was a surprisingly difficult transition—from a week of deep focus on my "internal processes" to a more direct engagement with external reality. I was now "on holiday" in the more traditional sense, which effectively released me from the "inner questioning" which had occupied my mind for the past week … Had it *really* been only a week? The intensity of the journey seemed to span something that felt more like years … And yet, here I was, only a week later, contemplating a time already "past", and struggling to process its profound impact in an ephemeral "present".

Finally I did make the transition, recognising that this family week was resonant with the depth of other precious relationships—in particular, with my son. In this mood of heightened awareness, I could relish the closeness with my family. Late at night, or in the early hours of morning, I would indulge in luxurious moments of quiet reflection on the terrace overlooking the magnificent mountains. At such times, it seemed as though the world around me was echoing my own inner peacefulness. I would watch, as the fading or dawning light magically effected the disappearance or re-emergence of the mountains, in inevitable accord with nature's supreme and ultimate authority. Despite a sense of my own fragility in the face of this incontrovertible power,

I could also connect with a deep feeling of harmony—which seemed to emanate from an unfamiliar recognition of my own power for personal agency.

And still, so many years later, I often retreat in my mind to that terrace, dominated by the power of the mountains. It has become a deeply spiritual connection, through which the paradox of my own frailty and strength can resolve themselves into something which is, perhaps, as a close as I can come to a feeling of inner harmony.

And so, despite its inevitable sorrows, I took home a gift from this extraordinary holiday experience—not only evidence of my inner strength, but also the promise of "endings and new beginnings"—of which Anna's perspective would continue to remind me ... at least, when I would allow myself to be open to hearing the message in her words.

* * *

Following the summer break, my sessions with Anna began again in early September. With the re-building of her house now in its final stages, I knew of Anna's plans to move back into her home during August.

I clearly recall the huge comfort which this news afforded me, and during the break, my mind would often conjure up a picture of the scenario which I imagined Anna to be engaged in. Despite any obvious evidence to suggest her discomposure, I knew that Anna and her husband had been living in the small flat containing her consulting room during the re-building process. Throughout this time, my mind had played fast and loose with every imaginable "difficulty and inconvenience" which I convinced myself they must both be experiencing—and which I believed Anna was "hiding" from me.

But as our sessions began again, I comforted myself with the thought that Anna was "back where she belonged"—even though this no longer represented the home which signified my first safe refuge. I had chosen not to re-visit the site for many months. Instead I think I chose to focus on the positive hold on life which Anna so often subtly conveyed, so that I could internalise some of this for myself.

But now that this period of internal and external turmoil had ended, I knew that I needed to take one final look—so that Anna's "new home" might occupy some place in which I could reconcile it with the memory of the "home" that I had lost. Soon after our sessions began again in September, I left early one day, intent on allowing myself enough time for this important diversion.

In contrast to the previous vision of devastation, the surreal sense of space had been transformed. Anna's house now rose majestically above the level of the characteristic single-storey buildings in the lane, its white-painted exterior and large windows inviting natural light in a way not obviously attributable to her former home. And in spite of its distinctive size and character, it somehow contrived to maintain a softly harmonious quality which avoided any clash with its surrounding environment.

But my first, rapidly formed impressions were abruptly curtailed by events. I had parked my car within viewing distance of Anna's house, in the hope of finding time for a more leisurely view … when suddenly I was confronted by the sight of Anna emerging from the house with a "friend". I watched uncomfortably as they stood for a few moments in conversation. Though overcome with feelings of guilt, I couldn't leave without drawing attention to myself by starting my car engine. Once Anna had returned to the house and her friend had departed, I turned the car around and left in time for our session.

It was horribly disturbing, to watch Anna arrive in anticipation of our meeting knowing that she was totally unaware of what had just occurred. I couldn't wait to offload my guilt, and was fully prepared for some comment containing at least a hint of recrimination. I should have known better. The only aspect that interested Anna was the feeling which it had aroused in me. Though complex and conflictual the most pervasive feelings were guilt and fear—that Anna might perceive what I had done as evidence that I was "stalking" her. It was enough to ensure that I resisted all further urges to visit the home where our relationship had first begun.

* * *

Surprisingly, the dust settled quickly on this disconcerting incident. As September advanced, and our sessions slipped back into their familiar rhythm, I continued to hold onto the inner strength that I had brought back with me from holiday. It was a unique sensation, in stark contrast to the feelings with which I generally greeted Anna on our return from the long summer break, and I was eager to regale her with the many experiences that had opened up for me. In this spirit of self-belief, I had proved that life could continue to feel hopeful even after the pain of endings, and that I could survive these sorrows without being drawn to thoughts of death. I had begun to experience something, which beckoned me towards a future that felt both inviting and exciting in its quality of "newness".

It was perhaps inevitable that this newfound resourcefulness would lead to thoughts of ending my analysis, and I certainly recall raising this question with Anna shortly after our return. But Anna was used to this by now, and recognised that behind these thoughts had formerly been an "infant anger" at having been "abandoned" during the break. Remembering the empathy with which she would respond at such times, I learnt that the angry feelings of the "outraged child" need to be sensitively acknowledged and validated—and, above all, allowed to be heard. The client's "rational adult" can then be reminded that holiday breaks tend to remove us from the reality of life, clouding our judgement on important decision-making. And so, without negating or dismissing the client's thoughts, the possibility of "allowing things to settle down for a few weeks" can be considered, before returning again to the question of ending. So despite the apparent evidence that my ego had strengthened during this break, Anna remained firm in her encouragement that we allow time to reflect before making any final decision.

As Christmas drew near, Anna finally agreed that it was appropriate for us to consider again the possibility of ending our work together, with my conviction on this question having remained undiminished over several months. However, we both recognised that Christmas was not a good time to end. My first approach to Anna had been just before Christmas—and with the deaths of both my parents over this period in earlier years, difficult feelings inevitably surfaced at Christmas time. And so, after careful consideration, we agreed to bring an ending to our work on February 16th 2006.

Little did we know that this "first ending", which began in such an optimistic spirit of celebration, was destined to become a drama whose consequences would resonate for many months. With no knowledge of the bitterly painful period that lay ahead for me, the stage was set to provide the final piece of evidence I still needed, to convince me that "in endings lies the promise of new beginnings".

CHAPTER NINETEEN

With Christmas over, there was no way of escaping the hard reality of what I had chosen to do in ending my analysis. By the time New Year arrived, I was far removed from the mood of celebration which had been such a strengthening aspect of my summer holiday experience. All former optimism had been replaced by deep misgivings, and as the New Year got underway growing doubts and fears increasingly emerged as anticipatory grief at my ending with Anna.

After the conviction I had carried for so many months, it was hard to believe the sense of foreboding which now replaced so much former certainty. In fact, I tried hard not to believe it. My decision to end was based on convincing evidence of my readiness—and there was now no going back on an event for which we had both been preparing for six months. Anna's recorded reflections are a reminder of the thoughts behind our agreement to end in February:

"What was happening was that you were ending your role as a relationship counsellor, and you talked about this as having 'completed the circle'. So that seemed to suggest that our ending wasn't a bad idea, because it felt like a phase of work had finished … because it felt like Gemma had been 'put to bed'—which indeed she had. And that completed what you had come with—your attachment to Gemma. So we decided to end soon after you'd finished the relationship counselling, which was only a couple of months later."

It all made such logical sense. And as testimony to my belief that "the wheel had come full circle", I showed Anna the outcome of my final visit to the tattoo parlour: the circle of thorns, engraved in symbolic celebration around the top of my left arm, and containing one red rose.

But as the date came ever closer I could maintain very little hold on logic, nor on the evidence of internal strength which had so convincingly supported my decision. The "inner voice" now resounding in my head was relaying a precisely opposite message. My whole being yearned with unspoken longing to hear Anna tell me, "I don't think you are ready to end after all", and to offer me a way out of the fearful predicament I had created. During our later recordings, Anna revealed two important considerations. First, despite her initial reservations, it had been the evidence of my own firm resolution over subsequent months that had finally convinced her that I was ready to end this period of analysis.

Second, it became clear over the years that ending with Anna would always be accompanied by painful associations with loss and death, no matter how hard we worked to prepare for this event. Often I remember acknowledging that I would never be "one of those patients that walked away from therapy in a spirit of triumphant achievement." Though my own clinical practice had by then provided evidence that endings could be "celebrated" as well as "mourned", I could only admire my clients' ability to achieve something so far removed from what I could achieve for myself.

And so, we both prepared for the fact that the process of mourning would inevitably surface most acutely as we neared the ending. The danger was that the grief would swamp me completely, drowning out any sense of being able to hold onto Anna as a strong "internal object", whose love and safe-holding might continue to exist "inside me" without the need of her physical presence. Reflecting back on that first ending, I recall the creatively empathic way in which Anna strove to leave me with "concrete evidence" of the depth of our relationship.

In anticipation of our final session, we discussed her thoughts about giving me photographs of her own paintings displayed in her consulting room. This was her recognition that I needed "something concrete" to hold onto, signifying the specialness of our relationship as contained within that space. Though it only emerged years later, Anna recognised that our relationship had always been marked by my need to express my transference towards her in concrete terms—by giving her "objects". Subsequently these "gifts" came to include the extensive collection of poems and letters, and ultimately her acceptance became the evidence I needed of her willingness to contain and hold me safely. In our early sessions, when it had felt so profoundly difficult for me to voice my thoughts and feelings, I believe that Anna recognised the writing as a pre-verbal "infant need" for her safe-holding as my "mother".

The subject of whether or not therapists should accept gifts from clients is a contentious one, particularly in analytic circles. I therefore feel bound to defend Anna's decision—since within the context of this narrative, she is not able to do this for herself. On many occasions I could sense Anna's discomfort. But in exploring the significance which these acts of giving held for me, I believe she understood that her acceptance was helping to strengthen the transference which was a vital aspect of the deep analytic work in which we were engaged.

Not that these "gifts" always signified a positive transference. Some of the darkest poetry which I needed Anna to "hold" for me indicated a challenging negative transference which I was unable to voice for fear that it would damage her. Had she not understood the unconscious process behind this unspoken need, I am convinced that a refusal to accept these "concrete objects" would have become evidence that my internal world was indeed "too awful" to be capable of containment by *anyone*, and that my deepest fear of being beyond help had been realised. Before our first summer break, I clearly remember the relief when, in recognition of this need, Anna asked if I wished to "take something" from her consulting room—"to hold onto during our break." I was offered several choices. Finally, from a bowl of "wooden fruit" that had often attracted my attention, I chose a "wooden pear". It was the first of many such occasions, and although unsure what attracted me to this particular object, it accompanied me everywhere while Anna and I were apart. I would often hold it lovingly, fondling its sensuously curved shape which, with hindsight, I believe symbolised the reassuring "roundness" of a loving and embracing mother in its suggestively feminine form. In recognising the power which this object held for me, I have translated Anna's empathic understanding into similar offers to my own clients, at times of deep distress or emotional fragility prior to a long break.

It was Donald Winnicott whose work with children led him to study the child's capacity "to be passionate about *things* as well as people".[1] The prime example of this—which I recognise well from my own experience of working with nursery age children—is the strong attachment which a child may develop towards a toy, blanket, or piece of cloth which they carry with them as a symbolic representation of "mother" when she is absent. In elucidating this aspect of Winnicott's work, the Jungian analyst Anthony Stevens reminds us that Winnicott's study of this phenomenon led him to define them as "transitional objects", whose use "represents the beginning of the capacity to use *symbols*":[2]

> Transitional objects are symbols of the mother. They are of special value to a child ... when feeling lonely or anxious, for the very good reason that they possess the magical power of rendering the absent mother symbolically present. Winnicott points out that by using symbolism in this way 'the infant is already distinguishing between fantasy and fact, between inner objects and external objects ...' For it is true that transitional objects are *not* internal objects, since they exist outside the child. They are equally *not* the mother or the breast for which they stand as symbols. They are *intermediary* between the inner subjective world of the imagination and the outer objective world which is shared with everyone else. They also become invested with those emotions which are normally associated with the presence of the mother and with physical contact with her. They are thus the first indications of the individual's emerging capacity to live what Jung called *the symbolic life*.[3]

However, in reflecting on my own experience as a teacher of very young children, I have been led to consider a further dimension to Winnicott's theory. Since the notion of "relationship" signifies a reciprocal process,

---

[1] Stevens, A. (1990). *On Jung*, p. 86. London: Penguin, 1991.
[2] Ibid., p. 86.
[3] Ibid., p. 86.

I believe I have witnessed evidence of an infant's need to reciprocate their own capacity to give mother a symbolic—and sometimes preverbal—representation of the two-way process implicit in this relationship, from as early as six months old. Thus, from my own observations, a six month old baby engaged in play will offer mother an object in a meaningful gesture, as if he were giving her "a present". An intuitive mother will respond in a loving, appreciative way, instinctively acknowledging that the infant is intending to give her "something of himself" to hold as a precious object. And from my teaching experience, this need continues to be expressed, at least through the nursery years, in the giving of concrete objects—though arguably, this might be considered to be a lifelong need, signified by the giving and receiving of gifts throughout the life span.

Later on, the "objects" which the child requires mother to "hold" have probably become paintings, drawings, or "works of art". I suggest that these are "transitional objects" whose concreteness has been *specifically created by the child* to express his need for the holding of a transitional object to be a *reciprocal* process, which will increase his security when separated from mother. Both my teaching and clinical experience suggests that the way in which mother receives these "gifts" is crucial in enabling the child not only to maintain a strong internalised object of the mother during periods of separation, but also expresses a need for evidence that the mother can retain a similarly strong internalised object of the child.

Although not having formulated this into a specific idea at that time, I have become convinced that the exchange of concrete objects between Anna and myself signified my infant need to be part of this reciprocal process of internalisation. This seems to me to be a sufficient defence against any disapprobation which might be levelled against Anna for her acceptance of such "gifts". From her close questioning of these acts of giving, I was quite aware of Anna's reservations. On at least one notable occasion, she discussed this question with me, attempting—with extreme sensitivity—to resolve my infant need to "give her things" by appealing to my adult mind. Since I did not consciously wish to cause her discomfort, I subsequently made efforts to limit this urge to "special occasions", when it might appear more acceptable. But I could never finally rid myself of the urge to express our relationship through such concrete acts of giving. I am acutely aware that in writing this book, as my final gift to Anna, I am continuing to express this need. And Anna's gift to me of the recorded reflections, which have enabled me to write this history, suggests her appreciation that its "concrete symbolism" represents a joint process of "internal holding".

*　*　*

I do believe that I struggled valiantly to manage that first ending with Anna, in spite of the fearful doubts which plagued my mind as I anticipated it. I put various strategies in place, in an effort to bolster my flagging courage. One of these was to ask Anna if we could "listen to some music together" in that final session. Though willing to agree to this, she explained that I would need to provide the CD player as she didn't have one in her consulting room. Especially for the occasion, I bought a CD of Schubert's "Impromptus", so that we could listen together to the Impromptu No. 2 in E Flat. It is a piece of piano music that always has the power to transport me back to an evocative childhood memory. At five years old, I would sit watching my mother play this piece, her fingers appearing to fly across the keys, giving birth to a sound that seemed almost heavenly to my young sensibilities.

Since my earliest emotional connection to Anna came from the knowledge that she also played the piano, it was relatively easy for me to allow her to become "another mother" in the transference. And this shared connection with music had continued to play a vital part in deepening our therapeutic relationship. Had we still been meeting in Anna's home, I am convinced that I would have found the courage to ask if she would play the piano for me in that final session. Though I have no idea how she might have responded to such a request, it was what I really wanted. It was a scenario about which I had often fantasised, and the image was always a source of comfort. But now we were no longer in Anna's home, where I might enjoy the sight of her piano or notice how the diverse books of piano music would change with the passing of the seasons.

Deprived of this option, the best alternative I could conjure up was that we might at least *listen* to music together. In agreeing to this, I believe Anna understood it as my attempt to turn fantasy into reality, so that this vital connection could be symbolised in a memory to which I could return when she was no longer physically present for me.

Thursday, February 16th dawned dull, grey, and with the promise of rain. I remember feeling resentful. Even the weather was conspiring against any reversal to the mood of deep desolation which now suffused both my internal and external worlds. I had asked Patrick if he would "take me out somewhere" once my final session with Anna was over, as another strategy to help me manage the ending. He had agreed to keep the day free, and the plan was for him to drive me to Anna's consulting room and then wait for me, so that we could go straight off somewhere afterwards. I didn't much care where that "somewhere" might be—I only knew that I didn't want to be alone with my thoughts that day, and that Patrick's ability to stay "safely grounded" would help to support my forlorn and grief-stricken spirit.

In anticipating it, I had forced myself to imagine a bright sunny day. I conjured up a pleasurable picture of walking by the river, and then perhaps finding somewhere close by for lunch … But as the day arrived, and we embarked on that melancholy drive to Anna's consulting room, any hopes that the weather might lift my spirits dissipated into the dismally enveloping greyness.

Mostly I enjoyed the journey to Anna's place, and I would look forward to it. The route took me along several pleasantly winding roads, where a view of the river would suddenly become visible below grassy banks leading down to the river's edge. Often, if traffic allowed, I would slow down the car in order to enjoy the gentle calm of this river view for a few seconds longer. At one particular point along the road, I could catch a distant momentary glimpse of the back of Anna's new house, whose imposing height made it easily discernible. As well as the gently calming view of the river, the journey had also always offered me a welcome opportunity to prepare my mind in anticipation of my session with Anna.

But on that morning it was not a sight which afforded me any pleasure. Everything was shrouded in a drab greyness which seemed to drain the scene of any colour or light. Even the river looked "dead" that day. It matched the "deadness" in my soul, as I recognised with a frightening clarity that I would never be making this journey again in the knowledge that Anna would be quietly waiting for me at the end of it. It was a relief that Patrick was driving. The terrifying thought that I now faced a future with no possibility of ever seeing, hearing, or being in Anna's physical presence again was producing shock waves which resounded through my psychic structure. I had begun to recognise the familiar signs of imminent panic: somehow I needed to maintain a conscious hold on my internal strength if I was not to be overwhelmed by the painfulness of this final session.

We arrived about fifteen minutes early, so I knew from previous experience that I could soon expect to see Anna arriving in her car. We sat without talking, my mind immersed in an awareness that I was probably surveying this familiar scene for the last time. Despite my earlier misgivings about Anna's new premises, I had learnt to love the ebb and flow of human life along this small local high street. I had become fascinated by the way in which the tableau would change between mornings and afternoons, and I had particularly come to love this scene while waiting for my afternoon sessions. The timing coincided with the end of the school day, when the street would come alive with the bright liveliness of children and their mothers, talking animatedly about their day. In the summer months, this would include visits to the sweet shop for lollies or ice cream, while the mothers stood around in the warm sunshine, engaged in friendly conversation. The scene reflected a changing picture of life with the passing seasons. Not only this, it had taken my mind back to many precious and pleasurable memories of my own time as a mother and a teacher of young children. I felt a sense of privilege at having been allowed to observe this high street scene over the years … and on that particular day, I knew that in mourning the loss of Anna, I would also be mourning a multitude of other losses.

With horrible, stomach-lurching suddenness I was brought sharply back to the present by the familiar sight of Anna's car arriving. I looked at my watch … about five minutes to go until my finger would be pressing the buzzer, and I would hear Anna's voice through the intercom for the last time. I began to imagine what might be going through Anna's mind as she contemplated our last session together. I thought about what she might be feeling, in anticipating this session with awareness of its momentous significance for me. In those few moments for reflection, I felt confident of one thing: that Anna would recognise the pain of my grief as she had always done—with loving empathy, understanding, and above all, the warmth of her humanity.

I think my limited memory of that final session is evidence that I was in shock, and only barely able to function. I remember that we listened to the music together. I had lugged in my rather unwieldy CD player. In the event, I found myself feeling uncomfortable about the strange experience of having to set it up while Anna was watching and waiting behind me. It was not usual for me to be "messing about" like this in her consulting room, and I became conscious of how all these necessary preparations were actually distracting our attention away from the significance of this last session. By the time the music began to play, I was almost regretting my decision. It didn't fulfil my expectations as I had imagined, although our subsequent discussion about my choice of music reassured me that Anna understood the symbolic resonance with our relationship that it contained.

Sadly I have almost no memory of anything else we talked about that day. Not surprisingly, I had brought a gift for Anna—and I remember that she accepted it with obvious appreciation of the loving and grateful spirit in which it was given. I took away with me the photographs and CD-ROM which Anna had promised to make for me of her paintings in her consulting room—the "concrete objects" which symbolised the relationship we had shared together. As the session ended, Anna offered to share a final "goodbye hug". In that moment we stood and held each other in what felt like a mutually loving embrace. There was no disguising my own tearfulness at this parting—but in that fleeting experience of physical closeness, I also retain a profound sense of Anna's own emotional engagement with the significance that this ending held for me.

All at once, it seemed, our final session was over. As I left, unable to staunch the flow of tears, I could see Patrick in the car, reading the newspaper, and waiting for me with patient resoluteness. I assume that he had braced himself for the inevitable tears. Following a brief glance at my distressed appearance, he diplomatically chose not to make any comment or enquiry. As he slowly pulled the car away from this now bitterly familiar parking spot, I was overwhelmed by an urge to "get away" as quickly as possible. I didn't care where we went, or what Patrick had planned for us to do. I just knew that I couldn't bear to spend another second surveying the painfully emotive environment which I now felt was lost to me forever.

Despite Patrick's best intentions, the rest of our day together did not help to lift my spirits. He took me to Guildford—where we often enjoyed ambling around the shops and having lunch in a pub overlooking the river. But with grim inevitability, the weather that day continued with its determined "pathetic fallacy" to match my mood of mourning. By early afternoon it was unremittingly cold and wet. I asked Patrick to take me home, where at least I could continue to nurture my grieving soul in the warmth and comfort of privacy.

CHAPTER TWENTY

"Fog"

Who is lost?
Is it me or you?
I see you shrouded
In an ever-thickening mist,
Moving further and further away from me—
Too far to touch,
Too far to see or hear.

What is the shroud that envelops you?
Does it signify your death or mine?
Where are you now?
I am losing you ….
You are drifting, drifting ….
I am trying to follow where you go
But my soul is crying out in pain—
You have gone too far away for me to reach.
Soon you will be lost to me forever.

28th February 2006

This poem, written shortly after our ending, is just one indication of the period of intensely troubled writing which followed. Anna had agreed to some "shared communication" after an appropriate interval of several months had elapsed. But I was unable to contain the outpouring of grief-stricken words which followed—and since I could no longer express them to Anna, the need for her to hold them in written form became overwhelming. So despite our agreement, I emailed the above poem to her.

Though I wanted a reply, I knew that I had no right to expect one. And predictably, Anna chose not to respond. Notwithstanding my distress, I understood that she could not respond to emotional demands for support when a therapeutic relationship no longer existed to contain such a dialogue safely. I was pushing at the boundary of our agreement, and I now recognise that it would have been both unsafe and unethical for her to respond outside the safety of a therapeutic dyad.

Trying to find the strength to contain these painful outpourings, I looked for a way to "talk to Anna" without actually sending her every written expression of grief as it emerged. I started to keep a "diary" of thoughts and feelings, in an attempt to hold and process this material for myself. In between these entries I also wrote "letters" which allowed me to fantasise about the continued existence of our relationship. I sent a few of these carefully selected letters to Anna, hoping that their "chatty news" gave me a more acceptable pretext for communication—and Anna did respond in brief acknowledgement. But in re-reading them from a vantage point of greater objectivity, it is impossible to ignore the subliminal messages of mourning which lie barely disguised beneath their surface. Again, Anna chose not to be drawn into a dialogue on this hidden emotional content.

A far greater number of letters—handwritten in an untidy scrawl—were never intended to be sent. These contained the *real* expression of my anguish. By then I knew that attempting to communicate these feelings to Anna was neither acceptable nor appropriate. A period of desolate grieving followed, in which my only source of comfort was the "imaginary dialogue" which I continued to have with Anna through this solitary correspondence.

I came across the powerful evidence of my deep desolation in one dramatically scrawled and unsent letter. It reads like the desperate voice of the child, crying out in an emotional wilderness for her lost mother:

> Tonight I feel as though I have no home ... I am truly isolated, drifting on some vast nameless ocean, disconnected and rootless with no sense of where I belong. And that one safe place where I felt contained and understood is gone—because I chose to cast myself loose from it ... I continue to write, but I don't know anymore who I am writing to. The door is closed now. I have got the message. I will try to learn to live without you ...

It was a darkly emotional period, mirrored by the harsh and unremitting cold of those winter months which reflected so accurately my own desolate spirit. One of the diary extracts was written on a Thursday morning, at a time when I would previously have begun my journey to Anna. Years later, this particular expression of grief was revealed as having had a significant impact on events that were to follow:

> ... I should be nearly there now, but instead I'm watching the snow trying to fall outside my window. The weather is matching how I feel—a cold, hard wind is beating against my heart. I feel imprisoned in my loneliness and isolation. Even my tears are frozen today and unable to fall. That huge icy boulder has returned, blocking everything inside me. The pain is numbing. I wonder about your other client, who I used to see as she was leaving. Will she wear a coat today? Does the weather match how she is feeling too? She always looked sad and thoughtful. I wonder what you will do with our time? Perhaps you'll also just sit quietly watching the cold world outside your window, and perhaps you'll wonder about me. And perhaps I need to send this to you today. It might help to melt the ice in my heart.

My intense distress outweighing all other considerations, I did send this extract to Anna. Something in its despairing content clearly affected her. Contrary to my expectations, she chose to respond on this occasion—briefly, but with a message of undisguised empathy:

> Dear Naomi,
>   I am reading your diary, and you are in my thoughts with the struggle to manage this huge transition.
>
>   Fondly, Anna

Anna's words were an immensely comforting salve to the raw wound of my grief. I knew that she had heard and understood my pain, and in that moment of renewed connection she came "alive" for me again. This did not mark an end to my misery, which continued for many more weeks. But from a distance, it seems that Anna was now carefully noting the increasing despair conveyed through these occasional communications.

Only years later, during the course of our recorded discussions on this dramatic period, did Anna feel ready to reveal the disturbing impact of that diary extract in particular. We named it the "Snowy Day" entry, and Anna recalled reading it and subsequently taking it to supervision—because she felt the need to "talk it through with colleagues." Together with the poem entitled *Fog*, Anna's concern was that my grief appeared to be "escalating, rather than decreasing," and seemed in danger of becoming a serious threat to my psychic stability.

By the end of March, my desperate efforts to cope with these intense feelings of loss led me to formulate a "plan", which I hoped might offer a way of renewing our connection without actually being in Anna's physical presence. I wrote her a long letter expressing the huge emotional pain I was struggling to manage … a grieving process closely resembling my feelings after the death of my mother. I explained my need to write about these feelings, but that it seemed "an empty undertaking, if nobody is there to hear me." The idea I hoped she might consider was to allow me to write perhaps once every three or four weeks, and that she would respond "as my therapist." I was fully prepared to pay her fee for this arrangement, and I explained the reasoning behind my idea:

> … My excuse for this is that I feel it would act as a bridge between us which would help me to deal more gradually with our physical separation. It is this, and the loss of my space for personal expression that feels so devastating. Despite having worked together towards an ending, it feels too sudden and too final, and I am really finding it hard to cope with the emotional fallout from this … What I do want to emphasise is that this is not an attempt to evade our ending. It is really a hope that you will feel able to help me find a way through the painful process I am currently dealing with …

Later that same day, I received the following response from Anna:

> Dear Naomi,
>
> I have given careful thought to your suggestion, but I can see a lot of difficulties. One thing we discussed was having some spaced-out sessions. I would prefer this option. We could meet at first fortnightly, and then perhaps go three weekly or monthly as it seemed possible. We should meet to discuss this. It's not avoiding the ending. As you say, it's trying to manage it in a way that is tolerable. If you agree to this, I could see you after Easter, on Thursday, April 20th at 3.30.
>
> Warmly, Anna

It is impossible to put into words the gratitude and relief I felt. I had held onto my letter for several days before sending it, because I was so terrified of receiving an angry or rejecting response. Of course I much preferred the idea of talking to Anna rather than writing to her. But I couldn't allow myself the luxury of imagining that such an outcome was even a remote possibility. Now, following Anna's response, I could fantasise about sitting in her presence once again, hearing her voice, and experiencing the safe, containing resonance of her words filling me with the strength which I seemed so unable to find for myself. It was a joyous day-dream of "re-connection" after so many weeks of miserable isolation.

But even as I allowed myself the indulgence of such imaginings, I was acutely aware of some distinctly opposing thoughts which obtruded themselves into my mind. Despite my desperate need to re-connect with Anna again, it was precisely this sense of desperation which so scared me. I had always doubted my ability to manage a satisfactory separation, no matter what tactics we employed, nor how many discussions on ending formed a part of this process. With clear evidence that my feelings of loss had intensified instead of diminishing, I was now confronted with the reality that my worst fears had been realised. I was angry with myself at how badly I had managed this ending, in spite of the care and sensitivity with which Anna had tried to support me through it. And the horribly painful fallout from this episode continued to haunt me, heightening my fear at having to repeat the experience again—since the inevitability of an ending with Anna could only be "delayed", but never finally "avoided". How on earth, I wondered from the depth of my despair, would we ever find a way to overcome this difficulty? For now, my only consolation lay in accepting that I had been expecting "too much, too quickly". With the unwavering trust I continued to maintain in Anna's therapeutic skills, I took comfort from her words—that this was *not* about "avoiding the ending", but about "trying to manage it in a way that is tolerable."

The second difficulty I had to face lay in telling Patrick. Though aware of my grief, I sensed that he viewed the ending of my relationship with Anna as an achievement. Understandably, he had never fully appreciated the need for my therapy to continue for so long, especially since he was aware that it had not always been a source of comfort. But I didn't expect Patrick to understand the complex and idiosyncratic nature of the analytic process. How could he have done, without having been through it himself? In addition, there was so much evidence of my "recovery": I had successfully completed my initial training, set up in private practice, and my client numbers were increasing at a reassuring rate. From his perspective, I was clearly both inspired by and deeply engaged in my new profession.

I could quite understand how Patrick might be disconcerted by my return to analysis, while apparently successfully engaged in performing a similar therapeutic process with my own clients. And I knew that Patrick would not be alone in this. A number of close friends, colleagues, and also my own children, had applauded the ending of my analysis as an achievement and a cause for celebration—even while understanding that it involved a process of grief. I dreaded having to confess to them my failed efforts to cope, and these thoughts certainly heightened my anxiety … but I couldn't allow my feelings of humiliation to be a deciding factor. If Anna felt sufficiently convinced of the need for us to "re-work" the process of our ending, I was not going to let my sense of failure get in the way of agreeing to this decision.

* * *

My diary for 2006 suggests that I kept Thursday, the 20th April totally free in anticipation of my meeting with Anna. I remember it as a strangely unsettling experience. Despite my longing to be with her again, I was full of fear. Only nine weeks had passed—and yet, to me, it had felt more like nine years. So much distressing emotion had emerged during the period of our separation—but even some of my more outspoken communications had only obliquely touched the surface of my distress.

I was dogged by a mortifying sense of failure. Though this meeting promised an end to my emotional fragility, I was forced to recognise that there were no certainties about the outcome. Maybe Anna would be angry with me for my bad management of our carefully prepared ending?

With these deeply troubling questions, I was surprised at the sense of comfort that enveloped me as I entered Anna's consulting room—though this did not last long. As I sat down on the couch and began removing my shoes—in familiar expectation of curling up with my feet tucked under the cushions—I was stopped by Anna's instruction to "stay sitting up." Surprised and unnerved, I looked at Anna's face. She looked strangely stern—almost forbidding. My fear that she might be harbouring anger towards me instantly doubled in intensity.

Later, I understood that her response had nothing at all to do with anger. In line with her "invitation", this was not intended to be "a therapy session", but "a meeting" to discuss possible plans for the renewal of our therapeutic relationship. Subsequently I recalled an almost throwaway remark which Anna let slip towards the end. She told me that, had she been a Kleinian analyst, "an ending would have been an ending"—in other words, there would have been no possibility of a renewal of the relationship. I found myself wondering whether her comment reflected some kind of inner questioning about the appropriateness of what we were doing. But in any event, it at least allowed me some explanation for her unaccustomed severity.

But unnerved by Anna's tone and body language, I rapidly dissolved into a distressed and tearful recounting of my inconsolable grief following our ending. My recollection is that the extent of my distress made any further mention of "spacing out our sessions" disappear from the agenda, and by the end of the session, Anna had suggested that we resume regular weekly meetings.

From the time that we resumed our relationship, my urge to write down the experience of our re-connection increased. This reflected the release of creativity which our relationship had always held for me, and which would continue up to and beyond our final ending three years later. At some point, Anna gave me the news that she planned to retire in April 2009. But strengthened by my relief in being allowed to return, three years felt sufficiently far off for me to ignore its implications for the present.

Following that first session, I was driven to write her a lengthy "Reflection" which included the following thoughts:

> ... Above all, it is the feeling of "healing" which is most powerful. Though I tried to bury the thoughts that are now demanding expression, I never stopped "watching you" in my mind. You became a silent figure, often turned away from me with your eyes averted, and I watched you silently getting on with your life ... The only thing that connected us was the silence, and this was far from comforting. But today has changed all that and here I am again, forced from sleep by the powerful urge to find my voice—to put into words the painful process of these past weeks—because now I know you are there to hear and make sense of it all ...

Reflecting my past and present analytic experience, this letter signified the more deeply congruent expression of feelings which would mark the next stage of our work. Remembering Anna's earlier words—that "endings" also held the promise of "new beginnings"—I recognised that this renewal of our relationship was not merely a continuation of our earlier process, but paved the way for a vitally new process of self-discovery.

CHAPTER TWENTY-ONE

I am certain that I had no concept of the challenges about to confront us in this final stage—rather, my mind was full of the positive prospect of what we might achieve. In this spirit of optimism, I really *did* believe that any serious threats to our therapeutic relationship were a thing of the past.

No doubt Freud would have pronounced this as "wish-fulfilment", but now a vitally new ingredient had been thrown into the melting pot: the subject of Anna's retirement. Though I tried to convince myself that it was sufficiently distant not to evoke concern, my unconscious refused to allow me to dismiss its significance so lightly. With no choice about prolonging my analysis beyond a three-year period, there was a finite quality to our relationship—and the anxiety this engendered surfaced almost instantly in a disturbing dream:

> My daughter Rebecca was a bereavement counsellor. She asked Patrick and me to look after her children while she was working. We said we would take them to the park, and Rebecca agreed to meet us there after work.
>
> We went to the park, and her three children—boys aged between seven and ten—were climbing a tree. Suddenly a woman appeared.

She had wounds on her cheeks as though someone had sliced off pieces of flesh, but the wounds weren't bleeding. She was agitated, and told us she had been attacked in the park by a man with a knife. Just then, Rebecca appeared and began talking to the woman. They went off to look for the man, and Rebecca asked us to follow behind with the children. We told the boys to come down from the tree because we had to go. Then we realised that one child was missing. The boys told us that he had run off, but they didn't know where. I began to feel anxious because of the man with the knife, but we decided not to say anything to the boys about this. We would follow Rebecca in her search, and look for the missing child on the way. By now, Rebecca was already a long way ahead.

After walking around for some time we found the missing child. He had climbed another tree and was calling to us. This was a huge relief, and we decided to tell the boys about the man with the knife so that they would appreciate the danger and stay close to us. They became very worried about what might happen to their mummy if she met the man with the knife. We tried to reassure them by saying that we would keep Mummy in sight, and would take care of her if the man appeared.

Eventually Rebecca and the woman stopped to talk to another woman who pointed to the gates of the park, suggesting that the man was now outside in the street. Once outside the park, they stopped to talk to another woman in the street, who also pointed ahead. She seemed to be saying that the man was not far away now. I began to feel very frightened … and then I woke up.

It was impossible to ignore a dream which contained such disturbing imagery, and had surfaced immediately following my return to analysis. Nevertheless, I chose to ignore any thoughts which threatened my comfort at being back with Anna. It was our recorded reflections that gave us an opportunity to consider the dream's import retrospectively, in full knowledge of what subsequently transpired. Having read the dream aloud, Anna shared her thoughts:

"Rebecca is working as a bereavement counsellor in the dream—and you had got into an acute state of bereavement following our ending. I wonder whether 'the park' with its 'gates', and its suggestion of 'inside and outside', is about being back inside the therapy? ... Because you'd just come back—so you're *in* the park now ... And there's a danger in the park—because when you came back you learnt that I would be retiring. So you knew you were coming back for a limited period of time, and needing to make sense of what had happened when we tried to end, so that we could end again. So the cut-off was there right from the start of this new phase."

This certainly resonated with me, but also raised a troubling question:

"Do you think 'the man with the knife'—and the wounds he inflicted—represent 'the cutting off' then?" I asked Anna.

For me, Anna's reply was destined to become a defining interpretation, to which I would often return during the course of writing these final chapters of my analysis:

"I think 'the man with the knife' represents a very sinister, attacking figure that we had to deal with and face in this second part of our therapy. And I think that this concerned your feelings about ending—that I *could* retire—and everything that this stirred up ... I think he's a figure from the shadow that attacks—that he's attacking you and me, and our relationship and what's going on between us ..."

I felt bound to agree with this insight, since I knew that the presence of this image was destined to haunt the next stage of our work—as a truly fearful figure, whose existence would later be embodied in some of the darkest poetry to emerge from my unconscious. His first appearance certainly indicates my unconscious need to confront and integrate this threatening presence, which I had split off as "too terrible" to bear recognition at that point.

"... And then he goes *outside* 'the park'," Anna continued, "... So there's a question of whether he is 'inside' or 'outside'... And there's certainly a feeling that he's got to be found and faced—which indeed we did."

This "confrontation" was something I recognised as vital, even then. But I was puzzled by his appearance as a man, and needed Anna to explain his emergence as an "animus" figure:

> "Well … it's to do with the shadow being the opposite from the non-shadow figures—and the shadow often appears in dreams in the opposite gender," Anna explained.

Anna suggested that the dream image of my daughter might signify an "anima" figure standing in compensation to my "animus shadow". From this perspective, I understood that her presence could indicate an unconscious attempt to balance this conflict of opposites—to bring into conscious awareness this split-off aspect of my shadow. As Anna commented:

> "She's the one that does the 'managing', so I think she stands for the 'mummy' part, while you're working on the 'child' part in yourself."

As our dialogue continued, Anna reflected on the significance of the dream in relation to both my past and present analysis. Since the challenge we both faced was the inevitability of our final ending, the way in which the dream reflected my difficulty with "endings" was a necessary consideration:

> "… I've often talked about the part of you that relates through 'merging'," Anna reminded me. "It's not all of you—but a *part* of you does do that … And since this is a fairly 'merged' dream we are left wondering: Is Rebecca you or is Rebecca me? Are the children my children or her children? … So there's something about coming back into therapy and 'getting in the park' which brings about a kind-of 'merging'—which is where you needed to be because it was the only safe place … Having felt so abandoned and excluded when we tried to end, when you come back, your need is to 'get right in there'—because our next task was going to be to separate out again more successfully … Does that make sense to you?" Anna queried.
>
> "Yes it does … because I know that I felt in danger of falling apart," I conceded. "So yes … getting 'close together' again was …"
>
> "…. was *paramount*," Anna added emphatically.

In these last months, we were still in the process of working through the written material which had surfaced following my return. And so we continued with some further thoughts on where this might take us:

> "I think that your connection with 'the man with the knife' will help us to make more sense of some of the very dark, later poems," I suggested.
>
> "Oh certainly," Anna concurred, "… because 'the knife' has been a theme throughout our work together …. It's almost a title—*The Knife and the Butterfly*—because it's such a strong theme …"

Anna's reflections were a reminder of the symbolic significance of these two images: the "knife" as a symbol of my self-attack during my early months in analysis, followed by the tattooed "butterflies", whose symbolic resonance with life and beauty had enabled me to bring an end to thoughts of suicide and self-harm. As a consistent theme throughout our work, their inherent conflict is effectively a metaphor for my long battle to hold the tension between them in my internal world. It is evident to me now that this particular extract of recorded dialogue has offered me opportunity to reflect on the next stage in my analysis from a more detailed theoretical perspective.

* * *

Recently I have come to recognise "the man with the knife" as a daimonic figure who emerged in dreams once the loss of Anna and our continuing relationship threatened to become permanent. Thus, while breaks in our work invariably caused emotional disturbance, sufficient ego strength gradually developed to prevent my psyche from being overwhelmed by the loss of Anna's physical presence. But with the news that she planned to retire, I was forced to confront the reality of her loss forever. I now appreciate how the initial sense of desolation, followed by this news, both represented *real* encounters with the threat of a permanent loss.

The fear that this generated provoked a trauma which caused my psyche to react as if threatened with annihilation. Since it was in this dangerously fragile condition that I had first approached Anna for help, the recurrence of this fear was a warning of the danger of re-traumatisation. And it was seemingly against this renewed threat that my psyche rose in angry defiance with determination to survive—symbolised by the terrifying image of "the man with the knife". Having announced his existence, he became temporarily relegated to a subliminal "twilight zone" until the time for Anna's retirement became a reality that could no longer be ignored. This became the catalyst for him to rise again in vehement and undisguised attack of our relationship. As Anna has further suggested in a recent correspondence, the image of "the knife" was an indication of how, for me, "separateness felt like being 'cut apart'—always brutal and damaging," adding that "the power of the dreams and affects in our work always felt bigger than the ego defences to me." Remembering Anna's words that "the cut-off was there right from the start of this new phase," I can now see how the emergence of this threatening dream image at this point makes psychological sense.

Since my analysis ended, I have better understanding of the huge analytic challenge that Anna faced in managing a tolerable ending. Nevertheless, there is something about this sinister attacking figure, which puzzles me when I try to make sense of it in terms of my personal history. A clinical stance would suggest a much earlier trauma, almost certainly linked to very early (even pre-verbal) infancy, and indicating an intense fear of abandonment. My difficulty is that my recollection of childhood contains no obvious history of abandonment which might conveniently explain the origin of this traumatic reaction. Rather the contrary; I have clear memories of being loved and cherished, seemingly contradicting any suggestion of "traumatic abandonment". And yet ... there is no denying that this deep fear can still haunt me, its acute re-emergence in adult life having arisen in response to my fear of being "abandoned" by Patrick early in our marriage. Nevertheless, it is true to say that I did have some less than happy childhood experiences that perhaps have a quality indicating the potential for a fear of abandonment to have been repressed into the unconscious—so as to have become, in the words of Donald Kalsched, "associated with *unthinkable despair*".[1]

These musings have led me to a thought which may explain my heightened sensitivity to this threat. The reader may remember the description of my early childhood as a lonely and isolated time—largely as a result of my parents' sense of alienation at finding themselves

---

[1] Kalsched, D. (1996). *The Inner World of Trauma: Archetypal Defenses of the Personal Spirit*, p. 16. Sussex: Routledge, 2010.

living in a community with which they felt little sense of connection. Since friendships with local children were not encouraged, I took comfort in the solitary activity of reading, through which my loneliness could be hidden in a rich and vibrant internal world, peopled with characters from fiction who became, to all intents and purposes, familiar childhood companions. A fluent reader by the age of five, my earliest reading material mainly consisted of fairy tales. I still possess an illustrated and beautifully bound edition of Grimm's Fairy Tales, inscribed by my father with a birthday message on my seventh birthday. When I look at this book now—900 pages long and quite dauntingly "adult" in its presentation—it surprises me to recall the excitement I felt to be the proud possessor of such a magnificently weighty volume. I remember devouring every page of this momentous mythical "history" of mankind's struggle with the limitations of his human Being, in the face of his battle against daimonic forces, both internal and external, which threatened to consume him.

I wonder now whether the undiluted diet of atrocities depicted in these fairy tales provoked in my childish mind a deep fear of man's vulnerability and of his capacity for evil. Contained within these stories was the "evidence" that even loving fathers, mothers, siblings, grandparents, could be coerced into betraying their loved ones by evil influences they could not control. And even worse, these stories seemed to provide proof that "loving parents" were capable of the most profound dereliction of their duty of care, by the deliberate abandonment of their children into a world rife with these threatening forces of evil.

This may be an over-emphasis of the power of fairy tales to seriously subvert a child's sense of security in their "real" world. Nevertheless, I clearly remember that reading Grimm's fairy tales in particular, led me to question my mother anxiously on subjects which certainly suggest that my sense of security felt threatened. Foremost amongst these anxieties was a fear that I was "adopted", and that this had been kept secret from me—because something in these stories led me to perceive "adopted children" as being especially vulnerable to parental neglect.

Following my mother's confirmation that I had *not* been adopted, I needed further reassurance that she had "wanted me to be born"—to which she also assured me that my birth had been both "wanted" and "planned". This question was followed by another: would they have preferred me to have been a boy? I have no doubt that my mother's loving efforts at reassurance indicated her intuitive understanding of the insecurity that lay behind my anxious questioning. And although I never doubted my parents' love, something concerning the inherent vulnerability of all human beings, which included my parents, left an indelible mark on my childish ability to "trust" that even they could withstand the unknown and threatening forces of evil, which I now feared might lie hidden and waiting to attack beneath the surface of our apparently secure family existence.

Was this a fear whose origins began with the battle between "good and evil", so graphically illustrated in these fairy tales? Or was this an "inherited legacy", contained in the fear of displacement, insecurity, betrayal, and abandonment which lay hidden in both the personal and collective unconscious memory of my family's Jewish history? In a recent correspondence with Anna on this question, her reply contained the following reflection:

> I agree that, looking at your history it is hard to pinpoint reasons, except that perhaps, with rather fluid psychic boundaries you absorbed material which was not then processed, by you or your care givers. This would certainly be reinforced by fairy tales, which are said to be "containers" for primitive anxieties—but I have often wondered about that … I always thought there was something of the archetypal experience of the Jewish people which got in here … That might seem fanciful, but it is in the collective memory—and your family must have been touched by it, even if unconsciously.

Finally, I have no way of answering this question with any degree of certainty. Whatever the origins of my fear of abandonment, I am certain that it was this which became activated by news of Anna's retirement. And the traumatic reaction it provoked led "the man with the knife" to emerge from my unconscious, and engage us both in a battle for the survival of our relationship which would continue over many months.

* * *

I can now understand in theoretical terms that the major depressive disorder, which first led me to seek Anna's help, was caused by the sudden emergence into consciousness of "possession" by my animus complex. It was the shadow of this complex that had led me, all those years ago, to adopt an implacable position of control over Patrick after his infidelity. In *A Critical Dictionary of Jungian Analysis*, Samuels et al. describe how "Possession by either anima or animus transforms the personality in such a way as to give prominence to those traits which are seen as psychologically characteristic of the opposite sex." Thus, "a woman subject to the authority of animus … is managerial, obstinate, ruthless, domineering".[2] So although I could understand my controlling behaviour to have developed as a defence against Patrick's betrayal, the feelings of guilt and worthlessness which followed precipitated a trauma which threw my psyche's capacity for self-regulation into chaos. As Stevens[3] points out, though the psyche as an efficient homeostatic system has the capacity to heal itself, "… it is in the compensatory function of the unconscious that this power for self-healing resides." This ability of the unconscious to create "symbols" which have the power to heal and strengthen the ego, as well as to nourish the growth of the personality, resides in the psyche:

> Just as the body possesses control mechanisms to keep its vital functions in balance, so the psyche has a control mechanism in the compensatory activity of *dreams*.[4]

And so, returning to "the man with the knife", I must consider why a dream symbol whose purpose implies the potential to reunite and heal conflicting complexes within the psyche should emerge as a daimonic, attacking figure of evil. How could this threatening figure be acting in defence of my psyche when, as Anna pointed out, his "intention" was to attack not only the two of us, but also our therapeutic relationship?

In attempting to understand this threatening dream image, I must return to Donald Kalsched's inspirational insight into the self-care system of severely traumatised patients, and of how this endeavours to save the personal spirit from annihilation.[5] As mentioned earlier, I must emphasise that my own life experiences do not resemble the traumatic experiences of Kalsched's patients. Nevertheless, as Anna pointed out, there can be no qualitative definition of what may cause any particular

---

[2] Samuels, A., Shorter, B., & Plaut, F. (1986). *A Critical Dictionary of Jungian Analysis*, p. 24. London: Routledge, 1997.
[3] Stevens, A. (1990). *On Jung*. London: Penguin, 1991.
[4] Ibid., p. 49.
[5] Kalsched, D. (1996). *The Inner World of Trauma: Archetypal Defenses of the Personal Spirit*. Sussex: Routledge, 2010.

event to be experienced as a trauma. So what may simply be a disturbing or disruptive episode for one person will produce a traumatic response in another. It has taken me many years to accept that my response to ending with Anna indicated that a traumatic reaction to a much earlier fear of abandonment had become activated. And since I have no conscious "knowledge" of the origins of this fear, I must finally live with the "not-knowing", and crave the reader's patience in asking them to do the same.

Kalsched clearly demonstrates from his clinical work that this sinister image can appear as "a true *agent of death*"[6] by nature of his disintegrative psychic activity, and emanates from a much deeper, primitive layer of the psyche than either the shadow or anima/animus complexes. To this primitive layer belong primordial images which derive from the *collective* unconscious rather than the *personal* unconscious, and this imbues them with attributes universal to all cultures throughout history. In addition to being unconscious, they are charged with a compelling force which operates independent of the will or personal agency.

With its capacity for "unfeeling, murderous acts",[7] this figure suggests a personification of the dark side of the Self. But if "… the Self is imagined as the supreme authority, the longed-for transcendent unity of life, a unity of opposites …",[8] how then do we explain the emergence of destructive, attacking, and daimonic figures who, as Kalsched points out, "hardly seem to be 'transpersonal guides' along the path of individuation"?[9]

Finally Kalsched considers that "The answer to this question is straightforward enough".[10] From his clinical experience, he has concluded that Jung's description of "the compensatory dialectical process between conscious and unconscious"[11] occurs in cases *where the ego is fairly well-established*. But in contrast to this, Kalsched asserts:

> It is otherwise where the ego has suffered severe trauma and is therefore only provisionally established, fragile, riddled with

---

[6] Ibid., p. 27.
[7] Ibid., p. 28.
[8] Ibid., p. 96.
[9] Ibid., p. 96.
[10] Ibid., p. 97.
[11] Ibid., p. 97.

> anxiety, and in a constant struggle to survive ... In this case, for reasons that are not altogether clear, horrific and destructive imagery of the Self predominates. We might distinguish this Self as a *survival Self* in order to distinguish it from the *individuating Self* found in psychological health ... these very attacks are the Self's (often misguided) 'efforts' to preserve the personal spirit of the individual from the unbearable affect of the original trauma ...[12]

Looked at from this perspective, the threatening dream image of "the man with the knife" seems to have emerged—in Kalsched's words—as a "Protector/Persecutor" figure in defence of my psyche. This would certainly explain my need to "merge" closely with Anna when the thought of her retirement—with its inevitable demand for both physical and psychological "separation"—became a serious threat to my psychic survival. As Kalsched explains:

> In psychotherapy with trauma victims, it seems that as the unbearable (traumatic) childhood experience, or something resembling it in the transference, begins to emerge into consciousness, an intrapsychic figure or 'force', witnessed in the patient's dreams, violently intervenes ... This figure's diabolical 'purpose' seems to be to prevent the dream-ego from experiencing the 'unthinkable' affect associated with the trauma.[13]

With the benefit of our recordings, I can now consider Kalsched's explanation alongside Anna's perception that "being back in the park" (i.e., my return to analysis) represented "a danger"—because her impending retirement now signified a definite end to our relationship. If I accept that this situation was sufficiently dangerous to trigger an original, if unknown, early experience of traumatic loss/abandonment, it is understandable that this would signal the emergence of the Protector/Persecutor in defence of my psyche. Kalsched outlines the analytic process necessary for a "working through" of this defensive

---

[12] Ibid., p. 97.
[13] Ibid., p. 14.

mechanism,[14] which, in its most extreme form, can lock the patient forever into a devastating cycle of resistance to psychotherapy:

> For experience to become *meaningful* requires that bodily excitations, including the archaic affects of infancy, be given mental representation by a transitional parental figure so that eventually they can reach verbal expression in language and be shared with another person. This process of mediation of archaic affects, their eventual symbolization and shared expression in language, is the crucial element in the personalization of all archetypal affects, including those of early trauma.[15]

This description has resonances with the analytic process in which Anna and I were engaged during the final stage of our work. From the moment of my return to analysis my unconscious went into overdrive, as the regular outpouring of dreams threw up more and more symbols indicating the unbearable fear which had been activated by my experience of "losing" Anna. These "unthinkable" fears found expression in symbolic dream imagery which was the raw material generated by my unconscious. In her role as the "transitional parental figure" to which Kalsched refers, I needed Anna to understand the threat of psychic danger, and to find a way for me to express something which my conscious mind resisted as intolerable. In Kalsched's view, this "working through" is essential if the daimonic archetypal defences are to be finally humanised and integrated into a more healthy psychological development:

> In Jung's language, we might say that the original traumatic situation posed such danger to personality survival that it was not retained in memorable *personal* form but only in *daimonic* archetypal form ... As archetypal dynamism it 'exists' in a form that cannot be recovered by the ego *except as an experience of re-traumatization*. Or, to put it another way, the unconscious repetition of traumatization in the inner world ... must become a *real* traumatization with an object in the world if the inner system is to become "unlocked".[16]

---

[14] Ibid., p. 26.
[15] Ibid., p. 37.
[16] Ibid., p. 26.

In re-reading Kalsched's writing, I can now understand why this final stage of my analysis *needed* to involve me in experiencing our final ending as something at least equating to re-traumatisation ... Only this time Anna would be by my side, helping me to contain the acute anxiety as it surfaced, so that—in Kalsched's words—it could be "'incarnated' in a human interaction" which would enable it to be "recovered by the ego". This was a vital aspect in enabling me to integrate this sinister, attacking figure, whose daimonic archetypal energies had continued to feed off my repressed fears. This formidably long process of recovery would seem to be vital in enabling the transcendent function to achieve its aim, since in Jung's words:

> One does not become enlightened by imagining figures of light, but by making the darkness conscious.[17]

---

[17] Stevens, A. (1990). *On Jung* p. 45. London: Penguin, 1991.

CHAPTER TWENTY-TWO

Shortly after my return to Anna I watched a documentary on the 1944 Warsaw Uprising. This depicted how, as the Nazis began to take over the city, people tried to escape by crawling through the sewers to reach unoccupied areas. The documentary film included original footage portraying this, as well as interviews with survivors of the horrifying mass slaughter of those two months. I found it deeply disturbing, and though I have no recollection of discussing with Anna any possible connection with my collective unconscious memory, I believe it was this that provoked another disturbing dream:

> I have a strong sense of danger. Something threatening is happening in the world around me but I'm not sure what it is.
> I need to go to my mother who lives in a house in the remote countryside, but for some reason I know I can't go there by road. I have to find a 'secret' way of getting there unseen.
> I find myself crawling through a long, dark tunnel which I believe will lead me to my mother's house. It is tiled and the walls are wet and wide, like a sewer pipe. I know I'm getting near the end of the tunnel but there is no light. Suddenly I reach the exit and realise that

it is blocked with tons of earth. There is no way out. I have to go back. I feel very frightened about what has happened to my mother.

Then I find myself talking to you in your consulting room. I'm telling you about what happened and asking you what I should do, as I'm very worried about my mother's safety. You are very firm and tell me that I *must* find a way of getting to my mother, even if it means clearing away the tons of earth myself. You seem to be asking me to do the impossible. I feel even more frightened and helpless. Then I woke up.

Now into the second stage of my analysis, Anna asked me for my thoughts on this dream. Even then, I felt uncertain about putting into words something which still provoked a fear of "hidden danger":

"Well ... I think it may be saying something about my fear ... around ... all my shitty stuff ... and expecting you to manage it ..."

My voice was a barely audible whisper, painfully emphasising my anxiety about sharing this dark material. Anna agreed with my interpretation:

"... And in the dream you seem to be wondering how to *be* about it, and what you *could* say about it—or whether it had to stay 'underground'," she reflected.

"Well, if this stage *was* going to be different, then I *needed* to be able to do that ... But there's still anxiety around ..."

"... Which is 'the earth' blocking the 'exit'," Anna suggested.

"Yes ... and it's making *you* unsafe, as 'my mother' in the dream—but then you're actually telling me I *have* to do it ... that I have to 'unblock' whatever it is."

"I think that makes a lot of sense," Anna responded, "... And early on, quite a lot of what you really feared as being your shitty stuff *did* have to stay 'underground'. It was hard, or even impossible, to get to it—and so we never did 'clear' it ... And what worried you about the shitty stuff was that it could really 'destroy mother', and that something awful would happen to her."

Anna was right. We were both aware of the existence of this intense fear, and it is only recently that I have understood it in theoretical terms. In *The New Dictionary of Kleinian Thought*, I came across a passage elaborating on Klein's idea that neither the ego nor the self came into being in a state of integration, but that this process was a "developmental task"[1] that needed to be achieved. Klein's belief was that "Integration depends on love impulses predominating over destructive impulses. Hate can only be mitigated by love, and if the two are kept apart this cannot occur".[2] As an aspect of the analytic process, this is a task likely to be fraught with difficulties. In Klein's words:

> … the coming together of destructive and loving impulses, and of the good and bad aspects of the object, arouse the anxiety that destructive feelings may overwhelm the loving feelings and endanger the good object. Thus there is conflict between seeking integration as a safeguard against destructive impulses and fearing lest the destructive impulses endanger the good object and the good parts of the self.[3]

When I hit upon this passage, I could instantly recognise the loving and destructive impulses which had been such a tormenting factor in my own developmental process. But what I finally understood from this reading was that only by means of this process would I develop the inner resources to separate from Anna, so as to effect a tolerable ending which would leave my sense of self sufficiently intact and able to hold on to her as a "good object" in my internal world.

From other pieces of writing I had given Anna since our return, she recognised that I was still questioning whether she *could* hold the fear for me without being damaged:

> "At this point in the therapy—and earlier too—you could write things that you couldn't tell me … So it's as if you're almost writing them 'from the tunnel'—and I think that's still around really—your needing to send me emails telling me about the hidden feelings … You still need to 'write things from the tunnel', because of the anxiety you feel when you come up *out* of the tunnel."

---

[1] Bott Spillius, E., Milton, J., Garvey, P., Couve, C., & Steiner, D. (2011). *The New Dictionary of Kleinian Thought*, p. 373. Sussex: Routledge.
[2] Ibid., p. 373.
[3] Ibid., p. 373, quoting Klein, 1963.

I couldn't deny her insight into why "writing" had so often replaced "talking" for me, though Anna left me in no doubt that she understood my intense discomfort:

> "Oh sure—I absolutely know about that ... It can be *very* hard to find a way back—to come in cold off the street, and to talk about such very internal feelings ..."

Nevertheless, Anna also invited me to consider how much the original feelings might have got "tidied up" during the process of writing:

> "I used to worry that you were tidying the shitty bit of the feelings out of it—the 'rough edges' ... because it might have got tidied up so much that they didn't exist ... But actually your writing *does* convey these feelings ... So I think it's always been the way that you tried to get down to the level that you knew you needed to get down to—and without being able to do the writing, you weren't at all sure that we would get there."
>
> "No ... I *know* I wouldn't have been able to. There needed to be some kind of a 'bridge' between the speaking and the not-speaking," I stressed.
>
> "Yes, there did," Anna agreed. "... And that's really what we're up to now—because by going through it all, we're really finding a way of bringing it all together."

* * *

Then a series of "baby dreams" emerged. In Jungian terms, I had learnt to regard this image as a hopeful indication that I had begun the process towards individuation, though ostensibly this dream was no different in its depiction of my uncertainty at the prospect of coping with "new birth", which had been recurrent during the weeks following my first ending with Anna:

> I am expecting a baby and I have been told to go to my local hospital for the birth. I feel very anxious as I don't want my baby to be born there.
>
> I ask for your help. You are very understanding, and tell me that you will help me to have my baby and look after me so that I won't have to go to the hospital. But while we are talking I hear an emergency siren which is getting nearer. I become very frightened

because I think it is an ambulance coming to take me to hospital, and that you won't be able to stop this happening.

With my uncertainty as to whether or not this dream represented a positive depiction of "new birth", Anna gave me her thoughts:

> "I see the baby as *an integration* of both aspects—the hope and the good and the creativity. But then there are also the difficult bits—the yelling and the fury, and the shit as well—Something new to learn to manage all over again … and certainly giving birth isn't much fun, and you're worried about that in the dream … It suggests something about 'a midwife' to help manage both sides of it, I think," Anna proposed.
>
> "My feeling around 'babies' in my dreams has always inferred something more positive for the future …" I reflected.
>
> "Yes … I think it *is* a positive aspect of the dream—but that's only one side of it. You are worried that the baby will die—so you're worried that there could be a destructive element to it, and you're asking me to help you manage so that the baby can survive … to help you with the 'separation'—the birth and the separation."

Of course, my final separation from Anna still remained a crucial concern, and Anna was wise not to indulge in over-optimism in considering the symbolism of this particular dream. Only five days later another "baby dream" materialised—only this time it bore no resemblance to any of the previous baby dreams during the entire course of my analysis. Even the prospect of re-visiting this dream for our recording caused me anxiety, since it suggested something darkly alien had emerged from my unconscious:

> My client is a beautiful, pregnant young black girl. We agree to counselling until her baby is born. She arrives very distraught one day, with her mother. She tells me that she has given birth, but her baby was stillborn. Now her mother is asking her to do something she can't bring herself to do. She is too upset to tell me what it is. Her mother explains … In their culture, a woman is expected to eat the heart of her stillborn baby. This will signify that the baby continues to "live" inside her. Angry that her daughter is refusing to do this, she wants me to persuade her.
>
> I feel disgusted and horrified, but know that I mustn't show this. I ask the mother to leave so that I can talk to her daughter. When

we are alone I try to comfort the girl, telling her not to worry. The hospital won't allow this to happen and I promise to help her. Then I woke up.

* * *

"What do you think about this dream?" Anna asked me.

"I feel confused—and part of me doesn't want to look at it at all," I admitted.

"You're repulsed by it," Anna suggested.

"Yes …"

Feelings of repulsion had stifled my ability to speak. Anna noted this, and finally decided to ease my discomfort by breaking the silence:

"It seems to me that it's clearly about 'how do you internalise somebody' " she gently interpreted. "… How do you 'digest' them—how do you make them part of yourself. It's an image from a very primitive culture, where that would be thought about very *concretely* … I mean, cannibals wanted to eat the enemy because they believed they would take on their powers … And it seems to me that this dream is about your struggle to *internalise* … Because when we tried to end before, you felt as if you hadn't managed to internalise anything—that it was all an empty space, and you hadn't really managed to take it in and digest 'the heart'—the centre of it, the essence of it, and have it as part of yourself … So this dream feels like a very concrete representation of that to me."

It came as an immense relief to hear Anna interpret this repellent dream with such an innocent explanation, which also made perfect psychological sense. But it did not entirely answer the questions which disturbed my mind. I still needed to know why my unconscious had chosen to illustrate my struggle to hold onto Anna by throwing up an image of a black girl, whose cultural origins were totally alien to anything I knew or recognised in my external world. Who were these figures, and how was Anna a part of this imagery?

"Again, it's 'the other side'—the shadow side," Anna explained. "It's the *concrete* side as opposed to the *symbolic*, I think … So, thinking about Bion, it's a question of whether you can turn it from 'beta-elements' into 'alpha-elements' … And the thing about alpha-elements is that you can metabolise them and move them around—so you have them in a different 'psychic space', as opposed to a bodily space … It seems to me that this is quite a *concrete* dream, with the mother telling her daughter that she needs to internalise her baby—to have the baby inside her in order to move on …"

At the time, Anna's reflections embraced complex theoretical ideas about which I had no knowledge. So she gave me a simplified summary of Bion's theory:

"Bion's idea is that it's part of the task of mothering to convert what he calls 'beta-elements'—which would be the very fragmented parts of feelings, images, bodily sensations—parts of whatever experience of the outside world the infant might have inside them. But they don't have a 'shape', they don't have anything really … they are just a sensation, so they can't be made sense of … So they're 'beta-elements' … they are really held in the body, concrete and 'untransformed' … And so part of the mother's job in 'mothering' is to *feel* the beta-elements that get transmitted through projective identification and put into her body—because there's no other way to do it … So mother kind-of 'picks it up' and *feels* it—And her job is to recognise this as something 'human'—to give it a name, give it a shape—something that's humanly 'recognisable' … And in due course, that changes the way it can be conveyed and metabolised …"

This was an immensely helpful explanation, followed by further advice:

"The concrete has come up a lot in our work, so if you are going to be writing something about moving from the *concrete* to the *symbolic*, then you certainly need to look at Bion."

I have already written about Anna's understanding of my need to express transference towards her in concrete terms, by giving her "objects", and that it was her willingness to accept these objects which symbolised the containing quality of our therapeutic relationship for me. In Anna's words:

"From the very beginning, it felt absolutely necessary for you to leave solid objects with me … and it always felt like more than just wanting to 'give me a present' … to feel that you really did have a 'place' with me … because to 'trust' that you were in my mind wasn't enough ... Which is why, having demurred and having interpreted it a bit, I decided that it was really important for me to have them ... because it felt like you really needed to leave something solid with me—a 'concrete object' ..."

Anna alluded to Bion's "theory of thinking", from which he concluded that *thoughts* exist prior to the development of an apparatus which allows us *the capacity to think* in earliest infancy. The process by which emotional experience evolves into the capacity for thought led Bion to hypothesise the notion of an "alpha-function", whose successful development was entirely dependent upon:

> ... the necessity for the infant in distress to find a real person willing and able to take in and to suffer the emotional impact and disturbance of the projection of it, including the sense of concreteness and indigestibility, without refusing or running away.[4]

In developing this hypothesis, Bion added another dimension to Melanie Klein's theory of projective identification, in which parts of the self are "disowned" and attributed to another person. Klein's contention was that both "good" and "bad" aspects of the self may be projected. However, especially in infancy, projection is a defence which helps the ego to overcome the anxiety of "bad" or persecuting internal objects by expelling them into the mother. Bion writes:

> As a realistic activity [projective identification] shows itself as behaviour calculated to arouse in the mother feelings of which the infant wishes to be rid. If the infant feels it is dying it can arouse fears that it is dying in the mother. A well-balanced mother can accept these and respond therapeutically: that is to say in a manner that makes the infant feel it is receiving its frightened personality back again but in a form that it can tolerate.[5]

The mother's ability to "contain" these projections will enable the infant to reintroject the fears and frustrations in a more tolerable form. As the *New Dictionary* explains:

---

[4] Bott Spillius, E., Milton, J., Garvey, P., Couve, C., & Steiner, D. (2011). *The New Dictionary of Kleinian Thought*, p. 266. Sussex: Routledge.
[5] Ibid., p. 510.

> When the infant encounters a *'realisation'*—something that approximates sufficiently to an inborn expectation, for example of a breast—a *'conception'* is produced. Under good internal and external conditions the temporary absence of the breast can be tolerated and a preconception can mate with a *'negative realisation'* (i.e., an absent breast, a frustration) to become a *'thought'* of a breast. (p. 509)[6]

If the alpha-function process continues successfully, the infant will eventually introject not only the bad objects in more tolerable form, but the "containing/alpha-function" itself. In this way, the infant will have:

> ... the beginning of a means within his own mind of tolerating frustration and for thinking. Symbolisation, a 'contact barrier' between conscious and unconscious, dream thoughts and a concept of space and time can all develop.[7]

However, deficiencies in the mother's ability to act as a "container" for these infant projections could interfere with development of the alpha-function and the container/contained relationship. If the alpha-function fails, according to Bion's theory, this then gives rise to an accumulation of beta-elements, leading to a need for the psyche to expel them by means of "evacuation".[8] This led Bion to further conceive the idea of a "beta-function" whose purpose was to become "an apparatus for 'ridding the psyche of accumulations of bad internal objects".[9] This constituted a pathological form of projective identification, since total expulsion of such threatening stimuli served to *extinguish* experience rather than *transform* it. From his clinical work with deeply psychotic patients, Bion observed that the effect of such total expulsion rendered the beta-elements unavailable for psychic metabolization by means of analysis.

How does this lengthy theoretical explanation help to make sense of my dream's content? It is evident, even from a limited outline of Bion's theory, that it contains significant resonances with Anna's interpretation—specifically in relation to my need for her to contain its

---

[6] Ibid., p. 509.
[7] Ibid., p. 510.
[8] Ibid., p. 262.
[9] Ibid., p. 262.

"concreteness and indigestibility".[10] And Anna elaborated on my dream image of the black girl's "repulsion" at the thought of executing her mother's demands:

> "… That's a really repulsive thought for the girl—but she hasn't got a better way of doing it yet … And then we have the 'hospital' in the dream, and although there isn't a person, the hope is that somebody can help her to do it in a different way," Anna reflected.
>
> "Okay," I acknowledged, "… but 'eating' is about 'devouring', isn't it? And there's something about this image of 'internalising' that doesn't feel like a positive way to take in what I hadn't internalised when we ended before," I suggested.
>
> "Sure … because it's from the shadow," Anna explained. "But you see, the influence from analytic thinkers, especially Melanie Klein, talks about the infant having fantasies about 'eating the mother' when it is breast feeding—and in a way, the infant *does*! … And certainly when you're pregnant, the baby is 'eating' everything that it can get from you … So it makes sense to think that there might be a part of the very primitive psyche that sees it like that. What feels difficult about this dream is that it's a *reversal*—the suggestion that the *mother* should eat the *baby* … But animals do eat the placenta, and a lot of mammals do eat their babies … So at a very basic bodily level there's a lot in this dream about struggling with the idea of 'how do I internalise?' … I think the black girl is just representing a more primitive way of managing it in your mind—a 'shadow' part of yourself that's struggling to find another way to internalise 'the heart' of it … And you're 'the therapist' in the dream, perhaps standing for me, but wondering if you can utilise 'the therapist part of yourself'," Anna concluded.

This interpretation not only resonated with meaning, but also helped to dissolve my deep fear about this dream.

> "I suppose it frightened me because it's so very different to the familiar 'baby' dreams. I couldn't quite believe that it was my dream …"
>
> "… Because of its primitive nature?" Anna questioned.
>
> "Yes … It's hard to have to think of myself on that level. I felt almost ashamed to own it … And then, the sense of powerlessness

---

[10] Ibid., p. 266.

over my unconscious mind, that could produce a dream like that," I admitted.

"But we've all got that primitive mammalian part in our brain" Anna stressed, "… And no, you can't control it. Rather you can wonder at it … that your brain could produce such an image."

The two processes of internalisation (or "introjective identification", in Kleinian terms) and integration are closely linked, since according to the *New Dictionary*, the establishment of "a cohesive and harmonious world of internal objects" will strengthen the ego's integration and stability through "the process of introjective identification with loved objects".[11] By May of that year, there was evidence that this dual process had begun. Anna took a week off to make a trip abroad with her husband and some friends. I wrote her a "letter" in her absence, which I gave to her on her return. It began by expressing the loving feelings I experienced at picturing her in the sunshine, away from her patients, and "being who you really are when you are not with me." But this changes to sadness, as I sense myself "hovering on the outside of a group to which I can never belong …" However, by the final paragraph, my sense of "longing" has become an attempt to resolve this conflict between love and envy:

> … Then I begin to see a different perspective. When we are shut together inside your room, you are sharing something of yourself which your husband and friends can only dream about. Now I can imagine *them* on the outside, wanting to know more of what you share with us which excludes them. In the end, I realise that none of us can have all of you. I am trying to accept this, and to acknowledge that with so much "sharing", there must remain a part of you which you keep to yourself and refuse to share with anyone. This thought brings me really close to you. I feel I have contacted your isolation as well as my own, and that this helps to make sense of what joins and divides us. In my heart I treasure this sense of "connected isolation". I will try to hold onto it because it helps me understand.

---

[11] Bott Spillius, E., Milton, J., Garvey, P., Couve, C., & Steiner, D. (2011). *The New Dictionary of Kleinian Thought*, p. 376. Sussex: Routledge.

This shift in perspective suggests the beginning of more tolerable thoughts about separating from Anna—though I had worried that putting these thoughts down on paper might also constitute an effort to "convince myself". But Anna was not deterred from perceiving my letter as a significant development:

"... But you must have been able to access that feeling to be able to convert it into an 'alpha-element'," Anna emphasised. "Because that's what this is—it's really symbolic and conceptualising ... It doesn't mean that the other way of seeing it isn't still there ... but you can make enough sense of it so that you have this 'possible position' ... You're not always going to stay in it—and we know that you don't, because later the other side comes out again ... But this letter seems to be about really trying to feel the distance—that you're *not* there ... and so then you go with those feelings and make sense of them, which is different to trying to imagine yourself there ... Because that's about trying to 'short circuit' something—trying to deny anything to do with 'separateness' ..."

This explanation immediately enabled me to connect with the subject matter of dreams that had emerged in the early and middle period of my analysis:

"So that's what's come up in the dreams where I am with you in your home, and you are surrounded by your friends and family," I speculated.

"... Which was your way of avoiding the pain that it provoked," Anna suggested. "But the trouble with that is that it gets you stuck. So when we do stop working together, you haven't then got a mechanism to manage the separation ... And I think, from now on, you can come and go with this—which is what I would expect. It's difficult, and it's what the psyche does ... and the hope is that each time it happens, the 'path' from one to the other gets more 'trodden'—So when you get into that awfully bad place, you kind-of know that there's a way back."

"... So perhaps the reason why I don't feel totally convinced at the time of writing the letter is because I'm still 'experimenting' with the feeling ..."

"Yes ... indeed," Anna agreed.

This was a relief. I felt reassured that at least I wasn't engaged in some process of self-deception.

> "... And you don't just 'change' like that," Anna elaborated. "If you think about it neurologically, you develop some new 'connections', which is what seems to be going on here ... So you might go this way or that, but the more often you make this connection, the stronger that path becomes ..."
>
> "... And do the 'old connections' eventually disappear if they cease to be useful?" I wondered.
>
> "They can wither ... yes ... But I don't know that they disappear absolutely," Anna responded. "I think they can revive again given the right situation ... but they become less the way of choice ..."
>
> "... So perhaps that's what happens when people really shift their perspective into a different way of responding to a situation," I concluded, "... And then presumably if there was some massive trauma, the response might be to revert to that earlier defence."
>
> "Yes ... exactly."

It becomes evident from this second stage of my analysis, that my unconscious mind was intent on pushing me towards the uncompleted process of internalisation and integration which demanded to be resolved before our final ending. My loving feelings towards Anna needed to predominate over the destructive impulses, in order to be able to manage our final separation. As the *New Dictionary* defines: "The stably internalised good object is 'one of the preconditions for an integrated and stable ego' (Klein, 1955, p. 144). It acts as a focal point in the ego around which integration can occur".[12]

Anna's incisive reflections on my struggle through this process were correct. In the coming months I would indeed continue to "come and go" between the possibilities of the "new" and the "old" neural pathways, along which this formidable process of integration was destined to lead us.

---

[12] Ibid., p. 373.

CHAPTER TWENTY-THREE

Over the next year a period of intense self-reflection produced a volume of letters and "Reflections" to Anna following almost every session. It seems clear that the process of wanting to "analyse my analysis" had begun in earnest.

We returned to twice weekly sessions as I had begun to feel that weekly sessions left "too much for me to process." It was a paradox that I readily committed to this when I was also embarking on an apparently opposite commitment. On my return to Anna, I revealed that I was planning to apply for an MA in psychotherapy. The dilemma was, which course should I apply for? With my long-standing interest in existential philosophy, I was seriously drawn to study existential psychotherapy, but by then I also recognised my growing attachment to a psychodynamic perspective, which had grown from my years of Jungian analysis. I struggled with this decision, knowing that if I chose the existential course I would probably have to end analysis with Anna and change to an existential therapist—since this was a requirement of the course. Despite this, I finally opted for Existential Psychotherapy. Until the course began in January 2007, this uncertainty hung over us as a threat which could not be ignored. Eventually, several weeks into my first term, I received written confirmation that I would be allowed to continue my analysis with Anna.

The threat was over. But the unconscious process which had led me to a decision which jeopardized our analytic relationship became the subject of our later recorded reflections. As I recollected to Anna:

> "The awful thing was that, having got you back again, something else was now threatening to take you away from me … and I was responsible for this, because I'd chosen to do the course."
>
> "Well, that's right," Anna agreed. "And the first bit of work we did was about you trying to decide which course you were going to pursue … and so 'the man with the knife' was threatening a cut-off to our relationship from the very beginning of that time … And he's all over the place during this period, and coming up in unconscious images too," Anna reflected.

But what I needed to know was whether my choice to pursue this course contained some element of "self-sabotage". As I explained to Anna:

> "I haven't ever resolved why I chose to do a course that threatened our relationship. Was I doing it deliberately? My worry was that there was something 'self-punishing' about it … Because on occasions you said to me, 'You have a way of trying to deprive yourself of something when you have got it'. So if that's what I was doing, then what was my need to be doing it?"
>
> "Yes … sure," she responded, "… But the way it's played out seems to suggest a more creative way of integrating … that there was a need for you to do a course which was different to mine. I think your ego was saying to you—or your 'adult' was saying to your 'child'—'Come along, Naomi … You've got to do something more independent.' It was important enough for you to be willing to lose me as your therapist … There was something hugely important about it."

Anna had accurately highlighted my internal struggle with the conflicted parts of myself—the "adult" that felt deeply associated with existential ideas, and the "child" that was really attached to Anna and drawn to her different theoretical approach.

"Well, that makes sense in terms of where I am with it now," I reflected. "In the end, it *has* felt like a creative choice …"

"… Which is what most of me always felt," Anna responded. "… And your worry about whether you were self-punishing goes with your negative take on things," Anna suggested, "… Because if it was self-punishing, it would have felt very perverse … But no, it has actually felt very creative …"

* * *

I now wonder whether this self-imposed challenge signified an unconscious attempt to retain my sense of autonomy concerning our ending. This conflict began to take centre stage early in 2007, and by April the poems had emerged again after an absence of three years—unmistakable evidence of growing internal turmoil. The poetry became our focus two years later, when one of the poems, *Mothers*, became the first in a series written between May and July of that year. Within this grim record is contained the fear of my potential descent into a dark, emotional "death", which had grown from my terrified imaginings of a future in which Anna no longer existed as the "containing mother" who would keep me safe. Not wishing to subject any reader of this history to the full impact of the emotional destructiveness which these poems were intended to communicate, I must at least convey a flavour of their painful content, as evidence of my need to project this emotional pain onto Anna. To this end, two poems from this series are sufficient evidence of the violent internal disruption which I desperately needed Anna to contain, as I battled with my supressed anger at the thought of her retirement and our final ending:

> "Mothers III"
>
> I have two mothers—
> Both of them are dead.
> Neither can hear the voice of the child
> Crying in the dark.
>
> It is night for the child—
> But beyond the grave is a place of light.
> One mother lives there.
> This is the place of her living future—

But the child belongs to her dead past.
And the sound of crying
Has no voice that can be heard
In that life beyond the grave.

"Mothers VII"

I am the child who speaks
From beyond the grave.
I mourn alone
For the death of the mother
Who loved and left me.

Briefly, I tasted her love
In a shared story whose days were numbered.
Briefly I grew, in the numbering of those days.
Now I grieve,
That in my beginning lay the story of my ending.

My soul is searching
For the lost love of the mother
Who chose my death for her life.

In 2009, Anna invited me to reflect on my present response to this series of poems. What I expressed to her then—which still holds true—was how appalled I felt by this evidence of my desire to hurt and punish her for her decision to retire:

> "I feel shocked by what I've written. I can't quite believe ... not only that I actually wrote this stuff, but that I actually *gave* it to you ... It feels so very black ... and so vengeful."

Not surprisingly, Anna had a more understanding perspective on the underlying punitive intention:

> "What we talked about, and what I wrote in my notes, is that the 'punishing' aspect came from the *desperate* need to share the feeling ... because it felt so awful—and the only way to share it was to give it to me—to have me feeling really bad too ... It might have

been to punish me, but I think it was the only way to make sure that I could actually feel what you felt …"

"Yes, I'm aware of that," I responded, "But it doesn't make me feel any better …"

At this point in our recording, I hear Anna's tone change as she became aware of my growing distress:

"… Do you feel able to think about it? … Because when we first tried, the feelings were so enormous that it was really hard for you to share them, let alone think about them … But if you are going to put this into a book, then you need to be able to think about it … So I'm wondering whether you can reflect now on what were the feelings behind what you were driven to write?"

"… Well … there's certainly a fear of not being able to manage the feelings," I succeeded in acknowledging.

"… And with your lack of knowledge about my reasoning, the terrible thing for you was that I could have made that choice to retire …" Anna suggested.

"… Yes … And that then developed into my fantasy around what you were going to do, and why you were doing it—that you were 'cutting yourself loose' from us … and all that kind of thing …"

Anna fully understood this, but was keen to go deeper in helping me explore the psychological process reflected in these poems, and its significance in terms of my personal history. She asked:

"Looking back and thinking about it now, do you *feel*—not do you *think*—do you *feel* that actually it was essential to produce this kind of material? … that it was part of your process, and that without it you wouldn't have accessed some part of your psyche?"

"… Yes … it *must* have been essential, because as I said to you at the time, the poems seemed to 'write themselves'. It always felt as though they were driven by some unconscious force which was out of my control …"

"… So there was something *absolutely crucial* about what you certainly felt were 'unacceptable' thoughts and feelings having the light of day," Anna proposed. "And if I think of what I know about your history—your family, and your Dad especially, took a very 'civilised, rational' approach ... everything had a 'reason' and could be 'thought through', which might make it hard to say the 'totally unacceptable'. So there were quite a lot of 'totally unacceptable thoughts' that actually you couldn't express. And I think that in our analysis, it was vital for us to find some way to enter into that level ..."

"... And of course, saying something that was intended to be hurtful was not acceptable either," I reminded Anna, "... and that's what I seem to keep needing to do in these poems."

"Yes ... certainly in relation to our ending," Anna agreed, "... and because of how difficult that was for you, the poems gave you a medium through which to express all that ... And you grew up with the knowledge of a Grandma who, in the family story, did *deliberately* say things that were hurtful and difficult to Mum ... So what I'm thinking is that you've got 'a couple'. You've got Grandma saying the unacceptable, and vulnerable Mum who had to be 'looked after' ... and you take inside yourself *both* these images ..."

I was beginning to understand Anna's allusion to this family dynamic, and her reminder of how I had unconsciously internalised these two different ways of being from early childhood. Unlike the earlier occasion, when Anna had made the powerful connection with the way in which I had absorbed my grandmother's role model as "the controlling witch"—I was no longer traumatised by being reminded of this connection, though it still had a powerful resonance. Anna continued by elaborating on the possible implications of this important association:

"... Mostly you live from the 'must protect Mother' position," she suggested. "But you've also got Grandma saying the nasty things too ... And one of the things that regularly happens in analysis is that 'the voice of Grandma' will emerge ... but you don't *own* it, because it doesn't feel like you ... but 'she' writes her thoughts at night, because you've taken her in too ... because it's not something you can help doing ... Does that make sense to you?"

"Well yes ... she's the most obvious connection," I agreed. "... . But there just seems something so contradictory in needing to hurt somebody who's showing you love ... So then I wonder, was I trying to push you away and make you hate me, because that would make it easier for me to end?"

"Um ... maybe ..." Anna reflected. "... Though the question about hurting the person who you receive love from—that's not necessarily contradictory, is it?" she suggested. "... Because if you really feel loved, that is so precious that the thought that they could then take that away is appalling ... So the two feelings are both different sides of the same coin really ... And what I've put in my notes after you'd given me several more of the *Mothers* poems is, 'More poems, but she couldn't bear to read them ... Desperate at their destructivity, and that they would hurt and damage me' ... ."

An interesting interruption occurred at this point. Anna was unable to locate copies of this series of poems in her file—and yet she retained a strong memory of having read them, which indicated that they must be somewhere. Then her memory of their location suddenly returned:

"Oh, wait a minute ... I put these poems in *another* file ... Yes, I've got them all here ..." Anna announced, finally producing another folder.

I watched as she glanced through the poems again, no doubt to remind herself of their grim content ... and the brief dialogue which followed this "discovery" now seems to me to be particularly revealing, with Anna's words spoken almost as an expression of her private thoughts:

"I find that *extraordinary* ... that I put them in a separate place and kept them away from the main part of your work ..."

I didn't find this discovery in the least bit extraordinary. On the contrary, it made complete sense to me that Anna would choose to remove such destructive material to a separate place.

"Do you think that perhaps you *needed* these poems to be kept somewhere on their own?" I wondered.

"Yes, I suppose so ... because everything else is in this file ... And because you were really worried about whether they would contaminate or damage ... So I think I put the poems in a separate file to hold and contain them," Anna considered.

"Right ... So maybe you *did* have a sense of them being 'damaging'?" I invited her to consider.

241

"Oh well ... I can't pretend ...," Anna graciously acknowledged. "It was both 'good' and 'bad' ... and I think I *did* feel *plus plus* anxious ... Of course ... How could I *not* have done?"

Anna's honest acknowledgement of the anxiety provoked by this series of poems would prove to be well-founded when the eighth "Mothers" poem emerged:

> Today, I went to the grave
> Of my living mother.
> The grave was empty—
> I mourned alone, for the mother
> Who only chose to die for me.
>
> Somewhere, she continues to live
> In the lives of others—
> Somewhere ... where I cannot reach her.
> Who can place flowers
> Around the foot of an empty grave?
>
> Where is the place where I can grieve?
> Where are the mourners
> Who can share in my grief?
> My mother has left me her empty coffin
> To fill with my tears for her living death.

Late that evening, following the session in which I must have given Anna this poem, I was driven to send her a lengthy and desperate email which clearly indicated my returning suicidal thoughts. These extracts clearly convey the cry for help that I needed Anna to hear:

> ... What really hurts after today is this: that it doesn't seem to matter how much reparation I try to make, my badness it is still there, lurking threateningly beneath the surface ready to spring—like a crouching tiger. In my heart, I know that it is only my death that will lay this evil to rest ... and tonight this feels, once again, like the only way out for me ...

… What happened today has taken me back to my original questioning. I am trying to believe that I don't have the power to damage you … and a part of me *does* believe this. But my head is explaining that you are special—different to other people. You are trained to protect yourself from my damage … but others are not. And your ability to protect yourself does nothing to lessen my badness. So what really hurt today was the realisation that despite all my efforts to repair the damage of the past, the evil inside me is still there, fermenting away, and now surfacing in hateful, punishing poems directed towards the "mother" who saved my life. I am finding it hard to forgive myself for what I am doing and saying to you. And the fact that you can "manage" it without feeling damaged does not help to mitigate the loathing I feel towards myself. I hoped that my "goodness" would destroy my "badness"—but it hasn't, and all that disgusting stuff is still living somewhere inside me, infecting what you have done and leading me to punish you for not being ready to sacrifice your life for me. Anna, I can't describe to you how devastating this all feels to me tonight … If you can give me any words of comfort to hold me somewhere … anywhere … other than where I am now, I would be really grateful.

Early the next morning, Anna had replied to this desperate plea for help:

Dear Naomi,

As I know you know, the most damaging thing you could ever do to anyone—me, Patrick, the children and grandchildren, is to carry out your sentence. You are trying to control your fears around the capacity to damage by turning on yourself. But that could never redeem anything, just make those around you suffer with no hope of repair. Your poems are expressing your image that my retirement feels to you as if I had decided to die and leave you. This is not the case, but your telling me your thoughts and feelings does no damage at all. It opens up a possible road to repair. I will see you on Tuesday.

With warmest wishes,

Anna

What was it like for Anna to receive this written evidence of my desperation well outside the boundary of my session time? Even re-visiting this memory two years later was painful. But Anna's response only emphasised her empathic understanding of the need which had provoked the timing of this expression of despair:

> "What do I think about it now? ... I think it was absolutely vital! And I don't think any of this could have come out unless we had experienced those sessions when we were really thinking about 'baby Naomi', and we were able to really feel the love between us ... Because I think that was the catalyst for the other side of your feelings to emerge ... . What you've been really wanting to tell me in these poems is that *I* actually had the potential to do damage as well," Anna stressed. "And being able to express how this felt from where *you* were was an absolute *crux*. It was a vital part of our therapy for us to get to that place, for you to be able to *show* me what I was doing to you ... Because you had to have *me* survive the knowledge of how it felt for *you*, to make that survival possible for both of us ... . Does that make any sense?" Anna queried.

Yes, it did make sense ... but Anna's explanation did not help to mitigate the moving recollections of that period. And when I consider that this recording took place less than two months before our final session, it is perhaps not surprising that our exploration of this earlier crisis would touch on feelings of grief and loss which were a poignant aspect of what still remained to be faced in the present. As this session nears its end, I can hear how this juxtaposition of emotions became too much for me to contain. But in the midst of my tearfulness I also hear Anna's voice, lovingly yet firmly encouraging me to stay with her in the moment of this important dialogue:

> "... The worry for you is your *intentionality*—that you intended to hurt. I think that's what worries you ... Yes?"

Anna was intent on keeping me focused while I struggled to keep my tearfulness in check. But then another distraction shifted my attention away from her important "message". I looked at the clock, which showed that only two minutes remained until the end of our session. Anna immediately recognised my concern:

> "Never mind the time. This is important," she insisted.

I felt myself sink back into the safety and containment of Anna's strong holding, free to open my mind to the influence of the message which she seemed intent on conveying to me:

> "In therapy, I intentionally and knowingly set up a 'container' in which these things can happen ... And I do that *knowingly*," she emphasised. "... Because you're deprived of all kinds of information, so you don't know any of the things that would usually be a moderating influence ... And that is done so that we can get down to trying to see what's *underneath* the feelings that emerge ... So the fact that it happens here, in the therapy, is as much down to *me* as to you—because it's a shared thing ... Yes? ... Does that make sense?"

Though the pain was just barely below the surface, I felt myself gripped by the power of Anna's words. It was as though she was "willing me" to stay with her. I gave her sufficient indication of this for her to continue:

> "... So whatever you did to *me*, I was complicit in it," Anna asserted, "Because I could have stopped you earlier, but I made a choice to stay with it ... so I had my ways of managing it too ..."

There was something profoundly moving about listening again to Anna's voice, insistently accepting responsibility for her "complicity" in having allowed this dynamic the space to exist between us. By the following day, her message had sunk in. I was able to tell Anna that her explanation had helped me to appreciate that everything that happened between us was not just about me—it was about the two of us and a shared responsibility. "Absolutely!" Anna responded emphatically.

It may seem strange to the reader that the process of "analysing the analysis" could produce such a deep outpouring of desolation so close to its ending. But in analytic terms, this was the evidence that we were not avoiding the grief by hiding behind an intellectual analysis of my past process. At times, past and present grief necessarily became synchronised into a single process of mourning—and Anna had made it clear from the start of our "recorded analysis" that we would need to allow the space for this to happen. And so, as the need to return to a therapeutic focus would arise, Anna saw our work as helping me to confront the reality of my present grief, in order that we might find the words to express and share this together.

In our session the next day, as we continued to reflect on the series of *Mothers* poems, Anna drew my attention to the archetypal dimension which she considered they contained:

> "They remind me of some of the Old Testament Psalms which express similar feelings: '*Oh God, You've done terrible things to me. I've praised you all my life and look what you've done to me ... .*' They've got *that* feel to them—so then that makes me start to think 'archetypal'…"

Anna explained how archetypes contain both a negative and a positive pole. Hence the archetype of the "mother" will have a positive pole, conveying the sense of a loving, giving, and nurturing mother, and a negative pole conveying the opposite when the mother is felt to have withdrawn her love. These two poles often become linked together in the infant psyche. In Anna's words:

> "As soon as mother withdraws herself and is not there—so when she has another baby, or goes off with daddy, or goes into hospital—she can turn into as bad a mother as she was good. Because once the good is withdrawn there's only the bad. So the best mother will also have a negative archetype which can get constellated in various circumstances … So that's from the 'instinctive level'. It's what happens to the infant when the person that it really needs isn't there, and I think that a lot of this poetry is coming from that 'instinctive' place …"

I was able to make a connection between Anna's explanation and Kleinian thinking about the "good" and the "bad" breast. As "the provider of food and physical closeness",[1] it is the earliest function of the ego to "split" the breast into "good" and "bad" part-objects which will later become integrated.

> "Yes," Anna agreed. "… And Jung's idea is another way of talking about that 'splitting' … The neuroscientists tell us that the systems in the brain that regulate our feelings are divided into 'pleasure'

---

[1] Bott Spillius, E., Milton, J., Garvey, P., Couve, C., & Steiner, D. (2011). *The New Dictionary of Kleinian Thought*, p. 269. Sussex: Routledge.

and 'unpleasure' ... There are no grey areas in between. And that goes along with Klein, and with the positive and negative archetypal poles. So at a neurological level, it gives the theory a biological basis. And perhaps understanding it in this way can make it more digestible for you ... So that when you get into that awful place of feeling abandoned, you're really a 'conduit' for an impulse that's coming from the brain ..."

While this helped me to make sense of the "infant" response to my fear of abandonment, it still left me struggling on an adult level with the "shadow" which these poems contained. I thought of how "being frightened of our own shadow" is often expressed humorously. But as I explained to Anna, I could find nothing humorous in this saying. For me, the fear of my shadow and its potential for destruction remained very real. But Anna was also able to make an important connection to the archetypal dimension of this fear:

"... I think that when you are so in-touch with that collective, then the shadow can become huge ... And we've talked before about whether there's something about your Jewishness in that too. I think there might be ... and I think that for you, that could be even more powerful because it wasn't talked about or recognised. It was *there* ... It couldn't *not* be there when your Grandma was a German Jew ... I mean, historically, it wasn't very far away—but it wasn't acknowledged ... And so I think something of that flows through, which is why I think I found myself thinking of the Psalms. Because of course a lot of the Psalms were written by the Jews in exile. They were somewhere where they didn't want to be. It's in the whole Jewish history ... being in exile, being persecuted, and the feelings of loss ... the yearning for 'the promised land' ..."

I recognise that these words had an even more powerful resonance three years later than they did when Anna first pronounced them. Perhaps the distance from the emotional turmoil leading up to our final ending has allowed me to "hear" their message more profoundly—and also to fully absorb Anna's reflections on Jung's archetype of "the child":

"... When Jung writes about the archetype of 'the child', his idea is not of a child and its mother, it's the idea of an 'isolated' child ...

perhaps rather like the Messiah … And some of your poetry about 'the buried child' or 'the dying child' feels something like that—the negative archetypal pole … the child that isn't being nourished …"

Even from this distance I continue to feel moved by Anna's words, which further emphasised this important association:

"… Because if this connection makes sense to you, I think it might be very important to write about … Because the shadow, and how unbearable and terrifying it felt to you, brought you to the point of writing an email suggesting suicide … But then the Jungian way of thinking gives us this other way to understand it, because the archetypal phantasies, if they *really* take hold, are the stuff of psychosis … It's really as if you're contemplating that 'chasm'. And Jung also went there—except he went over the edge and brought himself back from it … But to me, that's kind-of where you are at this point, and that's what we're trying to metabolise … Which is why you were so terrified and I was so anxious, because it's scary stuff! And I think we were meeting twice a week then—so we didn't have three or four times a week to hold you … So it *was* very scary …"

By the time of this recording, in February 2009, I no longer doubted my deep sense of connection with the collective unconscious. By then I could recognise that aspects of my inner turmoil represented something much more than a "personal struggle with my badness" … though this was often how it felt at the time. But something in Anna's interpretation had given me a sense that I was being driven to express not only my own pain, but a much more universal and fundamental pain stemming from a collective unconscious connection with my barely acknowledged Jewishness. Through the medium of writing, I had found a way to bring the pain of this personal and collective legacy into the therapeutic space. And in Anna's words, she was then able to "know something of the feelings. Then, somehow, we could begin to understand it better, to *feel* it differently … and to start metabolising it …"

By early July 2007, perhaps in an unconscious process of preparing myself for our long summer break, a poem "Holding" suggested both greater ego strength and a renewed spirit of hopefulness:

> You and I stand together,
> On the edge of another place.

Hand in hand,
We are nearing the end of our journey.

Through all the years
I have felt your hand in mine,
Guiding me gently but firmly
To this final moment of our departure.

Together we have travelled the world,
From the darkest corner
Into the brightest light—
Two beings, who briefly became one.

The future beckons for both of us.
You point ahead, to a distant shining light.
You tell me it is time
To leave the old world for the new.

I feel your hand slip gently away from mine.
My heart yearns to bleed
With the pain of old wounds
As I watch you walk away.

But I see where you are going—
Not to a place of darkness
But into a world of light.
I know it as the light you have shared with me.

Briefly, but powerfully,
You illuminated my world.
Now I must keep the light burning
For myself .... in memory of you.

Two separate paths
Both illuminated with one light.
Two beings, briefly thrown together
By the chaos of Life.

I hear your voice telling me
I must follow my path ....

>And wherever it leads, I will feel
>The spirit of your hand holding mine.

"... And that's very beautiful," I hear Anna respond to my reading. "And for now, it feels like a place of calmness after all the great storms ... the 'still small voice of calm' ..."

"Um ... It wasn't a calmness destined to last very long," I reminded her.

"Well ... that's the thing about 'still small voices'," Anna remarked.

The faint edge of irony was not misplaced. Nevertheless, the spirit of renewed hopefulness would not be lost. It promised to lie in waiting—as somewhere I could return to when the time was right.

CHAPTER TWENTY-FOUR

As Anna would later remind me, the events of summer 2007 would continue to reverberate through the months ahead. Patrick and I planned to visit Lake Como in Italy, and to stay at a hotel in Bellagio with a view overlooking the lake. In order to maximise on this beautiful location we had booked a room with a large terrace, in anticipation of enjoyable sunny hours spent basking in our private view of the glorious scenery.

Little had we imagined that during our two week stay, the sun would only emerge briefly and deceptively in the morning. Along with the many other hopeful visitors, we would empty out of our hotel into the colourful streets of the little town. But by late morning, perhaps while enjoying a leisurely cappuccino in one of the inviting cafés bordering the lake, this sunlit scene would eerily transform itself in a matter of minutes into something more reminiscent of the Day of Judgement. While visitors hurried back to their hotels in an effort to avoid the "wrath to come", the sky would turn grey, then black, as thunder clouds rolled threateningly across the lake as if erupting from some mysterious location behind the mountains. The visual and emotional impact of this phenomenon, with its frequent recurrence during the holiday, left a lasting impression on my memory.

Contrary to my earlier imaginings, there was no basking in the afternoon sun on our private terrace. Under the imminent threat of the storm, the streets of Bellagio would rapidly empty of all habitation until it resembled a ghost town. By now safely ensconced in our room, hotel staff would appear, insisting on folding away sun umbrellas and terrace furniture in anticipation of the vengefulness of the impending storm. So instead of sunbathing, I would seat myself half in and half out of the terrace doorway, to gain some shelter from the inevitable downpour which followed—at the same time allowing myself a "grandstand view" of the incredible drama of the elements which became a regular afternoon theatrical performance. While Patrick did crosswords or fell asleep in the gloom, I would sit transfixed by the terrifying vision of this eruption of Nature's majestic power. Following shortly on the dramatic music of the rain, the storm would suddenly explode in disconcerting and discordant harmony. Not only could I hear this music growing louder, I could also watch its gradual approach. Beginning with a far-away sound and sight resembling a firework display from the other side of the lake, the dark sky would magically light up, illuminating this distant spot in isolated brilliance. This fiery display would then repeat its exhibition around the whole circumference of the lake, in concert with a background theme of rolling percussive thunder.

And then, with incredible force, this natural *son et lumiére* was suddenly happening above me, while the mountains—now shrouded in black shadow—had totally disappeared from view. What transfixed my mind at that moment was the sense that "I" was now at the centre of this storm, and a part of this incredible drama. Suddenly the force of the storm contained dramatic resonances with the "storms" which had erupted in my analytic relationship. Just as my fear of ending with Anna had broken out into angry poetry, so I also wanted to hurl my angry words at the storm, which implied another threat to my survival. But contained within its music, I could also hear something resembling the "music" that Anna and I had created—and this connection drove me again to record it in words. Then it seemed that I could hear Anna's voice being carried in the wind, challenging me to find strength through the power of what we had created.

In a now familiar pattern, the poetry that emerged appeared to "write itself". But I could recognise a difference in the strength which it conveyed. Although separated from Anna, the storm echoed the power of her words and the strength of her love. In that intense experience,

I *could* metabolise an internal concept of Anna's safe-holding as having the power to contain me for the future, despite her physical absence … and then surviving our ending became something I could conceive of as both "imaginable" and "possible".

At the same time another important idea seemed to take root—perhaps as a consequence of this increased sense of inner strength. Hovering in the terrace doorway while the poetry formed itself on the blank, wet page in front of me, I found myself picturing the mountain of words Anna was holding as evidence of the history of my analysis. I knew it must be equivalent to a "mountain", because I had kept copies myself, which now filled eight books of double-sided entries. I had never previously understood what lay behind my need to keep this written record of my analytic experience … until now. All at once, it dawned on me that what I wanted to do, perhaps more than anything else, was to write the history of my analytic journey. I can still remember the immensely satisfying feeling of being able to assume a purpose to the safe-keeping of all this material. But more than this, I recognised that being able to engage myself in this project would help to overcome the feeling that Anna, and our relationship, had "died" once we were no longer meeting. If I were to write the history of my analysis I would have found a way to keep this alive—not only for myself, but perhaps for other colleagues or patients to whom our story might have meaning and usefulness.

Throughout the symbolic resonance of these storms, the possibility that I might "write a book" became an increasing source of comfort and hope for the future as I contemplated my inevitable ending with Anna—now only eighteen months away. Nevertheless, I soon anticipated the difficulties in such an undertaking. My own therapeutic training had been very different to Anna's, and though I had no concept of the form which the book might take, I knew that I would want it to include the Jungian analytic perspective which only Anna could provide from having accompanied me on this journey as my analyst. Finally, I resolved to ask Anna if she would join me in writing the book after her retirement. I could see no other way of achieving my aim … and while acknowledging the uncertainty of the outcome, I was, by now, so enthused with the idea that I hardly dared to contemplate failing at the first hurdle.

* * *

I returned to my sessions with Anna full of excited if nervous anticipation. I was in no doubt about the enormity of the "question" I needed to ask her, and I felt fairly certain that she would not give me an answer immediately … unless, of course, she took strongly against the idea from the start. Since this was too dreadful to contemplate, I tried not to even consider it as a possibility.

It took time to describe the momentous impact of the holiday storms—how they had come to symbolise the recent "storms" in our analytic relationship, from which a new feeling of inner strength had found expression in the very different collection of holiday poems that I gave into Anna's safe-keeping. Gradually I found the courage to explain how this had led to my "revelation"—that I needed to write a book detailing the history of our analytic journey. With so much written material collected over our years together, I expressed my conviction that this must contain the "record" of my psychological and emotional process … And finally I asked Anna if she would consider whether we might "write this together", since I had neither a sufficient grasp of Jungian theory, nor her unique perspective as my analyst, to enable me to attempt this written history without her help.

I remember that Anna asked me a lot of questions: What form did I imagine the book would take? Who were the reading public it would be aimed at? When would I plan to begin writing? How long did I think it would take me to write? Did I intend to use my own name or remain anonymous? I did my best to respond as coherently as possible, but it wasn't easy with no clear plan at this early stage. However, I knew that the book's future form and structure depended on the part which Anna might be willing to play in helping me write it. And one intention *was* very clear from the start: I wanted it to incorporate a detailed account of Anna's analytic perspective and experience, so that ultimately it would combine our *joint* viewpoints—and as I explained to Anna, I believed that this had the potential to offer something unique.

As I had anticipated, Anna chose not to make a decision straight away; instead she promised to give careful thought to my idea. I was grateful that she had not instantly rejected my proposition, and also that her questioning and responses seemed to convey genuine interest. Now I needed to remain patient until Anna felt ready to give me her final decision. But with so much hanging on this, it was difficult to stifle the inevitable anxiety which was never far from the surface during those weeks of waiting.

By November, three months had passed with no further mention of the subject. Considering this a reasonable period for reflection, and with the end of 2007 in sight, I felt an increasing need to know Anna's decision before the year ended. So by mid-November I asked if she felt ready to give me an answer.

I have a clear memory of Anna explaining to me, with great sensitivity, that she had decided she did *not* want to make a commitment to our joint writing of a book. Mainly, she explained this decision in terms of having "no way of knowing" what might be going on in her life once she had retired. And since this was clearly a long-term project which I could not anticipate starting until late 2010, when I would have completed my MA Dissertation, she considered it would be irresponsible to make a promise she might not be able to fulfil. But finally she added the admission that she did not "enjoy" the process of writing in the same way that I clearly did. So although she had contributed chapters to books, and had written various papers for professional journals and conferences, she generally regarded this as a rather burdensome task.

The thought that "writing our story together" would feel to Anna like an unwelcome burden once she had retired came as a shock … and my wounded ego so distorted Anna's words as to convince me that this was what I had "heard" her tell me. This "information" now took on a life of its own by playing into the worst of my fantasies, until I became increasingly persuaded of a previously unthinkable fear—that Anna was choosing to retire because she had grown tired of the demands of her work, and now wished to "cut herself free" from the burdens which we, her patients, imposed on her. Furthermore, I assumed that Anna would want to "forget us all" … and that she would need to do this in order to enjoy her freedom. With hindsight, I believe it was this assumption which led the next storm of anger to erupt between us.

Shortly afterwards, the first in a series of very troubled poems emerged:

> "Animus Shadow"
>
> I hear footsteps echoing
> Down the long black street—
> A split second behind,
> Spitting at me from the wet pavement.
>
> I try to fix the sound into a sense—
> One or two? Me and another,
> Or another and me?
> Who is leading and who following?

My sense is of a half-presence—
A shadowy spectre,
Whose ghostly footstep can neither merge
Nor separate from mine.

Tied in disjointed harmony
We move together, yet apart.
I long to stop, to turn and confront him,
But fear to face what I must see ...

The black, mirror-image
Of my debased other-self,
Reflected up at me
From the filthy wetness.

Angrily my feet tread louder,
Marking my territory
Against the force
Of his threatened invasion.

But I feel my footsteps slowing,
Melting against my will
Into his inevitable rhythm.
We become one—as I know we must.

This is the painful merging
Of my split soul.
I stare into his ghastly face,
With its fearful smile of menacing recognition.

At the time of writing, this poem had no title. I had not the faintest idea of its meaning, nor the driving force behind its creation. All I knew was that, while writing it, I experienced a powerful sense of being "haunted" by something menacing. But by the time I gave it to Anna, I had concluded that it was an unconscious attempt to reconcile my anger towards her—in other words, it signified my psyche's struggle to integrate my shadow—now appearing in male form as possession by my animus.

This is reminiscent of the earlier association Anna had made with my maternal grandmother—but as the series of *Animus Shadow* poems emerged, the image of the "controlling witch" had transformed into a horribly deformed male figure of menace, who demanded with increasing vehemence that I acknowledge his existence as an evil aspect of my own being. As Anna later suggested, this was an indication that "the man with the knife" had surfaced once again from my unconscious. And with the second "Animus Shadow" poem, which emerged in December, the "dialogue" continued:

> "At last—we meet face to face."
> I heard his voice—
> Low, surprisingly quiet
> And strangely familiar.
>
> I dared myself to raise my eyes to his
> And meet his gaze.
> Staring into the deep black,
> I seemed to be swimming in a sea of night.
>
> "Do I know you?"
> I heard the faltering fear behind my words.
> "Can you deny it?" came the soft reply.
> "Do you pretend not to know your own child?
>
> I have waited all your life
> For the day of my birth—
> When I could emerge into the light
> And you would know me as your own.
>
> You gave me life,
> But I was conceived in shame.
> Now my birth has freed you—
> You can choose to shun or embrace me.
>
> But separate or together,
> I remain a living part of you.
> In shunning me, a part of you will die,
> For the mother cannot live
>
> Who knowingly kills her child.
> I only tell you what you already know—

> That you cannot be whole without me,
> Nor I without you."
>
> I stared at his black, misshapen form
> And my heart filled with tears
> At the sight of what I had created.
> I held out my arms to him.
>
> "Welcome home, my child.
> I am your mother,
> And I will learn to love you."

Even as this poem formed itself on the page, I knew that these words were no more than a hopeful promise of what I still needed to achieve through the integration of my shadow. There was a long way to go, and the battle between the love and rage I felt towards Anna would continue to explode in outbursts of intensely destructive poetry.

This challenging period became the subject of our recorded sessions. In Anna's view, "there was something else that needed to be created between us"—because the urge to achieve my writing project had now become a question of "all or nothing" for me. As she reminded me:

> "You couldn't think that we might find another way to do it—it had to be the way you thought, or not at all. And I have always thought that there was something about finding a way to soften the ending ... and in a way, there still *is*, because you've got the recordings, and you *have* found a way that you hope will make something unbearable bearable ... Because in my saying 'no' we had a real clash, and out of that got born a new creative solution which is what we've been doing ever since ..."

As Anna pointed out, we were back once again with Jung's idea of the transcendent function, which suggests a need for the positive and the negative to "crash together" in order for something new to be born from the conflict. As Anna explained:

> "... When this happens and they crash together, out of that comes some kind of chaos and then a solution ... So I think we were always going to have a fight about the ending ..."

"Well, it didn't occur to me that there *were* any other alternatives," I commented.

"No, sure … Why should it?" Anna acknowledged. "… And I didn't say 'no' immediately, because I don't like to say no on principle … I like to live with it, and feel it, and think about it … Because it *was* an attractive idea, and constructive in all sorts of ways … So I had to really think about whether it was a sensible thing to tie myself down to, knowing how much hung on it for you … knowing that this wasn't something I could 'play with'. Because if I played with it and then decided I didn't want to do it, that would have been an absolute catastrophe from which we *couldn't* have come back … . So I had to think about that, together with what was going on in my own life—which of course *you* didn't know but I *did*. And I got to the position where I didn't think it would be a responsible thing to promise you—for many, many reasons … . But of course, you *had* felt tantalised, because this had been around for three months until I was absolutely convinced that I had to say no … But in saying no, I created a limit and a boundary within which we then thrashed around and had a fight … and then something else came out of it …"

"Well, *you* created something else out of it—because *I* couldn't have done that …" I suggested to Anna.

"No …" Anna acknowledged, "… but I knew we had to do *something* with all the poems and all the work which you'd given me … that somehow we needed to integrate it, because that was what your idea for the book seemed to be about … So then I could see that there *was* something we could do …"

But this resolution was still in the future. As 2007 drew to an end, my rage against Anna reached its zenith just before our Christmas break, in "The Grave Digger"—a poem that continues to haunt me to this day with its virulent destructiveness:

> "Here's something you can do to help—
> Take this spade and start digging
> A trench—and make sure it's six foot deep.
>
> A weird one, this—
> Not your 'regular' coffin—
> Nothing 'sacred in the eyes of God'—

Just a pile of rubbish really—
A mountain of papers, neatly typed—
Look like poems to me.

Then there's a load of files,
Still in wallets and covered in dust—
Must have meant something to somebody once.

Strange, how things that once were important
Suddenly become meaningless.
Time to 'clear the decks' and move on, I suppose.

Someone's having a 'sort out', that's for sure!
Must have taken years
To fill these files.

Now there's no room.
Time to make space for something new—
Time to bury what's dead and finished with.

This took me by surprise though—
The body of a dead baby …
Looks deformed to me.

There's a story to tell here, I bet!
A painful birth best forgotten, perhaps?
Can't blame the mother really—

No future in pain and deformity, is there?
Best to bury what's dead
And get on with living—that's what I say anyway.

Suppose that's why I do this job really—
Helping people to dispose of the past
So that they can continue in the present.

Sad though, poor little mite!
You'd have thought it deserved better than this—
Abandoned in an unmarked grave.

> No mourners expected, so I'm told.
> Well, there's hardly time to love
> A thing that never drew breath—
>
> That died before it tasted life.
> Still, it doesn't seem right to me,
> To let a lost life pass unmourned."
>
> His spade stilled,
> The gravedigger contemplated the dead child in silence
> And said his own silent prayer of love.

I clearly recall that what terrified me most about this poem was the ease with which it surfaced from my unconscious. I had no trouble in recognising the dark forces at work in my psyche which had led to its creation—and I also recognised the "murderous rage" towards Anna which it revealed. I could have chosen to keep it from her, since I was in no doubt of the pain it would cause her to read it … but instead, there was a vengeful sense of urgency in my need for her to have it, to hold it, to read it—and for me to witness her pain in this process. Despite the years since this this episode, I still suffer at the recognition of what I so knowingly chose to inflict on Anna—and continue to wonder at the depth of her compassion, that enabled her to accept all the vehement destructiveness of my shadow in the face of the love she had shown me.

When the time came for us to reflect on this poem, Anna insisted on reading it aloud. It was torment to hear her voice reciting my words of destruction back to me. But since she had begun by telling me that "this is the poem I will remember," I sense that she wanted me to experience its full impact in order to reflect on it with hindsight. There was no hiding the tears which surfaced in recognition of what I had intended to inflict on her. It left me wanting to ask an important question:

> "I wonder what it felt like for you, to get that poem?"
> "Oh well … ." Anna reflected for some time before responding. "It felt like you wrote it from rage—so it felt like a huge attack … that's how it felt … And at that point I'd said 'no' to doing the book, so that then turned everything into 'rubbish' … that was where the feeling of attack was," Anna elaborated.

There was a long pause before I could contain myself sufficiently to reply.

"It wasn't *quite* like that for me," I managed to respond.

It was never Anna's assumption that she might have the final word on interpretation, and her response indicated her openness:

"No? ... So how *was* it for you?" she asked me gently.
"I felt there was so much more I wanted to say, but I couldn't do it on my own ... So it felt like condemning what we had to 'an early grave' ... And I know I've said this before—but my anxiety has always been that it would fade in time—eventually there'd be nothing ... just 'dusty files' ... So it felt really important to create something else out of that."
"Something of the 'written word' though," Anna replied, "... Because my point was always to consider that what's gone on between us isn't 'held down' in words on paper ..."
"No ... But as we both realised, it became something important for me to do very early on—so it wasn't really surprising that I needed this to continue ... And if we couldn't do that, then what we *had* done wasn't going to last ... It needed some more concrete form ..." I suggested.

The comfort of attending sessions three times a week is that it allows the opportunity to return quickly to unresolved aspects of the analysis left over from the previous day. When I returned to Anna the next day, I was able to elaborate on *The Grave Digger* poem—that I did not consider that it had originated from a desire to turn what we had done together into "rubbish", but from my fear of the *potential* for it to become "rubbish" if nothing more was allowed to grow from it:

"... I think that's a big difference," I suggested to Anna, "... But I don't know if it feels like that to you?"
"Well ... the way I'd want to think about that was the potential for it to become 'rubbish' in *your* mind ... that this was because of what hadn't been processed and integrated, rather than that *I* would turn it into 'rubbish' ... But it depends on what level you're

really thinking about it—whether you're just thinking about the 'bits of paper', or all the feelings and symbols and thoughts that are recorded on them … Because I'd make a distinction between that. And yes, sure, in the end 'notes' change their function, don't they? … So in the end, the 'bits of paper' become, for me, just the 'vehicle' that holds what's on them," Anna explained.

I recognised the accuracy of Anna's explanation—that the main purpose of analysis concerned what was produced "internally" rather than "externally". But my ability to trust this process not to lose something vital over time still left me questioning whether this was enough for me to continue into the future without a record of Anna's words to hold me. And if this *was* enough, then how could I explain my unconscious need to preserve all this written evidence? And so my reflections continued:

"… I still worry about what gets lost over time, and I've got this illusion—and I know it *is* an illusion—that because it's down in writing, it's going to be 'captured' … But of course, it can't capture *everything*—it can't possibly do that … but it feels sort-of 'safer' than trusting myself to hold everything that we've done together … So that's what I'm trying to say," I concluded.

"Yes," Anna acknowledged, "… And out of all the thoughts and feelings and interactions that got stirred up by *The Grave Digger* poem, we eventually arrived at this way we *could* re-visit it all … to have another 'take' on it, to metabolise it, to internalise it … And from that came all this recorded material and the possibility of whatever you're going to write—which was a way of keeping hold of what felt vital to you. Because whatever we do at this stage has got to have meaning, and be as much as it can possibly be under the circumstances for *you*," she emphasised. "… Because however I hold onto you in the end, is going to be part of *my* psychology … But how you're going to hold onto me, is part of *yours* … So that's how we arrived at this way of doing it …"

* * *

As 2008 got underway, the angry feelings gained a momentum that led my mind into evermore nightmarish fantasies. The writing during this period now depicted Anna "wandering happily off into the sunset of her retirement", while carelessly turning her back on my misery with relief and detachment. Other poems fantasised a scene set years into the future, in which Anna and I would accidentally meet again in some crowded venue—perhaps a railway station. Having glanced at me distractedly, she would walk away without acknowledgement or recognition. In re-visiting these poems it becomes clear that my rage was spiralling out of control, its destructiveness threatening to lay waste to our many years of therapeutic work through my fear of abandonment, and a desire for revenge. This was, indeed, a way of turning everything we had done into "rubbish" ... and it was this potential which Anna had intuitively identified in *The Grave Digger* poem. Of course, this violent expression of anger was also the written manifestation of my profound misery ... and Anna undoubtedly recognised that my urge to attack her, and our relationship, was hiding my desperate need for psychic survival.

This hurtful and injurious period finally ended shortly before Anna's suggestion that we record the final months of my analysis. The night before a session with Anna, a poem "May Mourning" emerged:

> I watch you come and go,
> Arriving and leaving,
> And fear to know
> What is in your heart.
>
> In the coming months
> Those remaining few of us
> Must metamorphose ourselves,
> And you,
>
> Into phantoms
> Of our former reality—
> Conjure you up in our soul
> And learn to continue a ghostly communication.
>
> Now, everything you share with me
> Speaks to me of separation.
> I sense you building bridges
> To help me cross the huge divide ...

But my dreams speak to me
Of homes boarded up, closed,
Disintegrating into the dead dust
Off what once was living.

This time next year,
We will slip silently into a death.
No Memoriam or Requiem—
Just our cremated ashes, blown on the wind.

My pain is this … .
That in my death
Is signified your life;
That in my grief
Is signified your joy;
That in my darkness
Is signified your light;
That in my loss
Is signified your gain;
That in my separation
Is signified your connection.

I see you celebrating
While I am mourning,
And I wonder how
To be re-born from the ashes.

As I read this poem again in the course of writing this history, I am not surprised that Anna's ability for compassion and empathy were finally tested beyond endurance by the escalating violence of an attack that had now lasted for seven months. In our session, as I reiterated again my fantasies about her "joy" at the prospect of her retirement, I heard her voice responding with barely suppressed anger. Her words interrupted my now-accustomed reverie, so that I felt forced to halt my own internal soliloquy in order to attend to what she was saying:

"There might be *other* reasons for my retirement …"

It was a deceptively simple reflection—and yet the subdued anger in her tone alarmed me by its unfamiliarity. I felt gripped by a fear of what might lurk behind the angry simplicity. Clearly she was trying to convey something important which was evading me.

"Now I'm *really* worried …" I remember saying.

My fear had instantly created another nightmare scenario that had not previously occurred to me—perhaps Anna was ill, and her decision to retire was a consequence of this? As my mind immersed itself in this horrible prospect, Anna's voice jolted me back into the present moment:

"Well … You *know* I have my elderly mother living with me …"
I was struck once again by the suppressed anger in her voice.

Did I? … It took only a few seconds to be certain that this was something I didn't know.

"No … I knew you had an elderly mother … But not that she was living with you," I assured her.

Having absorbed this, Anna's tone softened. She began to explain something of the situation that had influenced her decision to retire. What I learnt was that the plan had been for her widowed mother to move in with her once the new house was built. Now in her nineties, her future had become a cause for concern, and Anna's choice was to care for her mother at home for as long as possible. There were other family considerations which she also shared with me. Though these remain the most private recollections of that session, they would prove to be "revelations" destined to transform the future course of my analysis. With Anna's words, the energy of my anger dissipated, resolving itself into a magical renewal of all the loving feelings towards her which had lain buried beneath my rage for so many months.

This was a huge relief—to both of us. But from an analytic perspective, it raised questions about the way in which Anna's disclosure had "broken the frame" of my analytic process, and this became an inevitable subject for discussion in our recordings. As I explained to Anna, while I could fully appreciate the need for boundaries around self-disclosure, it was "not-knowing" the reasons for her retirement which had led my anger to escalate into something which ultimately threatened to destroy everything we had created. And Anna agreed that it was her recognition of this threat which finally led her to end it by revealing the most important reasons which had led to her decision:

> "Yes ... The 'not-knowing' dug a deeper and deeper hole. It got more and more down to that shadow part of you ... Well, I thought it was a very important part of your analysis for us to get there ... But it was getting repetitive, and we hadn't moved from it ..."
> "I was just getting increasingly stuck there," I agreed.
> "Yes, you *were* stuck ... And I thought it was time to give you enough information, so that we could then try to start doing something different," Anna explained.

It made sense that allowing me to remain stuck in a destructive process was unlikely to lead to a satisfactory ending. But Anna's explanation had raised an important question which I felt impelled to ask her:

> "I don't know whether it's appropriate to ask you this, but I know you will tell me if it isn't," I began hesitantly. "... I wonder whether you would rather *not* have had to tell me the reasons for your retirement?"

Anna paused for thought, and her response clearly indicated that this was something about which she was still undecided:

> "... I'm not sure ... I'm still thinking about it," she acknowledged.
> "... I mean, from my analytic position, it broke the frame—but as you know, I don't necessarily think one has to stay absolutely stuck in a position ... and sometimes you might need to break the frame in therapy for a very specific reason ... I suppose I wonder where we would have got to if I hadn't done that," Anna reflected.
> "No ... I can't imagine either," I admitted.
> "I don't *regret* doing it," Anna pronounced firmly. "Whichever way I look at it, I think it was necessary. I think it would have been sadistic, actually, not to have done it."
> "... And maybe masochistic as well?" I queried.
> "Well, yes ... indeed," Anna agreed. "... I think it would have been perverse in the end ... And I do think that some therapeutic positions *can* get perverse ... And I think, when I finally told you,

it was quite an emotional response … And of course this process is *about* 'emotion' …" Anna admitted with disarming honesty.

Of course it was about "emotion"! We had both been caught up in all kinds of powerful feelings at the time of Anna's "disclosure"—and while I agreed with her that it *did* stop my process, I could also acknowledge the subconscious longing I felt at that time, for Anna to "make something happen" which would bring my destructive process to an end … something which Anna had also recognised:

"Well yes … you were terrified that it *would* end in destruction … And it was beginning to feel that it was going that way … And I'm really *not* a masochist," she emphasised, with that recognisable hint of irony in her voice. "… And since you were feeling increasingly bad about it, I didn't really feel there was anything to be gained by letting it continue … I needed to stop it, and I *could* … And that's just one of those decision … I don't know that I can really pretend that it was a 'clinical decision', because in the end it happened on an emotional level," Anna acknowledged.

"Well, I'm glad it did," I heard myself respond emphatically.

"Well yes … because we wouldn't be where we are now if you hadn't known the reasons for my retirement … I don't know where we would have been, but my feeling is that it wouldn't have been very good …"

"No … I feel that too … Because you helped me to make sense of something incomprehensible—and it can feel very … well, I don't quite know how to put it … it can feel quite 'infantilising' actually—to have something as important as that kept from me, and allowing me to regress into all kinds of 'child' stuff …" I expressed to Anna.

"Well yes, it *is* 'infantilising'," she agreed. "However, the theory would be that that's necessary for us to get into the unconscious process—and I think, if we're doing analysis, that's right to a certain degree … I think there were a whole load of things about my ending—about stopping and separating—that you needed to say. They were furious, upset, hurt things about feeling that I was being sadistic … I think you *did* need to say them … but not over and over …"

No … Anna was right. Enduring this storm of destructive rage for seven months was enough to convince us both that it needed to end, if we were to find a way of constructively concluding my many years of analysis. And now that the reasons for Anna's retirement were clear, our relationship moved into a different, more "equal" dimension. This did not mitigate my need to go through a profound grieving process, and Anna remained constantly on the alert for signs which indicated that it was necessary to allow a special space for this grief to emerge in our sessions.

By the time of our summer break in 2008, we had also resolved the question of Anna's contribution to my project. Though she was not prepared to join me in the process of writing, she offered to allow me to record our sessions for eight months, during which we would "analyse the process of my analysis" by means of the "mountain" of written material which I had placed in her safe-keeping over the years. Until our ending in April 2009, Anna agreed to meet three times a week, to complete this project with time to capture the essence of our relationship. During those months the words which had emerged from my unconscious took on a new dimension, as Anna helped me to understand something of the depth of psychological meaning in our work. Though my deep sadness at the prospect of ending never left me, I now knew I would have something to take with me which offered the promise of continuing what we had achieved into the future.

EPILOGUE

As I sit here writing the Epilogue to our story, I am reminded that it is more than four years since my final session with Anna. In re-visiting so intimately the loving and painful experiences of our shared journey, I recognise how this interval of time has facilitated the process of "internalisation and separation" that was Anna's ultimate hope for me. Hardly a day passes when I don't think of Anna with love. But now the strength of her containing presence has become a part of my internal being—something available to me despite her physical absence—and together with the knowledge that her life continues elsewhere, without me. Had I not been able to achieve this, it is certain that our final ending would have repeated the trauma of our earlier "first ending".

So what was it about this process that finally allowed me to separate from her, even as I struggled alone through my grief after our ending? I found myself recalling my earlier prediction to Anna—that I would never be "one of those patients who would walk away from therapy in a spirit of triumphant achievement." This memory took me back to my initial training, when my reading of a passage from Petrūska Clarkson's book, *The Therapeutic Relationship*, caught my attention by its particular resonance. Clarkson was writing about the "Person-to-Person" or "Real relationship", which suggests a move forward from the more regressed stage of the "developmentally needed" relationship:

> The person-to-person relationship is enquiring, encountering, where the client experiences a sense of the other as important as themselves—not only self-focused. The self needs of the client have been met and therefore they are ready, willing and able to move into and hear and metabolise it. The key is about genuine responsivity, and mutuality. Mutually satisfactory, mutually experienced as person-to-person. Mutually experienced as being met. Mutually assessed as reciprocal.[1]

But since the reparative work of therapy operates as a non-linear process, for some patients there will be distinct episodes of fluctuation, particularly when the work of therapy is drawing towards its end. I believe that the understanding of my own process, which grew from the insight gained from our recordings during those final months, gradually taught me to recognise and move into a "person-to-person" relationship with Anna once we were no longer together. Only then, it seems, could the reality of our "separateness" become something no longer "too unbearable" to contemplate. And once I had found the courage to confront this reality, it then became possible for me to maintain my emotional hold on Anna as a strong internal object, independent of her physical presence. In Clarkson's words, which had forged such an early and powerful connection in my mind:

> Every client will be different in terms of whether they need to separate while they are still in psychotherapy or whether perhaps they need to leave in order to become separate, and then to assume equality only years later ... People will have different timings—some need years before leaving home and becoming adults. It may be only in the next significant relationship or next therapy that the self fully evolves.[2]

With the period of intense anger now over, the months leading up to our final ending in April 2009 brought forth mainly dreams, in which

---

[1] Clarkson, P. (1995). *The Therapeutic Relationship*, p. 153. London: Whurr, 2002.
[2] Ibid., p. 154.

I conjured up scenes depicting Anna engaged in her future life, as I imagined it might be. These dreams suggested that the process of integration had begun, as I tried to imagine different aspects of Anna's future life reflected in her relationships with others. Though these dreams also expressed my fear of her being "crowded out", they nevertheless suggested an unconscious attempt to come to an emotional acceptance of the reality of Anna's separate existence outside the consulting room.

By the time of our final ending, I had been working as a psychotherapist myself for four years. I had always considered that the process of meeting for three sessions a week during this final period would have a different significance—and Anna fully understood this. But it felt gratifying to hear her express the thought that, "We moved from 'personal therapy' to 'training therapy'."

"Did it really feel like that to you?" I needed to ask her.

While I had intuitively sensed that this had happened, it was not a thought I had found the courage to express.

"Yes, indeed it did," Anna responded, "... particularly since last September."

In reality, it took many years for my understanding of the analytic process to develop. Once my training as a psychotherapist was underway, Anna became more willing to explain what was happening in theoretical terms. But even in the early years, I had felt a longing for a definitive theoretical explanation of what was happening in my internal world. Understandably Anna resisted this at the time, and often I experienced her resistance as defensiveness, or else I worried that she considered me "too stupid" to understand the theoretical perspective. Then one day, in response to my questioning, she explained,

"I never use 'theoretical jargon' with patients. It could feel deeply dismissive to hear their difficulties described in terms of theory."

She needed to be convinced that I felt differently—that I longed to learn from her extensive theoretical knowledge, so that I could understand and experience myself from this other and deeper dimension. By the time we began our recordings Anna had recognised this need—and having worked together through the crisis of my anger, I was now ready to look objectively and theoretically at my own process over the eight years of my analysis.

My most enduring memory of those final months concerns the way in which they signified a *shared* process of grieving. While Anna openly acknowledged pleasurable thoughts in anticipating her retirement, she also made no secret of the sadness surrounding her conflicted feelings. As evidenced by the recordings, the joint expression of mutual grief inevitably became the focus of many final sessions. In this connection, two recordings in particular stand out as moving and memorable examples of Anna's willingness to share her own grieving process in order to support and validate my own profound feelings of grief. These two consecutive sessions took place shortly before our last Christmas. As Anna would point out, our focus during the previous weeks had mainly concerned the positive developments to have grown from my analysis. While she did not question the importance of exploring this perspective, Anna recognised that it was only one aspect of the work we needed to do:

> "… at some point, if we're not just doing it to protect ourselves, the other side is going to come out … and now it *has* …"

This was a reference to the deeply distressed outpouring of my grief, which suddenly and unexpectedly surfaced during these two sessions. Barely able to speak through my tears, I hear myself attempting to describe to Anna the intensely physical pain that accompanied these feelings:

> "It's a really *horrible* pain, Anna … I don't know what to do with it …"

In deference to my acute suffering, I hear Anna respond softly, full of gentleness, love and empathic understanding:

> "The trouble with it is, that it's part and parcel of the depth of our connection and the places we've been together … Because if we hadn't been to such hugely powerful, loving places, the 'sad' wouldn't be so painful … It *is* painful—and very scary … but I suppose there is a way in which we also have to welcome it … It's a huge rite of passage—that immense 'before and after'—and

the 'not-knowing', because it *is* unknown. It's a total life-changing event ... and terrifying, because the unknown is always terrifying ..."

I knew that Anna was right: this was the inevitable price to be paid for the intensity of love that had been my experience of our analytic relationship. But it left me with a vital question that I hesitated to ask Anna:

"Well, you *can* ask it," Anna responded to my expression of doubt.

"I just wonder how *you* managed it, when you ended your own analysis ... Whether you've got a 'secret' about how to do it that you can share with me?" I asked her through my tears.

"Ah ..." Anna indulged herself in a few brief seconds for thought before replying gently. "No ... no 'secret' at all ... No, a handkerchief job for a year. There's no easy way that *I* found ... Except what I learnt is that I *did* survive it, though I couldn't imagine how I would do it ... and it took a while to get over the doubts about it ... It takes a long time to grieve," Anna finally added, "... And however much you grieve before you finish, you will probably still have to grieve a lot more ... So all I could hope for is that by next April, you will hopefully be strong enough to do that grieving for yourself—because nobody can do that with me, and I can't do it with you ... We both have to do that for ourselves."

I was relieved that Anna had chosen to respond so honestly to my question, and felt strangely comforted by what she had shared. As she would subsequently explain, her decision to answer my question with such congruence was an effort to assuage my many doubts about my own ability to cope, and the way in which I found myself needing to repeat the expression of these feelings, either in our sessions, or in some of the later poetry which emerged during these final months:

"... What I *really* want you to know is that it's not 'silly' or 'boring'— that the same thing *will* be coming up over and over ... I know that from my own experience, that it *has* to keep being referred to—it's about trying to manage something, and the way of managing it is that it has to be said over and over again ..."

As Anna would remind me, "Sometimes there's nothing new to say, Naomi—but it still needs saying."

Some of these reflections materialised as a result of two poems entitled *Celebration Song* and *Duet*, which emerged at this time, together with the many doubts that I expressed about my need to "keep saying the same thing again and again". But what Anna recognised in these poems was something significantly different—that they denoted my attempt to hold the tension of opposites which was such a demanding aspect of my grieving process:

> "However we try to end the therapy, if it's about anything, it's got to be about holding the tension of opposites—it's *got* to be ... It's got to be about a feeling of 'celebration' *and* a feeling of 'death'—and that's what you're describing. And in *Celebration Song* you write about 'the child'—and that's hopefully the 'third' that can come out of this—that it has the possibility to produce something else, which is 'the child' that you write about ..."

By mutual agreement, Anna and I both agreed not to record our final session on the morning of the 9th April 2009. Though I did write my own detailed account of that deeply emotional meeting, I must trust that the reader will understand my reluctance to make public the details of such a private and intimate episode. My hope is that I will already have shared enough of what passed between Anna and me in our preparation for this ending, to enable the reader to share sufficiently in the sorrow and celebration which must inevitably accompany the end of such a lengthy and life-changing relationship. Anna was right: while it had been a privilege to be able to share some of our grief together in advance of our ending, a long process of solitary mourning was to follow ... from which, like Anna, I *did* find a way to survive, though without ever truly relinquishing a sense of loss. As I listen to Anna's words at the time of our final Christmas break, her anticipation of the process of mourning still to come is evident:

> "What I was thinking was—however much we go back and think about what's happened between us, however much we recall things now, however much we do, there's always a great deal that we can never consciously *know*—that we can't actually 'have it' as a possessed thing ... It's a way of trying to keep hold of the past, and that's why of course there's a great sadness in knowing that we *can't* ... It's only a 'representation', and that whatever

happened, the feelings, the history, the story—we have it *inside* us, but mostly it's unconscious … and because it's unconscious, it's not a comfort …"

And so, as with any grieving process that ultimately repairs over time, there are occasions when the painfulness of the loss will threaten to re-open old wounds which never totally heal. And I cannot deny the recurrence of these feelings during the years since my ending with Anna. But in her unique gift to me of our recordings, Anna gave into my safe-keeping the potential for our work to continue to live and grow—in ripples which may spread out into the wider world, beyond the confines of the analytic consulting room in which our story was first born. The analytic relationship is the story of "the child" grown into adulthood, and ultimately Anna understood that this development was "held", as far as the limits of consciousness will allow, within my written material and the recorded history of my analysis. And thus, it seems appropriate to end this story of our analytic journey with Anna's recorded words:

"… In a way, that's the best thing that I could ever give you to hold onto. It's a shared thing—something that we hit upon together … Anything else is silent …"

POSTSCRIPT

Do you not see how necessary a world of pains and troubles is to school an intelligence and make it a soul?

—John Keats, *Letters of John Keats*, 1819

A testament to the author's life is an important postscript to this remarkable piece of work that I feel ill equipped to write. I want to express my love and admiration for my dearly beloved sister, the author, and pay tribute to this unique and astonishing achievement.

It has been a privilege but nonetheless disturbing experience to have been allowed a glimpse into the inner world of someone, who having stood at the edge of despair, teetered but remained upstanding, and survived with the support of the containment offered by a skilful practitioner of Jungian analysis. But having come through a dark and painful emotional death into a place of knowledge, resolution, and tranquillity, sadly for us all, she now faces yet another devastating challenge. My sense is that the reader will be shocked and dismayed, and for what follows I ask the reader's indulgence.

As a psychotherapist I have read many admirable and interesting accounts of the experiences of highly respected practitioners, describing their successes and failures, and the privilege of working in this special space. Equally I have read many accounts from the perspective of consumers describing the process that "saved" them, that gave them back their sense of self or opened the doors to a new and better future; or that damaged them and from which they were re-traumatised. There is no account, to my knowledge that has described so movingly the experience of "the patient" (not my chosen word) from the perspective of a person who is able later to reflect on the experience as a practitioner themselves and describe understanding on both a personal level that is raw and an intellectual level that succinctly describes the process of analysis. Whilst describing the innermost experiences of mental illness, this work is underpinned by a comprehensive knowledge of the theory. Additionally there are important reflections, insights, and interpretations from my sister's analyst concerning various stages and aspects of the therapeutic relationship later discussed during the recorded sessions that followed. I express my personal appreciation to her analyst who held that safe space for so many years when my sister was severely at risk.

The book is peppered with the poems that provided a vehicle for sharing otherwise inexpressible torment as well as optimism and hope. These poems stand on their own as creative expressions, but in the context of the memoir enlighten and inform the reader in a way that prose alone cannot.

So now I have the unenviable task of telling the reader that shortly following the completion of this manuscript, my sister was diagnosed with terminal cancer. There is an obvious irony in contemplating the inevitable, at a time when life has once more become precious; particularly when what this book describes is the black hole from which my sister crawled back into the light, and from where her footing faltered for so long.

Now the fight is against time and there is a quickening pace of an unstoppable force to contend with. My sister's motivation to complete the editing process and preparation of this manuscript has been remarkable, and the small way in which I have attempted to assist her, I hope has meant as much to her as to me. It has certainly eased something, to the extent that I felt that at least I contributed some constructive support, particularly since we live on opposite sides of the world. But this has been a shared task during which I hope she feels that I have truly heard her story and have walked alongside her process as best I can in retrospect.

I am truly grateful to have taken this voyage of words and meaning. Sensing every breath, feeling the mortal wounds—and whilst this has been a holding space for anticipatory grief, for who knows what will follow, I take solace in the knowledge that this road can now be shared with many colleagues and fellow analysands, and hopefully will help them understand the nature of the analytic process.

This is one remarkable individual's experience of that process that she has opened herself up to share with us and now forms part of what is her legacy to us all, but is particularly dear and special to me.

> *Out of suffering have emerged the strongest souls; the most massive characters are seared with scars.*
>
> Kahlil Gibran (1883–1931)

Corinne Henderson
Sydney, Australia

ABOUT THE AUTHOR

After a career of more than twenty years as an Early Years Teacher, in her fifties, **Naomi Lloyd** became a psychotherapist. A Diploma in Integrative Counselling was followed by an MA in Existential Psychotherapy and a Diploma in Clinical Supervision. Naomi worked in her busy private practice; as a voluntary bereavement counsellor; and taught existential psychotherapy to Diploma Course students. After retiring from private practice, she continued supervision and voluntary bereavement work. Until her death, Naomi lived in southwest London with her husband, not far from their two grown-up children and two grandchildren.